Abram Goldberg was born in Łódź, Poland, in 1924. Following the Nazi invasion, Abe and his parents were imprisoned in Łódź Ghetto. In 1944, Abe and his mother were sent to Auschwitz, where his mother was gassed upon arrival. Abe was sent to a series of camps before being liberated in 1945. Abe met his wife, Cesia, in 1946. In 1951 they moved to Melbourne, Australia, where they had two children and ran various restaurants, including the iconic Goldy's. Abe has been volunteering at the Melbourne Holocaust Museum since 1984 and remains a member of the executive board. He was awarded an OAM in 2013.

Fiona Harris is an award-winning writer, creator and actor working successfully across a range of media and has written and co-written over a dozen books for both adults and kids. She co-wrote the internationally award-winning comedy web series *The Drop Off* with her husband, Mike McLeish, which was adapted into both a novel and a telemovie that was broadcast by Channel 9 in 2021. The novel's sequel, *The Pick-up*, was released in 2021. Fiona is currently working on a new adult fiction book with Mike, due for release in 2023.

The Strength of Hope

A Holocaust Survivor's Guide to Love and Life

ABRAM GOLDBERG
with FIONA HARRIS

For my parents, Chaja and Herszl, the family members I lost and the six million people who were murdered by the Nazis during the Second World War.

First published by Affirm Press in 2022
Boon Wurrung Country
28 Thistlethwaite Street
South Melbourne VIC 3205
affirmpress.com.au

10 9 8 7 6 5 4 3 2 1

Text copyright © Abram Goldberg and Fiona Harris, 2022
All rights reserved. No part of this publication may be reproduced without prior written permission from the publisher.

 A catalogue record for this book is available from the National Library of Australia

ISBN: 9781922806314 (paperback)

Cover design by Christabella Designs © Affirm Press
Typeset in Baskerville MT Std 12.5/19 by J&M Typesetting
Proudly printed and bound in Australia by McPherson's Printing Group

Contents

PROLOGUE: AUSCHWITZ 1996   1
1. ELSTERNWICK MELBOURNE 2021   4
2. THE GOLDBERGS   10
3. FIGHTING FIT   21
4. RISING TENSIONS   28
5. DEPORTED   38
6. HOME AS A GHETTO   50
7. ILLEGAL ACTIVITY   70
8. BARBARISM REVEALED   77
9. ALL GONE   90
10. SEEDS OF HOPE   94
11. MUM & ME   101
12. THE HORROR   110
13. AUSCHWITZ   118
14. AN UNLIKELY ALLY   127
15. RIDING MY LUCK   134
16. LIGHT AT THE END OF THE TUNNEL   140
17. LIBERATION   147
18. HEADING HOME   151
19. SEARCHING FOR SURVIVORS   156
20. A MISSION WITH MUMEK   168
21. BELGIUM   180

22. CESIA PART 1   183
23. THE SMALL GIRL WITH THE DARK CURLS   189
24. A GRAND AFFAIR   196
25. REUNITING WITH MY SISTER   202
26. TOWARDS A NEW LIFE IN AUSTRALIA   210
27. FROM PRESSURE TO PRESSER   219
28. FAMILY LIFE   225
29. I AM A FATHER   233
30. EAT, DRINK & BE MERRY   241
31. STRENGTHENING COMMUNITY   254
32. JEWISH HOLOCAUST CENTRE   260
33. FACING THE PAIN   271
34. CESIA PART 2   280
35. A LONG AND FULL LIFE   283
36. ELSTERNWICK MELBOURNE 17 JANUARY 2022   292
37. CHARLIE   302
38. HELEN   306
39. CESIA PART 3   309
EPILOGUE: 2022   311

PROLOGUE

AUSCHWITZ 1996

I throw back a glass of whiskey to steady my nerves. Cesia's eyes are full of tears and she's trembling. I squeeze her hand to let her know that I feel what she is feeling. I remember what she is remembering.

Our children, Charlie and Helen, are here too, and Charlie's father-in-law, Borje, has driven down from Sweden to chauffeur us around. He has parked the car a little way back from the entrance to the camp and although Cesia's knee is giving her a lot of pain, she is determined to walk.

The quietness and the beauty of the clear blue-sky day is unnerving. As the memories and visions begin to flood back, I close my eyes to let them in ... the cattle trucks lined up along the tracks, their human cargo inside, the gaunt faces of painfully thin people staring through barbed wire with haunted, empty expressions, dogs barking, people crying, shouting and talking in anxious whispers. People's nerves were at breaking point, and I can still feel the atmosphere of terror all around me – and the smell. A most terrible smell. A smell I now know was burning flesh. When a voice rises above all the others in my mind, I recognise it instantly: my mum. This is where we shared our last precious moments together, where she spoke her final words to me.

'Abram, do everything humanly possible to survive. And when you do, wherever you find yourself, you must tell people what happened here so it can never happen again.'

A hand slips into mine, bringing me back to the present. Cesia stares at me with deep sadness in her eyes. She knows where I've been these last few moments.

'Come,' she says quietly.

My wife can hardly take a step without wincing these days but she refuses help. This is something she must do. All these years later she is going to walk into this place a free woman.

The five of us make our way slowly down the rusted railway tracks as Cesia struggles to recall details.

'Did I get off the train here? Or here?' she says softly. 'Did we line up on this side or that?'

Helen takes her other hand and clutches it tightly.

'*Raus! Raus!*' Cesia says as a memory comes into sharp focus.

I recognise the words as the ones the Nazis shouted at us as they slid open the heavy doors of the cattle trucks, 'Out! Out!'

'I thought we had entered a lunatic asylum,' Cesia tells our children, tears streaming down her cheeks.

'This has been the saddest day of my life,' Helen says.

Charlie agrees but is also angry. He can't believe how close the town is. 'Why didn't the people there do or say something?' he asks. 'They must have known! To say they didn't seems impossible.'

I say a silent Kaddish for the more than one million souls tortured, tormented and executed here, and we stand in silence with our arms around each other. Then I begin to talk. The words, slow at first, begin to pour out of my mouth and I can't stop them.

'That was where they lined us up … Here is where I watched my mother get taken away … That is where Mengele stood with his baton, waving us left and right.'

As the memories tumble out, our children cry and hold Cesia and me close. I know why I feel the need to say everything out loud. This was the promise I made to my mother all those years ago. That I would always tell. That I would always remember.

'Today is the exact date,' Cesia says, 'I arrived here as a fifteen-year-old girl.'

The pain in her knee is getting worse by the minute but she refuses to stop moving. Cesia continues into the camp, the same camp that took her parents away from her. Every step is agony, but the emotional pain is far greater than the physical could ever be. When we ask again if we should bring the car, she refuses.

'I will show these cruel beasts that I will walk how and when I want!' she says firmly.

Cesia's pride and determination is good for her children to see. Now they understand how their mother – a petite, shy teenager when she was sent here all those years ago – had the mental strength to survive this hell.

I am careful not to stumble on the bumpy, uneven road as we walk. I may be an old man now, but I walk taller and stronger than I ever have before, unaided and proud through the entrance. It is a far cry from how I first entered this place fifty-two years ago. A place so deeply embedded in my psyche that it will always be a part of me.

A place called Auschwitz.

1

ELSTERNWICK MELBOURNE 2021

Today is a good day because today I will see Cesia. For many weeks I've not been able to visit my wife at Gary Smorgon House, the care home she has lived in for three years, because of Covid and lockdowns. Cesia has not been able to visit me at home either.

Before the pandemic, I would see Cesia every week: at Friday night dinners with our family, on weekends when my son, daughter and I take Cesia out for lunch, or on drives to the coast or countryside. Sometimes our grandchildren and my great-granddaughter come along to spend time with their Bubba and Zaida too.

These times with our family are very special to Cesia and me, but get-togethers and trips like these have not been possible for many months now. Of course, we are not the only ones who have been separated from their loved ones. It has been hard for so many people all over the world.

Cesia and I speak on the phone every day, three or four times at least, but I miss seeing her face in real life; the same beautiful face I have been looking at for more than three-quarters of a century. 10 June 2021 was our 74th wedding anniversary, but of course we couldn't celebrate the way we would have liked, the way we have for many decades. For the first year since our wedding in 1947, Cesia and I were not with each other to raise a glass to our marriage. We resolve to celebrate together next year for our diamond anniversary because that's the sort of people we are – hopeful, optimistic and determined.

In less than two weeks I will turn ninety-seven years old. But how is this possible? How am I so old? It is a number that seems incredible to me. But I cannot complain. I have been blessed with a beautiful family, and a full and interesting life.

I may be old, but my memory is still strong. I remember so much about my early years, about my life before the war and how my mother's freshly baked honey cakes smelled when I was a child. I remember the way it felt to move my legs so fast, then leap into the air and vault over the horse at my gymnastics club. I remember that it felt like flying.

My vaulting days are well and truly behind me now, but the desire to run and fly is still there. Just last week at an appointment with my doctor, I used the handles of my walker frame to try and raise myself up into a handstand, and almost gave her a heart attack.

'Abram!' she scolded. 'Please don't do that!'

When I want to run and jump now I close my eyes and remember my active days in Łódź, Poland. I was a young, healthy, fit boy then. A boy who loved gymnastics, ping-pong and sport – a boy who had no idea what was just around the corner for him and his family.

Now, all these years later, I am still here. I have my health, my mind, my family and my Cesia. My wife turned ninety-two this year. She is starting to forget little things but she still knows us, her family. Cesia still knows me, her Abram.

And today I will see her again.

I was up earlier than usual this morning. Some people say I am fastidious – a man who likes order, routine, facts and figures – and they would be right. I have the same routine every day and have had for many years.

Every morning I wake early, around 6.30, shower (unassisted) and eat my breakfast, which is the same every day. I lay it out before I go to bed the night before – a bowl of crushed cornflakes (I don't like the big pieces), a pot of honey (because I need to be sweetened up a bit), one piece of bread for toasting (half with Vegemite and Swiss cheese and the other half with cherry jam and cottage cheese) and one big banana. This is followed with a cup of coffee. It is a healthy start to my day and keeps my stomach full until lunchtime.

When we first met, Cesia didn't even know how to boil a potato, but I taught her the basics when we moved in together. (She would say she taught herself, but we will have to agree to disagree. After seventy-four years of marriage, I know when to let something go!)

A carer arrives to my house after breakfast. I am lucky to have good carers who have become more like family to me. One of my carers, Andrea Santos-Mouthe, has been working with me for over five years now. We are very close and she, her husband, and two sons are like family to all the Goldbergs. Andrea first came to our house in 2015 to work with Cesia, six days a week, eight hours a day. When Cesia went to Gary Smorgon House, Andrea stayed to work with me. She calls me Zaida – the Yiddish informal title for grandfather – and we have spent hundreds of hours talking, laughing, and sharing our stories.

Another one of my carers is a woman named Basia. When she first started working with me, I asked where she was from as I recognised her accent.

'Poland,' Basia told me.

'Which town?' I asked.

She smiled. 'You would not know it. Nobody has heard of it.'

'Try me,' I said, smiling back.

'I come from a small town called Kolo,' she said.

'Kolo?' I said. 'The town near Chelmno?'

She was shocked. 'How do you know it?'

'Because I am from Łódź,' I told her. 'Just 80 kilometres away!'

We couldn't believe it. What a coincidence for us to meet all the way across the other side of the world! Since then, Basia and I have had many long and interesting conversations with each other, and I enjoy spending time with her. But neither Basia nor Andrea is coming today. Today it is my children who will take me to see Cesia.

I am dressed in my usual day attire of shirt, suit and tie, and when I sit on the bed to put on my Skechers I smile when I think of the moment I will see Cesia. I will reach out to hold her face in my hands, and she will smile, rub my face and stroke the back of my head. Maybe we will sit down to talk, or maybe we'll take our walkers and head out into the garden. As we walk around, we might talk about how our friends are dealing with lockdown, or what activities she has been doing in the home, or maybe I will tell her my big news.

'Cesia! I am going to be writing a book about my life.'

'Finally!' she will cry, clapping her hands together.

Many people, including my wife, have been pestering me to write my life story for years now. But I have always refused.

'A book of my life?' I would say. 'It is so long and there is so much to tell that I would need ten volumes!'

But now I have agreed. In preparation, Charlie, Helen, Fiona and I have been going through many old photos, some that are sixty, seventy, even eighty years old. Tiny black-and-white photographs from the past that spill out of cracked old leather-bound albums. Photos that are so old that the glue has worn away on the backs of them, so they are falling off the thin black cardboard pages. There are many photos in there of lost relatives and friends, but also many of Cesia and me. It is a shock to see how young we both were back then. Cesia Amatensztejn was only seventeen when I met her, and very different to me. Where I like facts and figures, and remember specific dates and places, Cesia is more emotional. Even now, she remembers the feelings from her past, much more than dates and facts.

In this book, I will tell stories about my life growing up in Łódź, Poland, about my teenage years before the war, and about life in the ghetto. There will be stories from my time at Auschwitz, from my exciting, sometimes dangerous, post-war travels through Europe, and, of course, the most wonderful story of all: meeting a young girl in Belgium after the war, and how we would go on to spend the next seven-and-a-half decades together in Europe and Australia.

At just one hundred and fifty centimetres tall, I may be a small man, but I have lived a very big life. For that I feel incredibly grateful. Some find it hard to understand how I have kept my positivity, and how I can see the good in people after what I went through. Maybe when you read my story you will see that I have always been a lucky man.

2

THE GOLDBERGS

I was the baby of the Goldberg family. The youngest of four siblings and the only boy. My eldest sister, Maryla, was seven years older than me; then came Frajda, four years older, and Estera, born two years before me. In those days many babies were born at home, and I was no exception. My mother and sisters were very happy to have a baby boy to fuss over, but I never liked being pampered. I enjoyed my mother and sisters' hugs, but I never wanted to be coddled. My fierce independent streak was there from the very beginning.

I was born in 1924 in Łódź, Poland. At that time, Łódź was a large and impoverished industrial centre – a textile manufacturing hub full of factories, large and small. It was home to some 700,000 people, a third of whom were Jewish, including the Goldbergs. We lived at 48 Zgierska *Ulica* (street), a main road, in an area that was 99 per cent Jewish and one of the poorer areas of Łódź. Our area had narrow streets, where the houses and buildings were all squashed up against each other. The six of us lived in a one-room flat on the third floor of one of those buildings, in an old, rundown wooden block. There was a shared common yard at the base of our building, which was paved with cobblestones and bordered by sheds and a large stable.

Our small flat was made up of two rooms, the kitchen area, and a little corridor that led to the front door. My parents shared a double bed, Maryla and Frajda slept on a day bed in the main room, and Estera and I bunked down on camp beds in the kitchen that were folded away during the day. When we were young boys, my friend, Shia Ajzenbach, rigged up a trapeze-type swing in our small corridor and we spent many fun hours trying out our acrobatic tricks. My mother and sisters got the fright of their lives some days when they arrived home to find two boys hanging upside down in the hallway, arms wildly swinging, but we thought it was great fun.

The Goldbergs were poor, but our mum, Chaja Goldberg, kept our tiny home spick and span and her four children clean and tidy. Mum was also an excellent cook. As far as my sisters and I were concerned, our mother made the best cheesecakes, honey cakes and sponge cakes in all of Łódź. Even though we weren't religious, my mother liked to observe Shabbat, the Jewish day of rest, and so we had a big family dinner every Friday night. She would make huge servings for Saturday too, and her pot of cholent – a bean, meat, and potato stew – was so big that it wouldn't fit in our oven.

Every Friday afternoon, before the lighting of the Shabbat candles, Mum would send me to see the baker when he had finished baking and his oven was still hot. For a small fee the baker would put our pot of cholent in his oven and leave it there to slow cook overnight. The next day, I was sent back to pick it up. We weren't the only family using the baker's ovens this way. In winter especially, many Jewish families took their cholent to the baker because, as a way of observing the Shabbat, religious Jews refrain from all work, including lighting fire and cooking.

The baker put a number on each pot before sliding it into the oven. Sometimes the numbers got singed in the oven overnight and the baker would accidentally give us the wrong one, but we never dared complain. Sometimes we were even lucky enough to be given one of the richer families' cholent pots, which was always bigger than ours.

My mum was a quiet, placid and affectionate woman. Family meant everything to her. She was an idealist, and a typical Jewish mother in that she endlessly fussed and worried over her children, especially her baby boy. Mum was so pretty, with soft, kind eyes and shoulder-length blonde hair that turned grey earlier than it should have. I adored my mother, and it was only as I got older that I understood how hard it must have been for her when we were little. She was a full-time mother and housewife, living in a tiny flat with four children, had very little money and a husband who worked long hours at his textile factory.

My dad, Herszl Goldberg, was balding, clean shaven and always neatly dressed. Despite his small size, he had incredible physical strength, as well as great mental fortitude. A softly spoken, gentle man who possessed an extraordinary inner strength, Dad was a strong revolutionary who would always strive to maintain positivity in any situation, no matter what the circumstances. *'Mir muzn zayn positive!'* (We must try to stay positive!) was one of my father's most common Yiddish phrases. 'We will find a way, I promise,' he would tell my mother if money was tight and we needed new shoes for winter. 'Everything will work out just fine, you'll see.'

My father was my hero. He worked hard to provide for us and was a conscientious man who fought for people's rights and equality throughout his life. At an early age, Dad developed a strong sense of social justice and knew that he wanted to spend his life helping the Jewish people. My dad was a man who led by example and early on I learned about the power of positivity from him, and it became the central lesson of my life.

Dad was born in 1887 in Łódź, at a time when the Polish Jews (then living under Russian rule) were exposed to a series of *pogroms* (organised massacres). In response to these massacres some two million Jews emigrated out of the region, but my father and his family stayed in Poland. Dad was always conscious of the poverty, injustices and antisemitism happening around him and so, when he was thirteen, he joined the Łódź branch of the Bund – a Jewish socialist political organisation founded in Lithuania.

The Bund was created to assist the Jewish workers and population. Bundists believed in helping to advance all of humankind and wanted to unite Jews in Eastern Europe in a class-based fight for economic reform. The Bund's philosophy was simple – God was not going to help the Jews, so they had to stop exploitation and antisemitism themselves. By the time my father joined the Bund it had expanded to Poland and Russia, and many young people flocked to enlist in SKIF – *Sotsyalistishe*

Kinder Farband (The Socialist Children's Union). My paternal grandfather almost became a rabbi at one point, and so he was very disappointed when his son renounced his religious beliefs and chose to become politically minded instead.

My mother was born in 1889, also in Łódź, and belonged to the women's association of the Bund from a young age too. Mum and Dad met at the beginning of the twentieth century through the Bund and fell in love, but their respective families were not happy about the union. My grandparents on both sides were religious and had already arranged for their children to marry different people within their community, but Herszl and Chaja were adamant they would only marry each other. Their parents tried to put a stop to the wedding, but Mum and Dad's minds were made up. They had so much in common, even then: they were two socially aware teenagers who had seen their fair share of Jewish persecution and discrimination, and wanted things to change. My parents were both stubborn, and that stubbornness is a trait that runs through all the Goldbergs, even to this day. Both were small in stature too – Mum was five foot one and Dad was five foot five – and my sisters and I all inherited their slight height.

I inherited my placidity, idealism and thick blond curls from my mother, and my strength and positivity from my father. My stubbornness I got from both. These were all traits that would go on to serve me well throughout my life.

At home, we all spoke Yiddish, which is a different language to Hebrew. Hebrew is a Semitic language spoken in its modern or ancient form, while Yiddish is a German dialect that integrates many languages, including German, Hebrew and Aramaic. It is written with the Hebrew alphabet but sounds German. The Yiddish language was developed in Europe one thousand years after the first diaspora, which is when Jews were exiled from Israel by the Babylonians. We also spoke Polish, as this was the language of so many of the kids in our neighbourhood, including our building caretaker's son.

I grew up with politically aware parents, so was aware of the ongoing threat to Jewish people from early on in my life. The growing antisemitism across Europe was a regular topic of conversation in our home when I was a young boy, and I spent a lot of time eavesdropping on the grown-ups. I didn't always understand everything that was being said, but from an early age my interest in these discussions was ignited. I would sit on the floor playing with a toy, but my young ears were always tuned in to whatever chat was going on at the kitchen table between my parents and their friends. Their conversations didn't scare me, simply piqued my interest. Already, I was starting to follow in my parents' politically active footsteps.

Abram is a biblical name that means 'exalted father', but the Goldbergs were not a religious family. My mother observed some Jewish traditions, such as lighting the candles on Shabbat and going to synagogue once a year on Yom Kippur, but my father, sisters and I never went with her. Even though we were a secular family, the Goldbergs were 100 per cent Jewish and proud of it.

We had at least forty or so relatives in Łódź – aunties, uncles, cousins, and grandparents – and most of them were also secular and belonged to the Bund. My grandparents, Zaida and Bubba, were the exception, and my paternal grandfather even ran religious studies classes from his home. It was tradition among observant religious Jews for boys to study all their lives and for girls to be raised by their mothers and to help in the house, so there was an expectation from my grandfather that I would attend these classes once I turned three. My Zaida was obviously hoping that I would fulfil the role that his own son had not. I can only assume that my secular parents felt some guilt or family obligation, because they agreed to let me attend these classes.

Therefore, at three years old, for five days a week, from 9am to 2pm, I took religious studies at my Zaida's house. When I first started going, I was so small that I couldn't see over my grandparent's kitchen table, and my Bubba had to put an upside-down pot on the floor for me to stand on. As would be true of any three-year-old, I wanted to be outside playing with my friends instead of sitting in a room listening to boring stories about God. But even at that age I understood how much it meant to Zaida that I was there, and how proud he was of me. I can still remember the way his crinkled, bearded face would light up when I walked through the door every morning. How he would point at me and bellow to whoever was in earshot, 'Look at my grandson!'

Of course, he was a smart man and knew I didn't want to be there. This is why, at the end of each day, he would give me a small bribe.

'Go buy yourself a chocolate ice cream,' he would whisper, pressing a few coins into my palm. 'But don't tell your Bubba!'

Bubba also knew how much I disliked these classes. When

she arrived to take me home in the afternoons, she'd wait until we were outside before pressing more money into my hand and whispering, 'Don't tell your Zaida!'

I was very happy with this arrangement and so never said a word to anyone. Even at three years old I knew that I was on to a good thing. Why would I jeopardise such a great deal and risk losing my stash of ice cream money?

It was the first time I learned the value of keeping my mouth shut for my own good.

Around the same time as I was beginning classes with my grandfather, my eldest sister, Maryla, got sick. My parents thought it was just a head cold at first, but the cold quickly turned into pneumonia, and soon after that she developed appendicitis. My sister had surgery to remove her appendix – a serious and dangerous operation in 1927 – and was then ordered to lie completely still for a long period afterwards. Soon after the operation, she fell into a coma and we were terrified she would never come out of it. Thirty days later she regained consciousness, but there was more bad news in store. My ten-year-old sister had lain in bed for so long that it had affected her spine and she was unable to walk.

My distraught mother took Maryla to a private Jewish hospital in Łódź to speak to the specialists there. They told her they couldn't help my sister but that there was a hospital in Vienna that specialised in spinal problems, and that she should take her there. My parents had a lot to organise before Mum could take Maryla to Vienna, including passports, finding the money to travel and organising accommodation. Once everything was arranged, Mum and Maryla boarded a train to Vienna. They left feeling hopeful that the doctors there would be able to help my sister, but on arrival they were told that the doctors there couldn't help my sister either.

My dejected mother and sister headed back to Poland, where my mother decided to try talking to the doctors at Poznaski hospital in Łódź once more. This time they met a surgeon who gave them the hope they had been longing to hear.

'Your daughter will walk out of this hospital by herself,' he told them.

And that is exactly what happened. Six years later.

Maryla was sixteen years old when she finally walked out of Poznanski hospital, having lost a significant part of her youth to this terrible illness. Even though I had visited Maryla with my parents as much as I could while she was in hospital, she was away for so long that my big sister felt like a stranger to me when she first came home. But it didn't take long before we were as close as we'd been before she left.

Through all the fear, worry and challenges my family faced during Maryla's illness, we never once prayed to ask for God's help. Despite everything my grandfather was trying to teach me in my religious studies, it was not the Goldberg way to ask God for help. Despite my grandfather's best efforts, I could not and did not believe in God, and by the time I turned six there weren't enough cash bribes or ice creams in the world to keep me interested in those religious classes.

One night, I told my parents that I had no interest in God or religion and didn't want to go to Zaida's for classes anymore.

They understood (how could they not when they felt the same way!) and so finally I was free. Of course, I missed the extra money and ice cream, but never once did I regret my decision to leave God behind. The only thing I felt bad about was disappointing my Zaida. When he passed away a few months later I missed him very much and felt grateful for the extra hours I had spent with him.

LESSON LEARNED

Sometimes the best thing you can do is to keep your mouth shut and your eyes open.

3

FIGHTING FIT

When Poland became independent after the First World War, it was made mandatory for all children aged seven and above to attend school. My parents enrolled Frajda, Estera and me in the Bund's privately run schools, where classes were taught in Yiddish, and my sisters both completed their schooling there. I, however, was only there for a couple of years. The financial burden of putting three children through private school was too much for my parents, so I was taken out and sent to the state primary school, where my lessons were all in Polish. But I continued to speak Yiddish at home with my family.

The Jewish kids at the state school were taught in a separate building to the Polish ones. Sometimes when classes were over for the day, some of the Polish kids, not happy about the 'dirty Jews' attending their school, would taunt and chase us Jewish kids. By that age, I had already endured my fair share of antisemitism. I'd had to pass the Polish school on my way to the Bund school for the couple of years I went there, so had heard these taunts before, but things got worse when I started going there. Most days I ended up in fights after school when these Polish hooligans shouted 'dirty Jew' and threw stones at me. But I always stood my ground and gave as good as I got, something my father taught me. From when we were very young, my father encouraged my sisters and I to be physically fit and strong, and to stand up for ourselves.

'Don't run away from your attackers,' he would tell me. 'Once you run you are gone because then they know you are afraid.'

'Okay, Dad,' I would say.

'They may be able to run faster than you,' he explained. 'Manoeuvre yourself so that you have a wall or something solid behind you so you can't be attacked from the rear. Ascertain who is the leader – usually the loudest – and attack him where it will really hurt, for instance the nose and eyes.'

Dad knew that Jewish Poles like my sisters and me needed to be able to defend ourselves in the antisemitic times we were living in. Threatening and dangerous encounters would always be a possibility for us, and his advice came in handy on more than one occasion throughout my childhood. One afternoon when I was walking home from school, a group of Polish boys started to chase me down the street. Remembering my father's words, I ran straight to a nearby wall and positioned my back against it, just as the boys advanced on me. They were much taller and bigger than me, but I went berserk, lashing out with my fists. I gave their leader a bloody nose and the others quickly jumped in, landing blows on my face and body, but I continued to defend myself as best I could. By the time they ran away, I was bruised and beaten,

The Strength of Hope

but proud that I had managed to stay upright.

Another time, our family went camping for the holidays. While we were there, a friend at the campsite told me someone had called him a 'dirty Jew'. He came to me, thinking I would be the boy most likely to do something about it. He was right. When my friend pointed the boy out to me, I saw that he was a full head taller than me. Undeterred, I walked straight up to him and told him to repeat what he had said to my friend.

The boy laughed in my face. 'I called him a dirty Jew!' He leaned down to pick up a rock, threw it straight at my head and split it open. It hurt a lot and I was dazed for a few moments, but the boy and his friends were still laughing when I launched myself at him. I could feel the blood trickling down my face, but it only gave me more incentive to give this boy a proper hiding. To the boy's surprise, I wrestled him to the ground and started pummelling him. People stood around, watching on in shock, but I didn't care. I knew that if we let this kid get away with calling us names, he wouldn't leave us alone for the whole holiday. Eventually the boy got up and ran away. He'd had enough of being humiliated by a tiny boy in front of a crowd. My friend and I didn't spot him again for the rest of the holiday.

I was nine when I started at the state school, and after a few weeks of fighting back, the bullies started to leave the tiny boy with his quickfire punches alone. Three other important things happened the year I turned nine: my sister came home from Poznanski hospital, I joined SKIF and a man named Hitler came to power in Germany.

Around this time I also joined the Morning Star Club, a

Jewish sports club in Łódź. It offered activities such as gymnastics, ping-pong, weightlifting, and soccer. I loved playing them all and made many good friends at the club, including a boy my age called Heniek Wajnberg and twins, Beniek and Heniek Dunkel. My mother did not want me doing these activities. She was worried I would suffer an injury and would have wrapped me in cotton wool if she could, but my father insisted I keep on with them.

I soon discovered that I had a natural talent for both gymnastics and ping-pong. Although I could barely see over the top of the table, I was placed in the Specialised Junior Ping-Pong Group and soon became the champion. I started winning gymnastics competitions too. Our coach was demanding and made us train thirty hours a week, which I see now was probably too much for a young boy, but I enjoyed every second of it and could feel my competitive streak growing stronger every week. One day I broke my left wrist during a gymnastics routine, but still went on to win a ping-pong competition that evening. My stubbornness, competitive nature and appetite for life would not let a bit of pain stop me from winning.

This stubbornness was on full display in 1936 when I was twelve years old. The Morning Star Club was holding its annual winter exhibition at the Łódź theatre, but on that day, I fell ill with a high temperature. My mother immediately packed me off to bed, ignoring my pleas to perform in the exhibition that night. My family had already purchased their tickets for the event and saw no need to miss out just because I wasn't performing, so they all headed out to the theatre that night, leaving me alone on my camp bed in the kitchen. The moment they were gone I leapt out of bed, pulled on my gymnastics outfit and – careful to avoid the same route as my family – ran the 5 kilometres to the theatre. I arrived just in time for the start of the exhibition, joining the rest of my class as they were making their way onto the stage.

You can imagine my parents' surprise when the curtains pulled back and they saw their 'sick' son jumping, flipping and vaulting his way across the stage. As soon as the exhibition was over, my furious mother dragged me out of there and marched me home, but when she checked my temperature, it was completely normal. She couldn't understand it!

I continued making a lot of friends at both SKIF and the sports club, including a boy named Abram Morgentaler, who we also called Mumek. Mumek was fit, strong and agile, and enjoyed being active like me, but unlike me, he had thick black hair and was tall. We had a lot of fun hanging out together during those years, both at the Morning Star Club and at SKIF. Between my commitment to these clubs and to school, this was a busy, but very enjoyable, time in my life. During the day, I would go to school, which finished at 2pm, and then walk home to do my homework. My father arrived home from work later that afternoon and we would all have dinner together as a family, before I would go out again to meet up with friends at SKIF, or at the sports club, depending on what night it was. Most evenings I wouldn't arrive home until after 10pm, when the gate to my building had been locked for the night. Instead of waking the caretaker, I would climb over the fence and quietly let myself into the apartment.

There, I would hungrily devour a plate of delicious food

that my mother had left out for me before going to bed.

One time, when the landlord was doing repairs on the exterior bricks of our building, the builders erected scaffolding around our block. I thought it would be fun to climb up that scaffolding, all the way to our flat on the third floor and enter through the window. I gave my poor mother the fright of her life when she saw my head suddenly appear outside the window, but she wasn't surprised. Mum knew that climbing, jumping, running and competing, both in and out of the sports club, were a big part of the boy I was.

My sisters attended the sports club too, but the boys' classes usually finished after the girls'. One night, our gymnastics class finished earlier than normal and, on our way home, a friend and I came across a group of Polish boys accosting my sisters. These hooligans didn't realise that my friend and I were walking just 50 metres behind my sisters and they got a big shock when we appeared out of nowhere and set upon them. My sisters watched and shouted with delight as the two of us beat those rude boys up for disrespecting and taunting them.

My active life had a big hand in building up my strength and endurance as a young man. This was good because life was about to get a whole lot tougher for all of us, although I couldn't possibly have imagined exactly what was to come, or how much my strength and endurance would be tested.

LESSON LEARNED

Being active is not only good for your fitness levels but can sometimes cure a fever too.

4

RISING TENSIONS

Meanwhile, as I went about my daily activities, life in Poland was becoming increasingly perilous. I had eavesdropped on many political conversations in my home over the years, so I was familiar with the word 'fascism' and understood its meaning. After Hitler came to power in 1933, I began noticing that discussions at SKIF meetings and at home were starting to revolve around Jewish people's rights, and the fact that they were being slowly but steadily stripped away. Being so young, I wasn't sure exactly how this was happening, but I knew my father and his friends in the Bund were trying to figure out how to help thousands of Jews who were being expelled from Germany.

By 1938 I noticed that these discussions, at home and at SKIF, were becoming more tense. There was a lot of talk about our right-wing government in Poland, and how antisemitism was on the rise. Things in Poland became worse just before the May Day marches on 1 May, when the government decreed that the Bund must march separately from the Socialist Party. Apparently, the authorities were warning parents to keep their children off the streets because there could be attacks from right-wing antisemites.

It was starting to dawn on me that not many other kids my age were exposed to these kinds of discussions at home. My political knowledge and insights made me different to lots of other kids in Łódź. Many children and teenagers at my school and in my neighbourhood weren't politically aware, or interested in such discussions. Another difference between the Goldbergs and other Jewish families around us was that we were politically, not religiously, motivated.

I knew that antisemitism was getting worse, and that things were starting to escalate, but felt safe in my little corner of the world. I had my family and friends around me, and although a small part of me feared for our future as a people, I felt sure Hitler's evil tentacles couldn't reach across the Polish border and into my haven of Łódź. When Hitler came to power in 1933 we knew that it wouldn't be good for Jews, but how could we possibly have imagined how truly terrible things would become?

We could feel the culture around us beginning to shift at the beginning of 1939. I heard my parents and their Bund friends talking about how difficult it was becoming for Jews to get work in Łódź. Very few factories would employ them, even those owned by Jews themselves, and ethnic tensions were brewing because most factory workers were Poles. Its manufacturing base made Łódź one of the fastest growing cities in Europe, and the Jewish factory owners didn't want trouble, which meant employing less Jews in their workplaces. I know the Bund fought against this without much success, but thanks to my father's connections in the Union, my sisters Frajda and Estera both managed to get jobs in the textile industry.

When I finished my primary school education in June 1939, I knew that I wanted to learn a trade when summer was over, rather than attend secondary school. Even if the war had not come along, it was becoming more difficult for Jews to even attend the state-run high schools. My sisters had encountered the same problem a few years earlier, which was why our parents sent them to the Yiddish secondary school.

But any thoughts of learning a trade were forgotten by the end of August. By then, the whole world could see that Poland was on the verge of war with Germany. That month, the Polish government called for volunteers to dig trenches and my father and I volunteered, along with tens of thousands of other Łódź residents. I was a strong, healthy fifteen-year-old and I wanted to follow my father's example and do anything I could to help protect our community should we be bombed.

Hitler invaded Poland on 1 September 1939. The air raid sirens started at around 5am, and shortly afterwards, bombs fell on the Łódź railway line and train station. The Germans did not bomb any civilian areas in Łódź, because of our large ethnic German population. In fact, Łódź was the least bombed major Polish city during the war, because the manufacturing sector was important to the Germans.

We were all fast asleep when the first bombs fell on the railway lines, 4 kilometres away from our flat. The sound of the bombs didn't wake us, and it wasn't until later that morning that we, and many others in Łódź, heard the news of what had happened.

Word began to spread and people on the streets started to panic. Not many people had radios, but the ones who did told everyone that the Germans were taking over the radio waves, while those who lived near the railway lines knew about the bombing that morning.

On every street corner that day you could hear the words, 'War is coming!' and people all over Łódź were having panicked discussions about what they should do. Withdraw money from their bank accounts? Pack up their possessions and get out of Łódź?

In the Goldberg house, our parents' decision was clear. We would stay. My father felt certain the Polish army would be able to resist and hold the Germans off. But over the next couple of days, returning refugees spread the news that the Polish army had been no match for the Germans, and that Warsaw had been bombed. We were shocked at how quickly our army had been defeated, but soon learned why.

Poland had a vastly inferior army, with an almost non-existent air force and only horse-drawn heavy artillery. Even the Poles' canons were pulled by horses and were no match for the German's panzers (tanks) and dive-bomber aircrafts. Although Poland had a standing army of one million soldiers, cavalry pitted against tanks and planes does not work. The Germans were so much more advanced than us, and we were completely blindsided.

The Nazis had refined the *Blitzkrieg* (Lightning War) military tactic. Through speed, superior equipment and warfare, as well as the element of surprise, the Germans created psychological shock and mass disorganisation in their enemies, and it was an easily won invasion. Even so, we were amazed by the speed at which it took place.

I had grown up believing in the Polish army, and always assumed they would protect us and keep us safe. Of course, I'd had no idea what our primitive army, with its people and horses, was up against. They had no chance of keeping the Germans out of Łódź, or anywhere else in Poland for that matter, and our army never stood a chance. To know that we had been so easily defeated was a devastating blow.

With this new information, we had another family discussion about whether we should now leave Łódź. But there was nowhere for us to go. Many men in Łódź had already fled to Eastern Poland, including my uncle, leaving their families behind, but Dad refused to do that. He would never leave us, and he had many friends in the underground who could help us get provisions if we needed them, so we decided to stay put.

The week from 1 September to 8 September was pure chaos. We heard that Britain and France had declared war on Germany, so at least we knew we were not alone, but there was a lot of fear, and no one knew what was going to happen. Many people started to leave Łódź, and on 6 September there were departures en masse. People were packing up their homes, and there was a flurry of activity on the streets, with hundreds carrying large bundles back and forth.

I saw many people crying in the streets that week, and parents having hushed, fearful conversations with each other, careful not to let their young children hear what they were saying. Rumours of the Germans sending the Jews to camps were rife, but no one knew anything for sure. All we did know was that whatever was coming would not be good. By that point our city had been abandoned by the police, so we had no choice but to wait for the Germans' inevitable arrival. A lot of people with relatives in smaller towns travelled to those places, and many decided to move to east Poland.

Every day there were more reports on the radio of the Germans coming closer and closer to Łódź with every passing hour. Then, seven days after the first bombs fell, the Germans marched into our town with their swastika armbands on full display. Łódź was officially under Nazi occupation, and my life had changed forever.

People started to panic straight away, grabbing whatever belongings they could carry and fleeing town on foot. But the German Stukas (dive-bomber planes) flew low over these runaways, spraying them with bullets. People had to dive into ditches and ravines, and hide behind trees to avoid the gunfire, but many were killed. These were the first of Łódź's citizens to be attacked and murdered by the Nazis.

In our newly occupied town, antisemitic laws were applied to Jewish people almost immediately. The Nazis walked the streets in pairs, alsatians at their feet and machine guns in their hands, plastering posters on our city's walls with proclamations regarding the new laws. We would be forced to wear yellow armbands and a curfew was in place from 6pm. Anyone caught outside after curfew would be shot. Jews were ordered to hand in cameras and radios, and signs reading *Juden nicht zugänglich* (no

Jews allowed) went up on shops and buildings all through town. Some even read *No Jews or Dogs*. The Poles too had to give up their radios, because the Nazis intended to cut off our entire city from any news about the war and how it was progressing.

Throughout all of this, my sisters and I took our cues from Mum and Dad, who remained calm. I'm sure our parents were more concerned than they let on, but they never showed fear in front of us. At home, my mother tried to keep things as normal as possible for us and Dad was his usual positive self. Frajda and Estera were nineteen and seventeen by then, and they too seemed mostly calm around me. Looking back now, I'm sure they were all doing their best to stay level-headed for my benefit. My sisters knew I could take care of myself and never sheltered me from the truth, but at fifteen years old, I was still the baby of the family. I'm sure my family tried their hardest to put on a brave face when I was around.

Ninety per cent of the ethnic Germans living in Łódź became Nazis overnight. Suddenly they were all wearing swastikas – the Nazi *Hakenkreuz* symbol – and every boy my age had joined the Hitler Youth and was going around attacking Jews on the streets.

The Nazis paraded through the streets two days after occupying Łódź, and I'll never forget the sound of their marching boots, or the cheering from the ethnic Germans lining the footpaths. As they made their way along Zgierska Ulica, they started shouting for everyone inside the buildings there to come out. My mother and sisters were terrified, but Dad told them to stay inside while he and I went out to see what they wanted.

When we got down to the street, many of our confused

neighbours were standing out there too, and we watched as the Nazis started pointing at people, selecting them for what job we did not know. When they pointed at Dad and me, we stepped forward. I wasn't scared but felt worried. What did they want? What were they going to do with us?

It was the Jewish police who gave us our instructions. We would soon learn that this would be the only way anything was ever communicated to us. In all the years they occupied Łódź, the Nazis never once addressed any of us Jews directly or spoke to us. All communication was done through the Jewish police, and it was these Jews who now informed us that we would be filling in the trenches around Łódź – the same ones my father and I had dug less than two weeks earlier. We weren't given shovels, or any other digging tools, so had to use our hands to fill in the deep ditches. The humiliation and degradation of all Jews was significant from day one.

I understood straight away that the Nazis were a different breed of bully to the schoolyard hooligans I'd dealt with in the past. I would never be able to stand up to these bullies in the same way. I would have to ignore my instinct to fight with my fists, and instead stay quiet and back down if confronted or attacked. In time I would learn that the only way to fight the Nazis was to survive, and to give those around me hope, but that realisation was a long way off in September 1939.

The Orthodox Jews were taunted and beaten as they filled in the ditches. The Nazis cut off their beards, as well as pieces of flesh, as they dug, humiliating them purely for their own amusement. I could see that it was taking every ounce of my dad's willpower not to lash out at the Nazis and help those poor men that day. Many of the Orthodox Jews in that street were murdered during this time, and those who survived returned home black and blue from the beatings they received. I managed to avoid being beaten over those first few days of digging, and apart from my cut and bleeding hands, I came through unscathed. It was the first time I would be lucky enough to avoid injury or death, but certainly not the last.

Further laws quickly came into effect. Jews could no longer attend school or work, and Jewish homeowners, particularly in the better parts of Łódź, were forcibly removed from their houses so they could be given to ethnic German citizens. We could no longer go to just any shop and buy what we needed either. We were only permitted to enter Jewish shops, but there were many Jewish bakeries and food shops in Łódź, and no one was thinking about buying clothing or expensive goods at that point anyway. We just wanted to know that we wouldn't run out of food. It was only later when Germans put restrictions on deliveries to these shops that supply was limited, and bakeries began to run out of flour and other ingredients. That's when everything became much more difficult. Thankfully we were never short of food in those early days because my father had his connections at the Bund and they looked after us.

The Germans viewed the long queues outside Jewish shops and bakeries as the perfect opportunity to target and attack Jewish people, usually the most obviously religious – the Orthodox Jews. They were more easily identifiable as Jews so it was harder for them to get supplies and go under the radar, unlike us, so Dad helped them. He was able to buy and deliver essentials to the Orthodox Jews in our building so they wouldn't have to risk their lives when they went out to the shops.

One day, soon after occupation, my father and I were walking down the street when we saw two members of the Hitler Youth attacking a couple of Orthodox Jews in the street. Without thinking, we immediately went to their aid and gave the two young Nazis a beating. The frightened boys ran away, and it was only afterwards that my father and I realised what a stupid thing we had done. We hadn't given it a second thought – we saw what was happening and couldn't stop ourselves from jumping in – but we quickly realised that the consequences could be severe.

We hurried home and didn't show our faces on the streets for a few days afterwards.

5

DEPORTED

The Goldberg family had reason to celebrate in November 1939 when Maryla married a man named Jacob (Jakub) Liwszyc. Jacob had been called up to the army when the Nazis invaded Poland in September, but once his unit was dispersed, he came to Łódź to be with his fiancée.

Despite my Bundist parents' objections, Maryla had become an active member of the Communist Party, and, like so many others already had, she and Jacob planned to escape to the Soviet Union. Many Jewish people believed they would be safer in the Soviet Union than in Łódź. They saw the Nazis as a much bigger threat to their safety than the Russians. Polish people had no fear of the Russians, and many were prepared to do anything they could to get away from Nazi-occupied Poland. But my parents wouldn't let Maryla leave Poland until she was first married, and Maryla agreed to their request.

Maryla's new husband, Jacob, had a brother, Aleksander Ford (born Mosze Lifszyc), who was a film producer in Poland, and had moved to the Russian-controlled east side of Poland when war broke out. It was he who arranged to smuggle Maryla and Jacob there after their quick wedding ceremony in Łódź. My parents were relieved to know that at least one of their children would be safe, far from the Nazis.

None of us resented Maryla and Jacob for leaving Łódź. We were happy for them to be getting out. It was hard for my mother to let her daughter go, but she understood that Maryla was a married woman and had to start her own life with her own family now.

Many young men and fathers had left Łódź for Russian-occupied Poland during this period, but a lot of them were starting to return, having arrived to discover that there was no accommodation or work for them there. Also, the Russians didn't want them. The communists hated the Bund because it was a socialist organisation and didn't toe the Bolshevik line.

Mum missed her eldest daughter but was comforted by the thought that we would soon join her in Russia. My father began making plans for the five of us to follow Maryla to Russia, but then people started coming back with stories of Bund members being arrested and killed.

'Do not go, Herszl,' these friends told my father. 'There are Jewish communists asking about you. They know you are a member of the Bund, and you will not be safe.'

This, combined with the fact that we did not know where Maryla and Jacob were living, and would have no place to live, was enough for my parents to decide that we should stay in Łódź.

In November 1939, the Germans destroyed the biggest synagogue in Łódź. They initially tried to burn it down, but it was too well-built, so they blew it up instead. Luckily the rabbis were able to smuggle out the holy scrolls before any of this occurred. I was very glad to hear this. We may not have been religious ourselves, but it made us so angry to see how the Nazis loved humiliating religious Jews. Every day for those first few weeks of the occupation, I would see these evil men beating them and cutting off their beards and *payot* (sideburns) in the middle of the street for everyone to see.

Even scarier was the first public execution, which happened on 11 November and took place in the square. Three people hung from ropes with placards around their necks that read *Bandit*. Dad was the only one from our family who saw the actual hanging take place, and when he came home that day I overheard him telling Mum about it in a low, distressed voice. Those poor people were left hanging for five days. I never knew the reason they were killed. Maybe they were just in the wrong place at the wrong time, or maybe the Nazis branded them 'bandits' because they believed they had broken the law. Either way, it was clear to everyone that anyone who opposed Nazis or broke the rules would meet the same fate.

Our house was around 150 metres away from this square, and when I was out one day I saw the bodies hanging there. It was a shocking sight and one I have never forgotten to this day. From that moment on we understood the brutality of the Nazis and realised there was no way out. It was clear to us that we would have to accept this new way of life and do everything we could to protect ourselves and our families.

But things took a turn for the worse at midnight on 10 December 1939. My family was asleep when we heard loud yelling and thumping coming from down on the street. The Germans had surrounded our 99-per-cent-Jewish neighbourhood and were going from door to door, waking everyone up. I heard their boots marching down the corridor outside our flat, as they banged on all the doors, and suddenly it was our door they were banging on.

My mother ran to open the door and found a large man in an SS uniform standing there. My father quickly ran up to stand beside her.

'YOU HAVE TWENTY-FIVE MINUTES!' he yelled at my poor frightened mother. 'TAKE WHATEVER YOU CAN CARRY AND BE DOWNSTAIRS IN TWENTY-FIVE MINUTES!'

Then he was gone, moving on to the next door to give the same orders.

We were all rattled by the late-night intrusion and orders, but with only twenty-five minutes and the clock ticking, we didn't have time to think. The five of us instantly grabbed and packed up whatever we could between us, mainly food and clothing. Money was not a priority. We didn't have much anyway, and being winter it was more important to take warm clothes and as much food as we could fit into bags. None of us cried during this. Maybe this was because we were in a state of shock, or maybe because we had been living under German rule for a few months at that point and knew there would be no point crying or carrying on. We just had to do as we were told and hope we could all stay together and be safe. I will never forget the sight of those soldiers outside our door, rifles at the ready, while the five of us gathered our belongings.

Twenty minutes later we walked down to the cobblestone

yard to join the rest of our bleary-eyed, scared and confused neighbours. None of us dared speak to or ask any questions of the Nazis who were standing guard and watching us so closely. Once we were all gathered, the soldiers began to march us down the street and onto the trams. Our block of flats was on the main thoroughfare and the tram line ran right outside our building, so we didn't have far to go. We were packed into the tram like sardines, and my father and mother pulled my sisters and me close to them. We travelled for around fifteen minutes to Radogoszcz – an industrial area in Łódź – where we could see that the Germans had erected a makeshift camp. Getting off the tram, we realised there were Poles in this place as well as Jews – I would later find out that this was the first concentration camp ever to be built in Poland.

All of us were herded into a large open area with no facilities, just holes dug in rows on the ground. We assumed these were toilets. Unfortunately, we were right. Soon after this we were directed into large empty warehouses and factories, where we all sat down to wait in the freezing cold for whatever was to come next. The five of us wrapped our arms around each other to keep ourselves warm and for some small comfort. We were all worried and confused.

What are they going to do with us? Where are they going to send us?

Mum and my sisters were putting on brave faces, maybe because they didn't want me to worry, but I knew them well enough to know that they were feeling as anxious as I was. There was fear too, of course, but mostly confusion because none of us understood what was happening.

We were kept in this place for around five days, along with thousands of other Jews and Poles. During that time, we learned to watch everything we did or said because people were being arrested and interrogated. My good friend Mumek's father was arrested for being a Bundist and a doctor – he was the head of a Jewish hospital for kids in Radogoszcz – and ended up being tortured. As a Bundist family ourselves, this was very worrying and upsetting, and so we kept our heads down and waited for whatever was to come next. We had no choice. The Germans were armed and had zero tolerance for unruly Jews. I think my parents felt relieved that none of our other relatives were rounded up and brought to this place when we were. They lived in a different area of Łódź to us and had escaped this incarceration.

After five long days, trains with cattle cars attached pulled up outside the camp area at Radogoszcz. We were once again rounded up and loaded onto the cars. These were goods trains, not passenger trains, so there were no benches or seats inside, just one bucket in the corner to relieve yourself in and another bucket full of water to wash with or drink from. They packed us in so tightly that there was no possibility of lying or sitting down. We didn't know where we were going but we travelled in this uncomfortable way for at least four days.

The five of us were small, which made it hard for us to get as much air as others, and the stench of excrement, sweat, vomit and urine was terrible. After a while it was hard to keep track of days and nights. We had no sense of time, locked in a dark carriage, squashed up against so many others. Most of the time we were silent, but many around us cried, especially the young children. I think we were all in shock at how quickly everything was happening. Our brains hadn't had time to process the appalling conditions and unbelievable situation we had found ourselves in. All we could do was comfort one another in whatever way we could and stay strong for each other. At least the five of us were together. That was the most important thing. Over those days and nights on the train, my mother would often squeeze our hands, or try to put her arm around us if she could, and sometimes she even smiled reassuringly at me.

'*Altz vaet zayn goot*,' my father whispered to us. (Everything will be okay.)

After the war I would learn that we were part of approximately 10,000 Jews deported from Łódź that day. Half were sent to Lublin and the other half to Krakow. We were on our way to Krakow; those sent to Lublin were subsequently murdered.

After this long, horrible train journey, we felt the train slowing until it eventually came to a stop. The doors were pulled open and we all took a deep breath, grateful for the fresh air. The guards began shouting at us to get out, so we piled out of the putrid, stale carriage, only to discover that they had taken us from one makeshift camp to another.

But we noticed one big difference as we walked into the camp. Unlike Radogoszcz, this camp was unguarded. It was still the early days of the war and the Germans were not as organised as they soon would be, so a few hours after arriving, we, and many others, walked out of the camp and into the city of Krakow. My father's objective was for us to find some Bundist friends to stay with while we figured out what to do. Thousands of Poles and Jews had been displaced and were also making their way into Krakow, hoping to find a haven. There were many people walking around on the streets, including those, like us, who had escaped from the camp.

Dad headed straight to the Jewish Council in Krakow and asked for the address of Max Alexanderovitch – a medical doctor and officer in the Polish army who was also a Bund leader. They gave Dad Max's address, but when we got to his house, his wife said he had been called away for army duty. She told my parents that I could stay with her and her children, a boy of eleven and a girl of nine, and Mum and Dad gratefully accepted her kind offer. Mum and Dad soon found another kind Jewish family – furriers – who offered to house my two sisters. Now it was just my parents who needed accommodation, and the Bund soon helped them find some.

Over the next five weeks, we stayed with our respective families in Krakow. The city was still under the general government's rule then, as opposed to Łódź, which was under the rule of the Third Reich. This meant that, although Jews were still being persecuted in Krakow and life for us was still restrictive, it was easier for us to get around because there weren't as many guards on the streets at that point.

Our family may have been living in separate houses, but we still saw each other most days and frequently had meals together. The Alexanderovitch family lived opposite Krakow's Wawel Castle, and the kids and I spent hours sliding on the frozen river that ran alongside the castle. Much later, the German governor used the castle as his headquarters for the duration of the war.

Eventually my parents decided we shouldn't be a burden on our hosts for any longer and started to think about where we could go next. If we stayed in Krakow, who knew how long it would be before we were all rounded up again and sent somewhere else? But we knew we couldn't go to Russian-occupied Poland either after what we'd heard, so there was no choice for us but to head back home to Łódź. The problem was we had no money and no papers, and it was illegal for Jews to travel on public transport, and even if we did travel illegally, a family of five would be very conspicuous on a train. My father also felt it was a dangerous time for two teenage girls to be out on the road. So, what to do?

Eventually my parents decided that they would leave my sisters safely in Krakow with their host family, while they and I travelled back to Łódź. The Bund would help us.

'It will be less dangerous for us to move around as a party of three,' Dad told my sisters. 'We will go ahead first and then, when everything is back to normal, I will come back to Krakow for you both.'

Estera and Frajda did not want to see us go but agreed this was the best plan. They felt safe with their host family and in Krakow. They had each other too, which was a comfort to them both.

The issue now was the logistics of the journey itself. Łódź was 260 kilometres away and Jews were forbidden to use public transport. Our Star of David armbands made us instantly recognisable. If we were caught without them, or on public transport, we would be arrested. But the Bund had close ties with the Polish Socialist Party (PPS) and so made all the travel arrangements for us. To begin with, Mum, Dad and I would all remove our armbands so we could travel by train in the dark of night, and local PPS Poles would buy our tickets. The train would take us to a station 30 kilometres from Krakow, and there we would begin the next leg of our long, dangerous journey home.

Some people might wonder how a fifteen-year-old boy was coping in the middle of such upheaval, fear and uncertainty. Was I scared? Panicked? Upset? The truth is, I was none of these things. Maybe I was simply too naive or ignorant not to be more distressed, but I was with my parents and that calmed me. They were the two people I trusted most in the world, and while I was with them I felt safe.

As we prepared to leave Krakow, I desperately wanted to ask my father what our travel plans were, but knew better than to ask such questions. I was confident my parents had everything under control and knew I should trust them. My sisters too felt that our parents believed they were doing the best thing for them. So in January 1940 we hugged Estera and Frajda goodbye, and I remember silent tears falling down my sisters' and mother's faces as they held each other. It was a very sad and emotional day for all of us, but we felt confident Dad would return for my sisters soon and that our family would all be together again. As we walked to Krakow station, the three of us removed our armbands before boarding the train.

'I'll tell you when it's time to get off,' my father whispered to me as we took our seats on the packed train. 'Until then, you must pretend to be asleep for the whole journey.'

I nodded, leaned my head against the window and closed my

eyes. My parents did the same. The lights in the carriages were off to save electricity so it was very dark. My father knew that if we were asleep, no one would talk to us or pay us much attention. We didn't want anyone looking too closely and guessing we were three Jews travelling illegally on public transport. Around 30 kilometres out of Krakow, the train started to slow.

'We will be getting off soon,' my father whispered in my ear.

The train reached the station and came to a stop, so we got off and walked down the platform. Here, Dad used a pre-arranged signal to let the waiting PPS members know that we had arrived, but I had no idea about any of this at the time, of course. It wasn't until much later that Dad told me about the secret signal and explained who the people waiting to meet us had been. The PPS members led us out of the station and to a nearby village where we spent the rest of the day hiding in a stable that belonged to a family we would never meet. I had been too full of nerves and excitement to sleep on the train so was very tired by the time we got there. My parents and I curled up together and fell asleep on piles of hay, the smell of horse manure all around us, until late that afternoon.

As darkness fell, a few more PPS members arrived to pick us up in a horse-drawn sled. The three of us climbed on and we set off through the night, travelling along back and side roads where no German patrols would stop us. Polish nights in winter were long and cold, and the thick snow slowed us down, but just before daybreak we arrived at another small village. There, we were taken to yet another stable to hide out for the day. This became our routine over the next couple of weeks. Travelling on horse-drawn sleds under the cover of darkness at night and sleeping in stables and barns during the day. We were lucky that these kind Poles, all of whom we would never meet, had agreed to help keep us safe on our travels. When there were only around 30 or 40 kilometres left of our journey, my father thanked the PPS members for their generous assistance and told them we could make our own way back from there now. Dad didn't want these people to endanger their lives any more than they already had. It was early February 1940, after many days and nights of travelling, when the three of us found ourselves on the road that led directly into Łódź.

Not once throughout the journey had I asked my father how much longer we had to go, or where we were on any given day. Kids didn't ask their parents those sorts of questions in those days. But as we approached the outskirts of Łódź, and I saw Radogoszcz station in the distance, I finally asked why he hadn't shared any travel details with me.

'It would have been too dangerous,' he told me. 'If we had been caught and tortured and you knew the names and places of people in the underground, they could have forced the information out of you.'

'I understand,' I said.

I was so relieved and happy that our travels were over and that we had almost made it home, but my happiness was to be short-lived. As we approached the city outskirts, we couldn't know that the Germans had spent the past few weeks turning our home into a ghetto and that, soon after we arrived, we would all be locked behind a barbed-wire fence for the next four years.

6

HOME AS A GHETTO

My parents and I were shocked to see the construction of the barbed-wire fence going up around the poorest section of Łódź, including our own street, when we arrived back. In December 1939, unbeknownst to us, the Germans had planned a closed ghetto in Łódź. The ghetto was 3.6 kilometres squared and encompassed the Old Town and Bałuty, slums that housed many poor Poles and 60,000 Jews, including the Goldbergs. In this part of Łódź, the streets were unpaved, narrow and full of rat-infested rubbish piles. Raw sewerage ran down the streets and many of the buildings had leaking roofs and water dripping down their dilapidated walls.

The ghetto, it had been decided, would be maintained on a simple barter principle: food and fuel would be delivered there in exchange for textiles and valuables. The only way the inhabitants of the ghetto would be able to travel around would be by the footbridges that spanned over the walled streets. The main connection to the outside world was a goods-loading platform along a railway line located just east of the ghetto in

The Strength of Hope

Radogoszcz, near the station.

As we tried to comprehend what we were seeing, the three of us headed straight to our home, where another unpleasant surprise awaited us.

Strangers were residing in our flat.

While we had been away, the Germans had begun moving all Jews outside the perimeter of the new ghetto inside. These relocated Jews were forced to settle their families in any empty flats and rooms they could find, and many families were forced to cohabit with each other. We weren't the only ones in this situation. A lot of other people returning from Krakow or eastern Poland were coming back to find people in their homes, but none of the people were any of those who had been deported along with us. When we'd been sent away back in December, it had been an indiscriminate sweep. I had recognised quite a few people from my neighbourhood on the train to Krakow, but, as far as I knew, we were the only ones from that particular deportation who ended up returning. It seemed that everyone had gone their own ways after arriving at the camp, and I would never see those Łódź friends and acquaintances again.

It was upsetting to find strangers in our home, of course, but especially for my mother. The home she had so lovingly created and filled with love and delicious food for her family, the home she had kept so clean and tidy, was no longer ours. My father remained positive it would be okay.

'We will be fine,' he assured us. 'I will find us somewhere to live and get our furniture back, I promise.'

My mother's sister and her six young children had not been

sent to Krakow with us. They lived in a different area and had not been deported that night in December, so were still in Łódź when we returned. Mum and I stayed with them while Dad went to speak to his friends on the Jewish Council to see if we could get our flat back. But despite his connections, my father was powerless to remove these strangers from our home. However, the council gave him a map showing which buildings in the ghetto still had empty rooms and, within a few days, we were assigned a small flat in a two-storey weatherboard building on Mianowskiego Street.

The building housed six flats in total and ours was on the second floor. It was one of the few buildings in the ghetto with a garden, surrounded by a high wooden fence, but best of all, my aunt and six cousins lived just 30 metres away in a small weatherboard house. Their place was on the other side of a cobblestone area, with a communal water pump in the centre, at the end of our fenced garden. My mother was happy to have her sister so close, and vice versa, especially because my aunt's husband had fled to Russia at the beginning of the war with many other Łódź men.

Our new flat was completely empty, other than a small stove in the corner, so our next priority was getting some furniture. Dad said it would take a few days to organise, so in the meantime, the three of us slept on the floor and borrowed what we could from friends and relatives.

A few days later, I gathered some of my friends together and, along with my father, we headed over to our old flat to try and retrieve some of our old furniture. In the end we negotiated with the new residents of our old home and managed to retrieve our sofa bed, a small wardrobe, our credenza, pots, pans, and utensils. We loaded these onto a large cart and pushed it up the street to our new home, satisfied that we now had all that we needed.

We were very lucky to have one large room between just three of us. Many families in the ghetto were forced to share one room with one or two other families. Sometimes there could be up to fifteen people living in just one or two rooms.

The moment we were settled in Mianowskiego Street, my father and other members of the Bund began working to coordinate numerous resistance and relief efforts in the ghetto. One of the first things Dad did was arrange for another displaced family to move into the empty room next to ours. The Wieners were Bundists too, and our families had been friends before the war. They were also fortunate that only four of them would be sharing the flat. Bono Wiener, who was five years older than me, his parents and Aunty Klara. Bono's older brother, Pinche, spent much of the war in a Soviet labour camp.

We had returned to Łódź with a plan to find out where Maryla and Jacob were staying in eastern Poland, so the five of us could possibly join them there when it was safe to do so. But apart from it still being very dangerous for Bundists, others told my father that the conditions in the east were atrocious: it was terribly overcrowded with overflowing schools and synagogues and no food, work or available accommodation.

'The communists are now arresting and shooting Bundists like you,' they told him. 'Two Bund leaders, Victor Alter and

Henryk Ehrlich, were arrested on the Russian side and have been sentenced to death.'

This news was enough to convince my father that we should stay. At least we knew Maryla was a communist, not a Bundist, and Dad thought it would be safer to stay in the German-occupied territory of Łódź than to head east and contend with the worsening and dangerous conditions there. At that early stage of the war, we were still naive enough to believe that staying in the ghetto with the Nazis was a better and safer option than falling into the hands of the communists.

As we were setting up our new home, thousands more Jews outside the boundaries of the ghetto were being ordered out of their homes and forced inside. Every day people pushed large carts up and down our street, making several trips back and forth to transport all their personal items from their old place to the new one. Of course, many did not want to leave the nicer parts of Łódź to relocate to the filthy, smelly streets of the ghetto, so they dragged out the moving process. But by 9 March the Germans had had enough, and this is when they stepped up their brutal efficiency.

Nazi soldiers forced themselves into people's houses, shouting that people had fifteen minutes to grab whatever they could carry and move inside the ghetto. Many were beaten or shot when they didn't move fast enough. The Kripo (short for *Kriminalpolizei*, the German Criminal Police) joined the Nazis in terrorising the people of Łódź. They had set up their headquarters in a red brick building, which we would eventually call the Red House, in the middle of town and opposite the large church.

That day, waves of people came down the street, pushing overflowing carts or carrying large bundles on their backs. Thousands of Jews, many weeping, rushed through the gates of the ghetto – old, young, tall, short, men, women, children, the elderly and the sick. Many of them struggled under the weight of their belongings and some carried virtually nothing, having been forced out with no time to grab a thing. This day became known as the 'Bloody March' and was a sign of the terrible things to come.

In April, the Łódź Ghetto was completely fenced off from the rest of the city, and on 1 May, the gates were closed, and we were officially cut off from the outside world.

Back on 13 October, the Germans had ordered the creation of a *Judenrat* (Jewish Council) to enforce German policies in the Jewish community of Łódź. In the weeks before construction of the ghetto began, they had called for all members of the Judenrat to assemble. Most members fled, fearing for their lives, but some stayed to present themselves, including a man named Mordechai Chaim Rumkowski.

This sixty-two-year-old failed industrialist was the oldest member of the Zionist Council. Before the war he had been director of the Łódź orphanage and was under suspicion of child molestation. Jewish elders in the community had begun looking into the matter, but once the war began the whole investigation went away.

The Nazis didn't want to bother themselves with the day-to-day running of the ghetto, so Rumkowski was appointed head of the ghetto's Jewish Council, which meant that he oversaw the implementation of all decrees coming from Germany. The only thing he was not approved to do was order a death sentence, but in every other area Rumkowski was given absolute power.

Rumkowski knew that the inhabitants of the Łódź Ghetto faced certain catastrophe once they were cut off from the world. Therefore, he tried to convince the Germans to exploit the considerable labour potential of the many skilled craftsmen of Łódź before it was sealed off with walls and barbed-wire fences in April. The Germans needed uniforms and other leather equipment, Rumkowski pointed out, and the many textile and leather workers in the ghetto could help suppliers keep up with demand. The Germans agreed.

It is true to say that no one can blame Rumkowski for what the Germans made him do in the beginning, but unfortunately it didn't take long for the power to go to his head. He appointed his cronies to the Council to cement his authority, and was eventually quoted as saying, 'Sometimes a dictatorship is the right thing to do'.

Rumkowski did indeed become something of a dictator as the weeks, months and years went on. One of his first orders was to produce a list of thirty names of former council members and political activists in the Łódź community. Twenty-seven of those people on the list were subsequently murdered by the Germans.

The Germans quickly figured out the potential of the many Jewish workers who were tailors, carpenters, metal workers, textile workers and cobblers in Łódź. They started to establish more and more factories in the ghetto, metal factories, carpet and furniture factories and shoe factories. Instead of bombing

The Strength of Hope

and destroying our city, they cut us off from the rest of Poland so they could create their own urban slave camp.

Although we were now living in a fenced-off barbed-wire prison, and had no freedom to leave, life returned to a strange kind of normality for a period. In those early days of the ghetto, people were still playing cards outdoors, kids still played on the streets and a couple of football teams even organised some games. I didn't play football and was unable to go to gymnastics because we no longer had access to our facilities, but I did play some ping-pong until I had to be home before curfew.

By the middle of 1940, hunger was widespread. A lot of people did not, or could not, work and were living on minimal rations. We were one of the lucky families, right from the beginning, because my parents had work at a time when many people didn't. Mum worked in a factory kitchen, peeling potatoes, and my father, again through his connections, was made responsible for looking after three buildings and received a small wage for this work. With both my parents working, we had enough money to purchase our rations. There were many others who were not so lucky.

There was initially some food smuggling that went on in the ghetto, but it was short lived. Both the Poles who were smuggling the food in and the Jews receiving the goods were shot if caught, and after a while no one was willing to take the risk. As hunger took hold in the ghetto, the people who suffered most were those women and children who had been left on their own. Women whose husbands were away, either because they were in the Polish army, or because they had fled with the retreating Polish army like my uncle had. Luckily for my aunt and cousins, they had my parents helping them out, but many other women struggled to feed their children and themselves.

The constant gnawing hunger that was to come hadn't yet settled in our bellies, so people in the ghetto still had strength at that time. We worked, came home and spent time with our loved ones, but of course we felt demoralised and were in a constant state of unease. My old life seemed like a dream, and I wondered if I would ever play in a ping-pong competition or do gymnastics with my friends again.

The poor conditions of the ghetto added to our despondency. Our area of Łódź was poverty-stricken and run down even before the war, but now that it was an overcrowded ghetto conditions became even more deplorable. It was always cold, both indoors and outside. There was no escaping it. It was the kind of cold that gets into your bones and no matter what you did it was impossible to get warm. We had no bath or shower in our room, so had to go down to the water pump with a bucket, collect water, bring it inside and heat it up on the stove so we could sponge ourselves down. This was much easier to do in summer of course, but very hard in winter when it was icy cold both inside and out. Lice were rampant in the ghetto as well, but my mother kept our place very clean so thankfully it was rarely a problem for us.

Every day was the same, and every night was long. We had not yet fully comprehended the evil of the Nazis in 1940 and many people took risks, desperate to find ways to survive and feed their families. They would steal food, sneak out after curfew, or try to escape over the barbed-wire fence, but these people were inevitably caught and the consequences were severe. The gate and walls were guarded by sentries who often would just aim and shoot at people to amuse themselves. Unlike other ghettos, it was almost impossible to escape, which is why it was called the 'hermetically sealed' ghetto. The very few who did manage to get over the barbed wire were usually caught.

I personally knew just one person who attempted to escape, a seventeen-year-old boy who lived across the hall from us. It was very challenging to get false documentation in the ghetto, but the boy looked more Aryan than Jewish with his blonde hair so decided to try his luck and see if he could pass as a German, non-Jew out in the world.

I didn't know this boy very well, as he was a couple of years older than me, but our mothers often chatted in the corridor outside our flats. I would never have dared to do anything as dangerous as what he was planning. Not only because I didn't believe I could pass as a non-Jew, despite my blonde curls, but also because I didn't want to leave my mother and father. I was still only fifteen years old.

When Mum told us that our neighbour had managed to get over the fence and escape, we were thrilled for him. It felt like such a victory for us all. But our happiness was short-lived. A few days later his distraught mother told mine that he had been caught with no documentation and was immediately executed. I don't know how she knew this, but she seemed certain of it and the previously happy woman I had known was never the same again.

By August 1940, the hunger had become so extreme that the Bund organised its first protest.

A broadsheet went out. It read:

All the starving Jews throughout the ghetto will assemble on Sunday, August 25, at 9:00 am at 13 Lutomierska Street.
Brothers and Sisters!
Let us turn out en masse to eradicate once and for all, in unison and by concerted force, the terrible poverty and the barbarian conduct of community representatives toward the miserable, exhausted, famished populace. Let every man do his humane duty to his kin and carry the cry:
Bread for All!
Enlist in the war against the accursed community parasite. We demand that soup kitchens be opened in the blocks.

Sundays were our only day off, but Dad and I planned to take part in the protest and Mum helped us make the placards demanding more bread and more work. The two of us marched alongside thousands of others, demonstrating against the appalling conditions in the ghetto. Our demands were directed at Rumkowski but were obviously meant for the Germans.

The Nazis and Kripo agents quickly shut the protest down, and many people were badly wounded. Luckily my father and I weren't hurt, but it was scary. That was our final act of innocence, believing that what we were dealing with had some sort of humanitarian conscience and that organising ourselves in peaceful resistance could appeal to it. But it was clear that any more organised protests in the ghetto would be too dangerous and the consequences too great. However, my father was not willing to give up entirely. Even in the face of such misery and

The Strength of Hope

hardship, my dad's positive outlook and fighting spirit did not wane.

'*Mir muzn shtendig gloyben mir valn iberleben*,' he would say. (We must believe we will survive this).

He was sure we could find other ways to fight back against our captors, and I was inspired by his positive attitude. Where religious families put their faith in God, the Goldbergs put ours in the human spirit. We were determined not to lose hope. Hope was all we had.

In late 1940 we received news from my sister, Maryla, that she had given birth to a son, Danek. At that time, people in the east were still able to write to those of us in the ghetto, and we were allowed to write back, but only on an open postcard and only in German. We knew that Maryla's letters were heavily censored, so when she wrote saying Danek had diarrhoea, we wrote back saying we had diarrhoea too. We knew that would get past the censor but hoped Maryla would understand that this was our way of letting her know we were not okay.

Meanwhile we had heard nothing from my other two sisters, Frajda and Estera, in Krakow. Mum must have been extremely worried, and there was probably not a moment of the day when it wasn't on her mind, but she never showed her distress or worry around me. I think she wanted to keep her fears to herself, so I wouldn't get upset, but I knew both my parents were constantly thinking about them and hoping they were safe, just as I was.

We shared our garden with the Wieners and we all knew how lucky we were to have it. Dad got a permit from the Jewish Council that allowed us to grow vegetables, and Bono and I helped him to remove stones and clean up the land so we could begin planting them after fertilising the soil. The only fertiliser we had available to us was human faeces, so we used this of course.

None of us knew anything about gardening, because we had never had a garden before, and we had a lot to learn. Growing food that we could eat as soon as possible was the priority, so the first thing we had to figure out was which vegetables grew the quickest and which ones would take a whole summer. Beetroot, carrots, and cabbage were the slowest to grow, so we utilised the space between those rows for lettuce and radishes, which grew in just six weeks. We also had a cherry tree, an apple tree and a pear tree in our garden. Fruit trees were such an anomaly in the ghetto that when Rumkowski's people heard about them, they came to pay us a visit. They inspected our garden, then instructed us to continue looking after the trees as best we could.

'When the trees bear fruit, we will return to collect it,' they told us. 'Of course, we will give you something in return.'

We knew better than to trust or believe anything Rumkowski or his men promised, so when the fruit started to grow, we picked it all and ate it ourselves, sharing it with my aunt and cousins too, of course, even though it was not yet ripe. When the Council members came back, they were annoyed to find no fruit on the trees. We played dumb.

'We don't understand what happened,' we told them. 'The trees haven't produced a single fruit!'

The winter of 1940 into 1941 was a particularly tough one. People everywhere were dying of hypothermia, and lung disease was raging in the ghetto. Children no longer played on the streets

The Strength of Hope

during the days. They were all in their cold, unheated rooms, lying underneath piles of rags in bed with their families, trying to keep warm. People had to wait a long time to bury their loved ones too. Not only was there a lack of skilled gravediggers but the ground was too frozen to dig into, so the line of dead bodies waiting for burial grew longer.

Many people had no fuel for fire, and the high wooden fence that surrounded our garden didn't last long. We pulled off the palings to use for heating and cooking. Some people ripped planks of wood off public fences, knowing they'd be sentenced to hard labour if caught but they were so desperate that they took the risk. The tables I played ping-pong competitions on, before the war, were now used for wood to keep people alive. Most people would come home from work, cook whatever meagre rations they had, eat, and then get straight into bed with their families to get warm.

I am sure the garden and fruit we hid from Rumkowski's men are the reasons we survived those winter months. We were lucky to have a little more than others, but I was still hungry all the time. I adapted to the constant hunger by forcing myself to stop thinking about food. Even when I was so hungry that it felt like my stomach was twisting itself inside out, I trained my mind not to think about eating. Most of the time it worked, using mind over matter to convince myself that I wasn't hungry. To this day, I still don't think about food, even though I know I must eat to live. Back then, I tried to convince myself that my appetite for life, and to keep living, was bigger than my appetite for food. I was determined to stay positive, and alive, for as long as I could.

In 1941, my neighbour, Bono, took me into the factory

where he worked and got me a job as a metal worker. This factory produced steel toe and heel caps for military boots and Bono worked there as a metal engineer. The two of us would walk to and from work together each day, and we were quite the sight. Bono was six foot one and I was five foot nothing, so we stood out on the ghetto streets. A few months after I started working at the factory, Bono was made foreman and asked me to be his deputy.

'I need someone I can trust,' he told me. 'Someone I can rely upon to run things when I am away.'

I was honoured to have been given such a big responsibility at just sixteen years old. And I soon realised Bono was away quite often, as he had many duties to fulfil as a SKIF leader.

One day, early in 1941, we noticed the Nazis setting up a separate area, 500 metres from our flat, behind barbed wire and deep ditches. We would soon find out that this was a camp for Sinti and Roma people, which the Nazis called the 'Gypsy Camp'. The Nazis decided to set up this separate area because in their racist worldview they demonised all Sinti and Roma as thieves who were unwilling to work.

We had no contact with the people in there, but we were so close that we could see and hear the appalling conditions of the camp. When a typhoid epidemic broke out in the 'Gypsy Camp', Bono and I heard terrible screams in the night. We didn't know if they were from torture, hunger or fear, but listening to the children screaming all night was the worst sound I'd ever heard. A Jewish doctor named Arnold Mostowicz was sent into the camp to try and contain the spread of the disease and did not expect to survive. Ironically, the SS officer in charge of the camp contracted typhoid and died, but the doctor survived and would go on to write a book about his experiences called *With a Yellow Star and a Red Cross: A Doctor in the Łódź Ghetto.*

The next insidious move by Rumkowski was to establish a court within the ghetto in March 1941, complete with his choice of judge. Most of the so-called criminals who found themselves in front of the judge were just trying to get extra money to pay for food rations. One woman was arrested for making and selling lollies because it was 'unhygienic', and another was arrested for taking a paling from a fence to use as firewood. A tailor who forgot to put a strand of thread back on the table before he left his shop and was searched was arrested for stealing. A carpenter who cut a strip of wood to fix his table at home was a thief. All these people, and those who committed similar crimes, were sentenced to hard labour within the ghetto or sent to the ghetto prison.

When we heard these stories of people being arrested and sent away for such trivial matters, it was a reminder to always be careful and vigilant. Living in the ghetto meant you always had to be on high alert. At any moment there could be a banging on your door, shots fired outside the window or a hand yanking you backwards off the street and a truncheon coming down on your head. We lived in a constant state of trepidation and staying aware of your surroundings was crucial to our survival.

'Keep your head down,' Dad would tell me. 'Stay alert.'

I was a strong, fit seventeen-year-old in 1941 but my life bore no resemblance to that of a normal teenager. I had no time or inclination to think about sport, recreation or girls. The only thing on my mind was food and survival, and I was exhausted all the time. I would work long hours in the factory all day then attend meetings with Dad, Bono and other Bundists before curfew.

Dad and I continued to actively participate in the Bund, along with Bono who was a leader of the Bund socialist youth group and who I looked up to and considered a role model. The Bund continued its secret operations in the ghetto and staying involved was also a way to stay connected to my father and to all the good work he was doing for the people in Łódź.

He delivered food rations to those who couldn't get out themselves, or to the Orthodox Jews in our area, who didn't want to risk going out on the streets lest they be harassed or beaten up. As it was my father's job to look after three buildings in the ghetto, he was always checking on the residents to make sure they had enough food and fuel, and if anyone was sick he would do everything he could to get them medical attention. I sometimes accompanied him when he visited these people, and it always gave me such a feeling of pride to see how much these people thought of my kind father and how grateful they were for the help he was always happy to give them. Not to mention the hope he instilled in them that everything would be okay.

'*Mir muzn zayn positive*,' he would tell them. (We must stay positive).

Meanwhile, Mum tried to maintain a sense of normality for our family, as much as she could, but anytime I left the flat, she would always tell me to be careful. Looking back now I can only imagine how worried she must have been about me, but most of the time she didn't show it. Dad and I tried to protect Mum from the appalling things going on in the ghetto as well. A lot of the time she didn't know what the two of us were up to with our Bund activities, or what terrible atrocities we were witnessing out on the streets. As much as possible, we wanted to protect her from the horrible truth. We also received a letter from Frajda in 1941, telling us that she was now staying in a small town near Krakow called Koszyce, and was well. This obviously reassured my parents and me and made us feel slightly better.

Dad would always try to keep our spirits up with his familiar refrain of, '*Mir muzn shtendig gloyben mir valn iberleben!*' (We must always believe we will overcome this!) He would tell us stories of people in the ghetto and the things they were doing to defy the Germans in their own small way. He told us about the teachers and parents who held secret gatherings for children after the schools in the ghetto closed in 1941. In these small groups, the children read and discussed books, continued with their studies, held recitals and put on small plays and readings. The adults knew how crucial it was to keep their children engaged with their studies, as well as distracted from the terrible circumstances around them, even though the punishment could mean death for their whole family if they were caught. My father knew how important it was for people to have something familiar to cling to in times like these. Rather than focusing on the negative and discussing the terrible specifics of what was going on around us, we talked only about how we could avoid deportation and starvation for as long as possible.

A newspaper was published in the ghetto, but as it was controlled by the Jewish Council it only detailed our daily provisions, the ghetto rules and names of people who had been arrested or killed for breaking the law. Nowhere in those pages was there any mention of what was going on in the rest of Poland, or of the death camps the Germans had begun to build. They wanted to keep us as ignorant as possible, completely sealed off from the rest of the world. Being as we were, 'hermetically sealed', we could not discover the catastrophic reality that was taking place throughout the country.

While my father was desperately trying to keep up our hopes, as well as those of the people around us, the Nazis were experimenting with different methods of mass murder to kill the Jewish people in a more efficient manner. Some of these experimental trials were taking place just 50 kilometres away from Łódź, close to a small village named Chelmno.

These trials began in December 1941, but none of us in Łódź had any knowledge of it for quite a while. Much later we would find out the gruesome and terrible details. We would learn that Chelmno was the first death site to be established in our area. The Nazis were using an abandoned synagogue as a holding pen and a partly-ruined manor house as a loading station for 'gas vans'. People rounded up and sent to Chelmno would be taken into the manor and told to undress. The unsuspecting victims were then sent down a corridor towards 'shower rooms' but ended up in the hold of the 'gas van' in the loading station. As soon as all space inside the van was taken up, the doors were closed and the van pulled away from the manor. Exhaust fumes were then pumped back into the van, killing the people inside. A forest 5 kilometres away became the site of the mass graves, hastily dug to bury the victims.

When the first large deportations from Łódź began in January 1942, all 5000 of the Sinti and Roma people living in the 'Gypsy Camp' near us were the first to be sent to Chelmno. Soon after this, large groups of Łódź Jews were deported and sent to Chelmno too. We had no idea at the time where they were going, only that it was somewhere 'to the east'.

The first time the people of Łódź got an idea of what might be happening at Chelmno was when clothing belonging to the deported Jews started turning up at a church in the ghetto that had been converted into a sorting station. Jews who had been given the job of sorting through the huge mountains of clothing and shoes started finding possessions belonging to their loved ones, and panic and fear spread through the ghetto. Were these people still alive? If so, why were their clothes and belongings sent back? Was it because they had been given prison uniforms at the labour camp so didn't need their clothes? Or was something worse going on?

None of us could possibly have known about, or comprehended, mass murder sites like Chelmno or Auschwitz at that point. We only knew Auschwitz as a military barracks and camp for soldiers, which it had been before the war, and had no idea it was now a place of true evil.

7

ILLEGAL ACTIVITY

As the war dragged on, Rumkowski's dictatorship in the ghetto became more tyrannical, and our underground movement was forced to become much more secretive as a result. Bono continued in his role as a leader in the Bund socialist youth group, while I carried out acts of sabotage like shutting down the power system in the factory to temporarily stop production and slow everything down. We knew these acts were dangerous and that we were taking a giant risk, but just as those teachers knew how important it was to keep a small semblance of a cultural life for the children, those of us in the Bund knew how crucial it was to give people hope. Without hope there is no life at all, and we never contemplated giving up.

More than anything we wanted a connection to the outside world, and the only way to have that would be through a radio. If we had a radio, we would be able to tune in to British radio, as well as the Polish underground broadcasts, and find out what was happening in the world. We could follow the progress of the war and find out if the Germans were winning or losing. We would know if the Americans and British were aware of what was happening to the Jewish people, and if there was any light for us at the end of this very long and dark tunnel. If we knew that the Germans were losing the war, we might be able to instil hope in those around us that this would soon be over. But the Germans wanted to keep us ignorant and cut off from the rest of the world, so it was illegal to own a radio in the ghetto. We knew it would be impossible to get access to one, so we decided that we would have to build our own.

Viktor Rundbaken was a clever Jewish electrical engineer who lived in Łódź and who would prove to be crucial in helping the Bund gain access to much-desired information from the outside world.

Viktor worked for the Kripo, doing repairs on their radios, and so midway through 1941, a plan was hatched between him and Bono. Whenever Viktor was called to their headquarters to investigate a problem with the Kripo radio, he would remove a component that was in perfectly good working order and tell the Germans that it was faulty. In front of them, he would then throw the component into the rubbish bin and request a replacement and the Germans, eager to have their radios working again, would approve these requests. Later, when the Germans weren't around, Viktor would return to the bin and retrieve the discarded component. After hiding it in the bottom of his toolbox, he would carry it out of their headquarters and hope that any inspection upon departure would be cursory. Viktor was a brave man. He knew the enormous risk he was taking by helping us in our quest to build an illegal radio, and that the consequences would be severe were he caught. Regardless, he continued to deceive the Kripo in this way until he had collected enough components to start building illegal radios for the underground.

In the factory where Bono and I worked, there was a smelter that was used to melt down scrap iron and other items. In 1941, Bono and I began to keep a lookout for discarded parts that we could give Viktor to contribute to the building of the radios. Smuggling these discarded parts out of the factory was tricky, but we came up with a solution.

Each of us who worked in the factory brought our soup to work in a metal pot called a *menaschke*. After eating our soup at lunchtime, we would wait until no supervisors were around, put the discarded parts into the bottom sections of our menaschkes and cover them with cabbage leaves. Bono would take his menaschke with one part hidden under the cabbage leaves, I would take mine, and we would walk out of the factory, through the gate and home. We were confident no one would stop us because 90 per cent of Jews in the ghetto carried a menaschke to and from work.

The whole process of building these radios was painfully slow. But at the end of 1942, after eighteen long months, Viktor had succeeded in building a handful of illegal radios that could receive overseas broadcasts. Bono was lucky enough to receive one of these radios and it was completely life changing for us. At that point we had been locked up in the ghetto for three years, so to have Polish underground and BBC broadcasts at our fingertips was incredible to us. Finally, we had a connection to the outside world and could find out what was going on beyond our barbed-wire cage. However, we needed be vigilant about what we disclosed to the people around us. The older members of the Bund, including my father, warned Bono and I not to tell anyone, not even our closest friends, about the radio. He knew that no one could be trusted to keep their mouth shut. Ours was one of around only six clandestine radios in the ghetto, so we knew how important it was that we keep it a secret.

It was too risky to tell a single soul, and so of course we didn't. But we did have a few close calls, like the day a friend came to visit Bono and me at our home. Bono's flat was closest to the stairs, so our friend knocked on his door first. Hearing no reply and finding the door slightly ajar, he pushed it open and walked inside, calling out to Bono as he went. There, right in front of our friend's eyes, was our radio, sitting out on the table in full view. He froze, stunned at what he was seeing, just as Bono's Aunty Klara walked into the room. She looked from our friend to the radio and frowned.

'You'd better run for your dear life,' she told him sharply. 'And don't tell anyone what you've seen, or Bono will kill you!'

Our petrified friend bolted from the room, taking the flight of stairs in a single jump. He knew Aunty Klara wasn't kidding about Bono killing him, so he literally ran for his life!

Another time, I was at Bono's when I spotted a man called Sutter entering the building across the road from ours. Everyone in our neighbourhood knew and disliked Sutter. He was a Polish-born ethnic German, and we all knew that he was working for the Kripo, even though he also spoke Yiddish. The Jewish police often conducted surprise searches and I guessed this was what was going on there. They had sent Sutter to do some snooping. I decided to stay at the window in case he decided to visit us next and discovered what was going on in our flat. Although households in the ghetto were only allowed one 40- or 50-watt globe each, Viktor had helped us take extra power from a pole outside our flats so we could run our radio.

Bono's mother had a small electric stove (also forbidden) and if Sutter saw it, he'd want to know where the electricity to run it was coming from. Any investigation into our electricity system would have resulted in the discovery of the radio, currently in the double drawer where Bono kept it hidden. It would have been a fatal discovery for all of us. I couldn't let Sutter find either the stove or the radio.

When I spotted Sutter, Bono's mother was cooking something on the stove. Before I even had time to warn her, I watched in alarm as Sutter walked straight back out of the building across the road and directly across from ours. There was no time to hide the stove, but I had an idea. I leapt up and over to the curtain in front of the stove that also divided the room in half. At the very moment he reached the door, I managed to sweep the curtain behind me. The stove was hidden behind my body, but I hoped Sutter would assume I was sweeping the curtain across to show him there was nothing in the room. By some extremely good fortune this action worked. From his position in the doorway, Sutter took a quick peek into the room and left. Mrs Wiener and I were beside ourselves with relief.

The radios incited the Bund to establish a new system of the organisation. Those of us in the ghetto who were involved in the Bund were split up into around twenty smaller groups. I was in the same group as Bono, and we would all get together once a week to hear him report on what he had been hearing on the radio. Bono told us what was happening on the western and eastern fronts, about the bombing of German cities, political news, as well as Jewish news.

Other members of the Bund had radios too, so the main topic for discussion at our regular meetings was how we could use the information we were hearing to help people in the ghetto to not give up, morally or spiritually. This was part of what we called our 'passive resistance'. The philosophy of the Bund had always been to not only look after one's own family, but to help those in the community find and keep hope too. Each of us in our group would memorise the information we heard from Bono in our meetings, then take it out into the ghetto to spread 'unconfirmed' rumours.

The long bread distribution lines were where gossip and information were exchanged, ideas were discussed, and hopes were shared. The ghettos' 'whispering telegraph' was how many people received their news and updates, and a new piece of information could be all over the 3.6 kilometres squared area within a matter of minutes. We wanted to be able to spread hope among the people in the ghetto, while keeping the source of this information secret at the same time.

As Bono and I walked the streets of the ghetto, we'd talk to people and enquire after their physical and mental health. The responses were mostly positive in the early days and weeks of the war, but slowly started deteriorating as weeks turned into months, then years. Nevertheless, we still felt we had a responsibility to try and keep up the spirits of those around us for as long as we could. Bono and I would tell people to 'not give up hope' and that 'we had to find the strength and the will to go on'. At that time, we all believed our incarceration would be temporary. We had no idea that that the war was going to last almost six long years, or that the Nazis' plan was the complete annihilation of the entire Jewish population in occupied Europe.

8

BARBARISM REVEALED

We received our first news of Estera in 1942. It was a postcard and very short and was addressed to 'The Eldest of the Jews – Chaim Rumkowski – to deliver to Herszl Goldberg'. At that time there was no mail coming into the ghetto at all so this was very strange.

It read: *We hereby kindly write to the Goldberg family, living in Litzmannstadt Bleigasse 30/1, to inform you that your relative Estera Goldberg, living in Koszyce, is healthy.*

The postcard was typed rather than handwritten, oddly worded, and in German, but it was all we had and so we had to hope that Estera had written it herself, that the information contained within it was true and that Frajda was with her. Koszyce was 47 kilometres east of Krakow, where we had last seen Estera, but we were not surprised to hear that she had moved. We knew the Krakow Ghetto had been established on 1 May and its Jewish people sealed behind barbed wire, just like us, and that all those Jews not born in Krakow had been forced to leave. We had no choice but to trust that this postcard was a true account, and not a ruse by the Germans to fool us into thinking my sister was alive when in fact she was already dead.

Conditions in the ghetto worsened in 1942 – the cold, the bread ration cutbacks and price jumps, the number of deportations and the hunger. Bread normally cost 300 or 400 marks in Łódź but, in 1942, a 2 kilogram loaf of bread cost 2000 marks on the black market, equal to two years wages. Hunger was now a permanent part of our life. We lived with it, slept with it, dreamed about it, and talked about it. Food was everything. In the Goldberg home, we were incredibly lucky to have our fruit trees, and some Bund members at the factory sometimes gave us a little extra soup on our lunch break. These small blessings were enormous in the scheme of things.

But many in the ghetto were not so fortunate and people were dying of starvation and malnutrition all around us. Bono's father was one of these unfortunate souls. He steadily began losing strength, eventually dying from starvation on 16 May 1942. Bono and I buried him together. It was a very sad time for all of us.

Some people knew that Bono and I were associated with the Bund and would stop us to ask if we had any news on how the war was progressing as we walked to work together. They had no idea we had a radio of course, but maybe assumed we had access to information they did not.

'Do you think liberation is close?' they would ask us.

'Just hold on,' we would tell them in Yiddish. '*Mir darfen kain moll nisht farliren hofenung*' (We cannot lose hope!)

We never told them what we were hearing on our radio in

case someone turned us in but would try and encourage these friends and acquaintances to stay positive and hopeful.

Our intention was to try and lift people's spirits, even during such horror and misery, and give them hope. Over the years I had learned from my father that people need to believe that life is not completely meaningless, so that was the message we tried to spread in the ghetto. That, and that we should never give up.

But there were times when I witnessed such cruelty in the ghetto that it was hard to keep my positive outlook. One day, I was walking home from work when I saw Chaim Rumkowski riding down the street in his horse drawn carriage. A young mother ran up alongside him, carrying one child in her arms and with two others beside her.

'Please Mr Rumkowski,' she begged, holding up her youngest child up to him. 'Can you do anything for us? My children are starving!'

I watched as Rumkowski leaned over, slapped the woman twice on the face and shouted, 'Go away!' before trotting off down the street.

I couldn't believe it. How anyone could treat another person that way, let alone one Jewish person to another? Why couldn't he simply have said, 'I am very sorry Madam, but everybody is starving, and I'm afraid there is nothing I can do to help.'

But to slap her? No human with a conscience could do such a thing.

From that moment I despised the man and kept my distance whenever I saw him on the street.

There were also small moments of hope that we clung

desperately to, like when we heard on BBC broadcasts that Germany was starting to suffer defeats in places like Africa. When we heard news like this it meant that we could discreetly spread it through the ghetto, without anyone knowing for certain where the rumour had come from, giving people the tiniest ray of hope in a very dark time.

But things were about to get much darker.

It was the end of 1942 when Bono listened, shocked, as the BBC broadcaster announced that nearly a million Jews had already been murdered. The broadcaster gave no information as to how these Jews had perished but when Bono reported these figures to us, we simply could not comprehend what we were hearing. The numbers were staggering. How was such a thing possible? And how could the world allow such a thing to happen? It was also the first time we heard that Auschwitz was a place of death.

After much discussion in the Bund, we decided to keep this information to ourselves for the time being, mainly for security reasons. If we told people, it would cause widespread panic in the ghetto and the Germans might suspect that people had illegal radios. That would incite a full-scale search and we could lose our only connection to information, not to mention our lives as well.

Therefore, rather than confirm this information as true, we spread rumours. Even though so many of us in the ghetto had witnessed the brutality of the Nazis, it was another thing entirely for anyone to believe they were capable of murdering millions of us in camps all over Europe. We knew this concept would be

The Strength of Hope

incomprehensible to most people and that many wouldn't believe what they were hearing whispered on street corners.

The next thing we needed to decide was what, if anything, we could do about this new and terrible knowledge. It was impossible for us to procure any weapons so we couldn't fight the Nazis physically. Even then, at almost eighteen years old, I knew I could shoot a Nazi if someone put a gun in my hands, but I also knew that the consequences of an uprising would be disastrous. Dozens, or even hundreds of people, including me, would be murdered as a reprisal. After the war I would learn that this theory was correct as whole villages had been wiped out in reprisal attacks by the Germans.

Instead, we told people the positive things we heard on the radio, like when the Americans entered the war and the Germans started suffering more and more defeats. This kind of information made it easier for people to believe that the invasion would come any day now. People in the Łódź Ghetto had endured so much, but we were strong. These people spent their days looking at endless death notices, dying of starvation, and walking around with swollen feet and swollen bodies, yet were you to ask them, 'How are you?' their response was always, 'We are going to survive this.' This was the attitude of many people I knew in the Łódź Ghetto. This was our strength and this strength kept us going.

Hearing about the death camps was the first time I had to entertain the idea that deportation could mean death, but it still seemed incomprehensible. Surely the BBC had been misled with these figures and this information?

Then, one day, I was to see with my own eyes acts of such evil and brutality that I couldn't help but wonder if what Bono had heard on the radio could be true.

I was walking to work on my own early in the morning on 1 September 1942 – the third anniversary of the start of war – when I heard German trucks rumbling down the road behind me. Ducking out of sight, I stood and watched the trucks, with flatbed trailers attached to the back, round the corner and pull up outside the hospital.

People on the streets around me noticed what was happening too, and we all watched Nazi guards jump out of the trucks and run inside the hospital. We instinctively knew that something bad was about to happen. There had been rumours that the Nazis wanted to liquidate the hospitals. We knew they wanted to evacuate them because of the number of patients – young and old – suffering from TB, typhoid and many other illnesses caused by malnutrition and starvation, but we could never have imagined the evil we were about to witness.

As the Nazis began herding the patients out of the hospital and loading them onto the trucks, news that sick people being taken from the hospitals spread like wildfire through the ghetto. Many people had relatives or friends there, so people from all directions began running through the streets towards the hospitals, desperate to save their loved ones or see them one last time.

People gathered in front of the hospital and the Jewish police standing guard tried to chase them away. But everyone wanted answers and began shouting at them.

The Strength of Hope

Why are they throwing sick people up onto the trucks like slabs of meat? Why are they using military trucks if they are taking the sick Jews to another hospital? Where are they being taken?

We could hear people inside the hospital screaming and crying, while many outside rushed through the doors and climbed in windows, desperate to save their loved ones. The Jewish police grabbed and caught the Jews who were trying to flee through the rear window of the hospital, as patients who could still move made attempts to save themselves. Some started jumping from the upper stories and climbing out of rear windows.

Then, the most terrible sight I had ever witnessed.

The Nazis began throwing babies and sick children out of the second-floor windows, down onto the trailers. There was not a sound from the babies and young children, only the sickening thud as they hit the wooden slats of the flatbed trucks.

I saw this evil brutality with my own eyes and still couldn't believe it. I watched in horror, and it is something I have still not recovered from seeing to this day. The true nature of the Nazis was on full display in the ghetto that day. Never have I seen anything like it since.

Later we learned that some sick people in the hospital tried to disguise themselves by putting on nurses' uniforms. But this caused more trouble later when the Germans arrived back with a list of every member of the hospital staff and discovered the patients' true identities.

I never imagined such barbarity and couldn't believe human beings could act in such an evil way. It shook me to my core. But unfortunately, it was the beginning of a phase in the ghetto that was so appalling and degrading that we would need to create a new language to be able to accurately describe it.

If I was demoralised after this horrific day at the hospital, I didn't have time to properly process it because life became distilled into one objective for us all after this: to survive.

Three days after the horrific events at the hospital, notices went up on all the ghetto walls. They read: *At 3:30 in Fireman's Square, the Chairman and others will speak about the deportation.*

Dad and I left Mum at home on 4 September and crowded into Fireman's Square, along with thousands of others, to hear what Rumkowski had to say. It was a stinking hot afternoon and Mum was so frail from hunger by that point that we didn't want her to have to stand in the hot sun just to hear whatever this latest bad news would be. Once we were all in the square, German soldiers surrounded us, guns at the ready. Rumkowski didn't appear until almost 5pm and by then, many people were so hot, fatigued and dehydrated that they could barely stand.

Rumkowski stepped up onto the platform and, as recorded by Alan Adelson and Robert Lapides (eds) in *Lodz Ghetto: Inside a Community Under Siege*, said the following: 'A grievous blow has struck the ghetto,' he said. 'They demand what is most dear to it – children and old people … The taking of the sick from the hospitals caught me completely by surprise. And I give you the best proof there is of this: I had my own nearest and dearest among them, and I could do nothing for them. I never imagined I would be forced to deliver this sacrifice to the altar with my own hands.'

But what was this? Murmurs started through the crowd as

Rumkowski paused and began to weep. I looked to my father and saw his worried expression. This was not a good sign.

'In my old age,' Rumkowski continued through his tears, 'I am forced to stretch out my hands and beg, brothers and sisters, give them to me! Fathers and mothers, give me your children!'

People all around us began to scream and weep, rushing towards the platform.

NO! Not our children!

We could not believe what we were hearing. How could he ask parents to give up their children? Was this really happening?

I looked to Dad again and for the first time in my life, I saw tears running down his cheeks. Seeing my father cry was one of the most unsettling things I had seen over the past three years. He was my touchstone, my rock, the man I looked to for guidance on how to think and feel. If he was strong, I would be strong. If he was unafraid, I would be too. But on that day in the square, I realised he was just as scared as everyone else. It was a startling and scary revelation.

Rumkowski continued to speak to the horrified, weeping crowd. He told us that all children aged up to ten years old, as well as the sick and the elderly must present themselves for deportation, and that from this moment on, everyone in the ghetto was in a seven-day lockdown. No one was to leave their homes for a week and during this time, Nazis would make their way through the ghetto, sweeping section by section, searching for any children and elderly who had failed to present themselves. Those found hiding would be taken away.

Chaos ensued. People began to flee from the square,

running home in desperation and panic, to hide their children and elderly relatives. Walking home, Dad and I passed distressed parents dragging their crying children down the street, searching desperately for somewhere to hide them and keep them safe for the next seven days.

As Dad and I walked, we talked about what we would do. We knew we would both be safe as we were considered essential workers, but my aunt, Mum's sister, had six children, all aged between four and ten – the ages of children that were to be taken away.

We needed to keep Mum out of sight too. Both Mum and her sister looked older than they were. Mum was only fifty-one, but ghetto life and starvation had taken a toll on her and she was weak, frail and had grey hair. The Germans would almost certainly take her for deportation, and we were not willing to take that risk.

'When the Nazis get near to our area,' Dad said, his expression calm, but his voice trembling, 'I will hide your cousins and aunt, and you must hide your mother, okay?'

I nodded, willing to do whatever he asked of me.

By the time we arrived back at our flat, my mother had already heard the terrible news. Some of my young cousins knew too. Mum and Aunty wept as Dad reassured them that we would do everything possible to keep them and the children safe.

The Germans were typically systematic with their process of searching for children and elderly over the next week. They cordoned off areas, and the Nazis swept through them one by one, and we knew they wouldn't reach our area for at least a couple of days. From our flat, we had a good vantage point and could see where the Nazis were in the ghetto, and when they were getting closer to our area.

A few days after the speech in Fireman's Square, we were able to estimate that the Nazis would be arriving in our area first thing the next morning and so kept lookout from the early hours of that day. The moment we spotted them, I took Mum downstairs to hide her in a large shrub in the corner of our garden and Dad ran to my aunt's house to take her and the six kids to his chosen hiding spot.

As soon as Mum and I had wedged our bodies into the back of the large shrub, I peered out through the leaves. From where we were in the garden, I had a direct line of sight to my aunt's house, which was around 30 metres away and across our yard with the communal water pump in the centre.

I kept my eyes locked on my aunt's back door, waiting for my family to emerge but seconds, then minutes passed, and they didn't appear. Meanwhile, I could hear wails and shouts coming from our neighbours as the Nazis got closer.

Where were they? What was taking them so long? Six children aged between four and ten were not the easiest group to get organised and out the door, but today was not a day to drag their feet.

Come on, Dad! Get out of there!

The Nazis came into sight, and I put my arm around my mother and held her close as they entered our building. Mum buried her face in my shoulder, her whole body shaking with fear, and as I held her, I kept my eyes on my aunt's house. I was desperate now for any sign of movement to reassure me that my father was going to get them out in time. But the door stayed closed.

Moments later, the Nazis walked out of our building, having found no one inside. Bono and his family had abandoned their flat for their hiding place too. I watched in horror as the Nazis walked across the cobblestone yard and straight towards my aunt's place. Mum put her face in her hands, not wanting to look and my heart was thumping so hard that I felt sure the Nazis would hear it. I watched in silent anguish as the Nazis forced their way into my aunt's house.

Movement, noise and then the sight I had been dreading: my father, aunty and cousins all being marched out of the house and onto the street to join the rest of those discovered that morning.

Mum still had her face buried in her hands so didn't see the terrible sight of her husband, sister, nieces and nephews in the hands of the Nazis. I was glad. I would find the right time to tell her, but that time was not now. Waiting for the Nazis and Jewish police to leave our neighbourhood, I tried to push my fears aside, collect my thoughts and plan for what to do next. When the lockdown was over, I would go straight to our Bund contacts to find out where the Nazis had taken my father. Dad had so many connections that I felt confident he would be able to bribe his way out of this situation and bring my aunty and cousins home.

Mum and I eventually felt secure enough to emerge from the bush and go back inside our flat. Once inside, I told her what had happened to Dad, her sister and the children. She was very distressed but also felt sure that my father would find a way to get them all out of deportation, just as I did. We had such an unwavering belief in my father that we refused to entertain the notion that he wouldn't be coming home.

At the end of the week, I ran all the way to the house of one of my father's contacts.

'Do you know where they took them?' I asked him.

He nodded. 'All those brought out of their houses were taken to the Jewish Prison.'

I sprinted all the way to the prison, elated at the thought of seeing my father again, but when I arrived, all the cells were empty.

'It's unlucky,' the prison officer told me. 'The day they were brought here, everyone was put straight on a truck and taken away.'

9

ALL GONE

I felt sure that my father would have tried to escape from the truck. At the very least I know he would have done everything in his power to save my aunty and her kids, because that's the kind of person he was. After leaving the prison, I went to talk to the people who lived next to my aunt's house. They told me what had happened on that terrible morning.

'When your father arrived to take your aunty and the children to hide them,' they said, 'the children took too long to get organised. We could hear your dad trying his best to get them to hurry up and leave but, in the end, it was too late. The Nazis were already in the door.'

I returned to our flat with a heavy heart. It was terrible to think of my father in the hands of the Nazis, but I wanted desperately to believe that he had been taken to a work camp, not places of death like Auschwitz or Treblinka, and that he was still alive. I refused to believe that my father was gone forever. I had to believe that I would see him again one day when this was all over.

Either way, my dad would not be coming back to the ghetto

before the war ended, and that was a very hard reality to come to terms with. Life in the ghetto would be very different with my dad gone, but the worst part would be telling my mum what I had learned at the prison.

'Your father will manage somehow,' Mum said, sounding surprisingly calm. 'He will be okay.'

My mother refused to accept that anything bad had happened to my father. She clung to the hope that her husband was still alive. We both did. Never once, after that day, did we talk about my father as if he was dead. Neither of us ever let go of the hope that Herszl Goldberg was in a labour camp somewhere waiting for the war to end so he could come back to us.

When Mum and I discovered that all our relatives who had been living in the ghetto had also been taken that terrible day, it was a shocking and heartbreaking revelation. Out of forty or so Goldbergs who had been in the Łódź Ghetto, Mum and I were the only ones left. It was too terrible and difficult to comprehend. We never learned the circumstances of our family's deportation, where they had been taken or what happened to them, but I would never see any of my extended family members again.

'What can we do?' Mum would ask me, as we huddled in bed together at night.

'We carry on,' I told her. 'We keep going, and maybe one day we'll see our family again.'

I wasn't sure I believed this but knew I had to stay positive for my mum. It's what my father would have wanted me to do. If he *was* still alive, Dad would want to know that I hadn't let either of us give up. It was just Mum and me now and we had to be strong for each other.

There were around 90,000 Jews still living in the ghetto in September 1942. It was illegal for children under the age of ten to be there, so any kids who had managed to stay hidden needed to stay out of sight or pretend to be older than they were. Everyone over the age of ten rushed to find jobs to avoid deportation, and everyone had a card that had to be stamped to prove that you were working. Mum and I both had jobs so felt relatively safe at that point.

Every day we comforted each other with reassuring words and hugs, but we never talked about that terrible day. We shared the one bed in our flat every night – one that we folded away during the day – and were both so tired from working that we usually passed out in seconds, too exhausted even to have nightmares. I knew how tired and worried my mum was, but she never complained.

If I wasn't working, I kept myself busy with the Bund. In our secret meetings we would discuss what had happened and try to make sense of it. Why did they take our children? Our parents? For what purpose? None of us could understand. So many people in the ghetto were grieving the loss of their loved ones. Losses that no one could make sense of. None of it made any sense at all.

I had always tried to emulate my father's optimism for life, and his intrinsic belief that everything would be okay, but those were dark days. It was hard to stay positive after losing my father and most of the time I felt numb. The man who had been such a huge positive influence in my life, the man who had taught me how to stand up for myself and fight for what was right, was gone. I missed him terribly. My father had always tried to keep other people's spirits up and give them hope, but I was struggling to find a way to do this now. How can you give hope to parents who have just had their children stolen from them? How could I give hope when I, too, was emotionally wounded from my own family being torn apart?

I thought about my father constantly. As I worked at the factory I'd think, if only I'd had more time with him. As I walked home from work I'd think, if only I could have saved him from that truck. As I lay in bed next to my mother at night I'd think, if only that truck hadn't left the prison straight away. If only ...

But as hard as it was to go on at times, I knew I couldn't give up. I had to look after my mum. She had only me now, so I had to protect her and keep her safe. This became my true purpose in the ghetto.

She was the only family I had left, and I was not going to lose her too.

10

SEEDS OF HOPE

Through the rest of 1942 and into 1943, Mum and I continued with our routine of working at our respective factories in the ghetto and making sure we had enough food to survive. The pain of losing Dad from our daily lives was so great that it felt impossible to find the energy to go on at times, but we knew we must. The winter that year was brutal, and it broke my heart to see my mother becoming so frail and weak at such a young age, but still she never complained.

At night, I would lie in bed and think about how much we had lost as a people, and how much I personally had lost as a young man. But I also told myself to stay hopeful. If my father was in fact dead, I did not want him to have died in vain. When I was a boy, he had taught me to fight with my fists, but now I was learning that sometimes it's better to fight with your mind.

From May 1943 to the beginning of 1944 there were no significant deportations from our ghetto. Jewish people from the cities and villages surrounding Łódź were being sent to our ghetto, if they were judged to be useful, to work in our factories.

We didn't know it at the time, but those who were not judged to be useful were sent to Chelmno and murdered. Soon there were no Jews left in the area, except for the Łódź Ghetto, and so in May 1943, the Germans destroyed the Chelmno site to get rid of the evidence of what had gone on there.

Mum and I were both hungry and exhausted by this point, but it seemed as if we had escaped deportation, unlike the rest of our family and so many friends. Early one morning in 1943, around 6am, there were five rapid knocks on our door. I recognised it as an arranged signal between Bono and I when he had news, so I was not worried. I opened the door to find Bono standing there with an excited gleam in his eyes.

'Quick, come to the garden,' he said.

We were down the stairs in a few leaps, and once we were out of earshot, Bono told me his news.

'I just heard on the Polish underground radio that the Warsaw Ghetto is fighting,' he said, unable to hide his excitement, 'and the Germans are in retreat!'

This was incredible news, and as we returned upstairs to get ready for work there was a definite spring in our steps. We collected our menaschkes from our respective flats, met at Bono's to hide our radio under cabbage leaves and a slice of bread, then headed to the factory. Bono would sometimes take the radio into the factory to listen to the news in an attic area. It was much noisier in the factory than in his flat, so there was less chance of anyone hearing it.

This morning we felt different to every other day, and people must have noticed the broad smiles on our faces. As we walked, we discussed how to inform our comrades at the factory about this momentous news. We decided to meet in a secluded part of the factory at lunchtime. As soon as we arrived at the factory, Bono grabbed my menaschke and took it straight upstairs to the attic to listen for more news about the Warsaw Ghetto uprising.

I told our Bund comrades that we would be meeting in our usual place at lunchtime and once everything on the factory floor was under control, told our supervisor that I needed to go to the storeroom for something. As soon as I was out of his sight, I rushed up to the attic to find out if Bono had heard any more news, but he had no more updates yet.

We could hardly wait for lunchtime. At 11.55am, Bono and I rushed to get our soup and went straight to our prearranged meeting place – an isolated corner of the factory. As soon as the rest of our friends arrived, Bono began to speak. I remember Bono's chest was puffed out as he provided the update. He sounded uncharacteristically formal, as if he was trying to contain his excitement while measuring every word.

'This morning I heard rumours that yesterday, 19 April, the heroic uprising of the ghetto fighters in the Warsaw Ghetto began,' he said. 'The Germans suffered many casualties and retreated from the ghetto. On this day we should feel inspired to continue our struggle and our fight for survival. Let us wish our brethren in Warsaw continued success in their fight against the German oppressors.'

Hearing Bono speak with such pride and admiration was stirring for all of us that day, and the news from Warsaw gave us all a renewed sense of hope.

Neither Bono nor I could sleep that night, so we sat and talked for hours. We spoke about how wonderful it would be if we could tell all the people in the ghetto about the glorious fighters of the Warsaw Ghetto, to give them the same hope we were feeling that evening. But we knew it would be too dangerous. We also shared our dreams for the future with each other, and for the first time in many months I could almost believe they could come true.

Conditions in the ghetto had been getting progressively worse for those of us who were still there in 1944. Over the past almost five years, nearly 50,000 out of over 200,000 Łódź residents had died due to starvation and illnesses brought about by the horrendous conditions.

I was fortunate to still be in good physical condition. Being an all-round sportsman and gymnast before the war had obviously helped, and my mother and I having access to the garden and fruit trees meant that we supplemented our basic diet with potatoes, beetroots, carrots, lettuce, apples and cherries. This was an enormous help. Fresh vegetables were of huge benefit to my health and wellbeing. It also meant that we were self-sufficient and didn't have to rely on measly rations.

We heard about D-Day – the Allied landing in Normandy on 6 June 1944 – on our radio less than twenty-four hours after it happened. In fact, we knew about it even before the Germans in Łódź did. We were elated, but again were careful not to make our joy obvious to the Nazis or Jewish police in case they became suspicious. Instead, we only told cell groups of five, just as we had with the Warsaw Uprising. Those were the people we trusted and knew to be discreet and careful.

But others in the ghetto heard about the landing on their illegal radios and some of them were not as discreet. As a result, the news quickly got out and euphoria began to spread among groups of people in the streets. Many assumed this meant the end of the war and of our incarceration and so couldn't help but celebrate. After so much hardship, terror and misery it was hard for some to hide their excitement, which was understandable, but the excited murmuring on the streets of the ghetto made the Germans suspicious.

It didn't take them long to figure out that the only way people could have heard about the landing was on illegal radios. After these people were denounced by neighbours and/or spies, the Gestapo immediately went into action, searching those people's houses for radios, arresting, and subsequently executing them. One guy I knew of killed himself because he was sure he wouldn't be able to withstand the Nazi's torture and didn't want to be responsible for turning anyone else in. It was extremely dangerous for us to keep our radio hidden during this period of course, but Bono and I felt confident that it was well-concealed and that no one else knew about it.

Much later, I learned that after the Allied landing at Normandy, the Nazis were concerned they wouldn't have enough time to liquidate all the remaining Jews in Europe and remove all traces of the atrocities. In the Łódź Ghetto alone there were still 70,000 living Jews, so the Nazis decided to bring back working crews from Yugoslavia to rebuild and reactivate Chelmno.

We were oblivious to any of this at the time of course, so there was a growing excitement among those of us in the ghetto who were aware of the Allied landing at Normandy. D-Day was a turning point for us. We had been living in the ghetto for five years by then and that day we truly believed it was almost over and that we would be freed from Nazi occupation very soon.

LESSON LEARNED

The most important thing to do as a human being is give others hope and kindness. To help people as much as you can. Otherwise, life is not worth living.

11

MUM & ME

Soon after D-Day, deportations started again when the Germans ordered every factory in the ghetto to make a list of people they deemed unfit for work for reasons of ill health, age or weakness. Those of us with radios now knew that deportations very likely meant death, and we assumed these deportations had started up again because the Nazis wanted to dispose of as many of us as they could before the Americans advanced further across Europe and into Poland. Rumkowski announced that, under Nazi orders, any individual whose name was on the list and did not present him or herself, would have their family's rations stopped. If the individual still did not appear, the whole family would be consequently deported.

When the lists were put out by the factories, there was panic on the streets of the ghetto and many families whose father, mother, brother, sister, son or daughter were on that list, went into hiding. By another stroke of luck, my mother and my names were not on any of the lists. More than 7000 people were deported from 22 June, right up until 24 July.

During this terrible period, I witnessed Nazis physically pulling children away from their parents in the streets. When the mothers or fathers ran after them, those parents were shot. This kind of thing was happening in front of my eyes, which was a terrifying thing to witness, and it was a fraught and scary time all round.

After the war, some people asked me why we didn't kill Rumkowski, but that would have been disastrous. You can imagine what the Germans would have made of that: 'See, the Jews even kill their own leader!' That would be a pretext to do even worse things to the Jews, and in any case, they would have replaced Rumkowski in the blink of an eye.

In early August, as people were still mourning the loss of so many loved ones, and grappling with the aftermath of the mass deportations, posters signed by Rumkowski went up announcing that Hans Biebow, the ghetto's chief administrator, was going to speak.

Biebow was a former coffee merchant who had connections to Berlin. Later we would learn that he had been making a personal fortune from the ghetto. The minister in charge of wartime production had persuaded Heinrich Himmler, a leading member of the Nazi party in Germany, to keep the Łódź Ghetto functioning because it was producing war supplies at virtually no cost. Also, the worker's 'wages' amounted to less than subsistence rations. The Germans kept the Łódź Ghetto operational for so many years into the war because they were making a lot of money from us.

When these posters appeared on the ghetto walls, we were

immediately wary. They were different from those we were accustomed to seeing in the ghetto, which usually told us what rations we would receive and gave instructions as to how a Jew should behave when seeing a German in uniform. But the only information given on these posters was that Biebow was going to speak to all the workers in all the factories.

On 7 August, the day of Biebow's speech, Bono, myself, and the rest of my co-workers gathered on our factory floor to listen to what he had to say. Biebow informed us that all the Łódź factories and their machinery, as well as 5000 factory workers per day, would soon be moved to a safer place outside of Łódź. He went on to say that we must present ourselves in groups, according to our factories, so we could be deported as a union to these new and 'safe' workplaces. Biebow assured us, hand on heart, that nothing bad was going to happen to us, and that they simply wanted to resettle us and then we could get on with our work in the factory.

None of us believed him of course. Even the many people in the ghetto who didn't have the inside knowledge of the death camps that we with radios had, knew by now not to trust the Nazis or believe anything they had to say.

Bono, I, and a few other Bund members got together to talk about this latest development to consider our options and talk about what we should do. We all agreed that the Germans were most likely sending us all away to be murdered and that we should hide. We also agreed that if we told people around us about the death camps, the news would spread panic, desperation and fear throughout the ghetto, which would be dangerous and could result in even more deaths.

Before we made plans for where to hide, Bono and I put important underground documents with detailed notes on life in the ghetto, as well as precious personal photos and mementos, into two different boxes and hid them in two different places. We buried one deep under a tree, and another near the filthy and pungent latrines, hoping the smell would be enough to put anyone off from searching there. Bono and I knew there was a chance that we might never see each other again, so we made an agreement that whichever of us survived after the war should return to Łódź to dig up the boxes. These boxes were evidence of life, and death, in the ghetto, and we wanted people to know what had occurred here, even if neither of us survived.

There were still at least 65,000 residents in the Łódź Ghetto in August 1944. The Nazis were hoping to deport at least 5000 people a day, with a plan to execute all of us at Chelmno, and then liquidate the ghetto. But they quickly figured out that this would be too slow and arduous a process, so decided that they would begin directing the remaining residents to another camp in southern Poland: Auschwitz.

Auschwitz had the capacity to dispose of 60,000 Jews much more efficiently than Chelmno; it had already successfully murdered 400,000 Hungarian Jews over a period of ten weeks. Of course, we didn't know any of this at the time.

Every day, people were turning themselves in at the Jewish Central Prison, but others were trying to find places to hide when they witnessed people being grabbed off the footpaths and out of their homes. There were lots of people who had been in hiding with their children since Rumkowski's terrible 'Give me your children' speech two years earlier, and who were now finding it impossible to hold out for much longer, and these people would eventually come out and present themselves for deportation. But as soon as Bono and I buried the boxes, I started looking for a hiding place for Mum and me.

A friend of mine, a carpenter, had built a bunker under the stove in his room and so I went to visit him to check it out. The stove stood on a metal plate for camouflage and fireproofing, and the bunker underneath could hold up to twelve people. I wasn't convinced that this this was a good idea, since Germans knew a lot about bunkers after the Warsaw Ghetto uprising and decided that we should find a hiding place that was up high, rather than underground. Being up high meant that we could possibly keep a lookout and know when the Nazis were approaching.

I started looking for high up places to hide and soon found a manhole leading up to a small space in the roof of a building across the road from our flat. The roof area was as wide as a small lounge room, but only 80–90 centimetres tall at the highest point, before the ceiling gradually slanted down to the floor at one end. Still, it was big enough for the two of us. We wouldn't be able to stand up, but we could lie down. The Germans never entered the ghetto after dark, so I knew I would be able to go out and find food and water for us every night, and that Mum could climb down to stretch her legs. The main problem was how we would climb up and down. The manhole was at least 4 metres from the floor and there was no wood left in Łódź for me to make a ladder. In any case, a wooden ladder would be too bulky for the small attic space. I was nineteen by this time and still strong but even I wouldn't have been able to pull it up and inside quickly if necessary. I eventually had the idea to make a ladder out of thick rope, which I found by scavenging and asking people for any remnants of rope they had. Mum helped me plait the pieces together to make it strong.

Now all I had to do was convince my mother to climb up there and hide with me. She wasn't very keen on the idea at first. Mum was incredibly frail and weak by this point, so the idea of climbing up and down a rope ladder for days, maybe even weeks, on end, was not an appealing one. But I told her it was the only way we could stay safe and avoid deportation.

'I will be with you,' I told her. 'I promise I will look after you.'

She finally agreed, and so on 9 August 1944, the day the liquidation of the ghetto officially began, Mum and I went into hiding in our small attic.

We couldn't stand in our small space, only lay down or half sit up, and used a bucket for a toilet. Each night, Mum and I climbed down our shaky rope ladder, to the top floor of the building, to stretch our legs and bodies, and then I would venture outside to empty our bucket and to find us food. There were always small bits of food to be found in empty houses and rooms. People who had been dragged out of their houses and transported had had no time to take it with them and so I would bring it back to Mum. I got us water from the pump across the road in our old cobblestone yard.

During the day, Mum stayed up in the roof, while I stayed

The Strength of Hope

on lookout. From the top floor of the building, I could see when the Nazis were making their way through the ghetto, searching buildings for any Jews who were in hiding. When they got close to our area, I would race back up the ladder and tell Mum that we needed to lay very still and quiet. Lying there on the floor, we could hear shouts of 'RAUS!' and 'If you are hiding, we will find you!' drifting up from the street. There were gunshots, screams and children crying – this was the worse sound by far. A lot of the people in hiding had small children and their screams and cries upon discovery could be heard all through the street and in our tiny attic. It was terrible.

We existed this way for four weeks, and as the days and weeks passed, my poor Mum found it harder and harder to climb up and down the ladder. I helped her as much as I could, but the distance from the floor to ceiling was so high that I constantly worried she would fall off the ladder and onto the hard floor below. Mum was not only exhausted from the grief of losing her husband, children and the rest of her family, she was physically weak and emaciated from lack of nourishment. I was able to go up and down the ladder quite quickly and would leave the attic a few times a day to keep lookout, but Mum was up in that dark narrow space all day. Finally, one night after we had climbed back up into the manhole together, my mother confessed that she couldn't take it anymore.

'Abram, I am going to hand myself in for deportation,' she told me, gripping my hand, and looking at me with kind, tired eyes. 'But you must stay hidden.'

I stared at her, shocked. I hadn't told Mum about the death

camps because I hadn't wanted her to imagine my father and her sister being taken there, let alone her two daughters, but now I wondered if it was time to tell her. Maybe it would be the only way to convince her to stay hidden with me.

'You don't know what will happen,' I said. 'We could be murdered if we present ourselves for deportation.'

But my mother was adamant. By this stage her poor body and mind had had enough suffering and she was willing to take the risk.

'I cannot stay here any longer,' she said. 'I have to go, but you stay here, please.'

I knew that if we presented ourselves, we would be taken to Auschwitz. I knew this, not only from the radio, but also because my connections in the Bund had told us that when the trains arrived back in Łódź to take more people away, cleaners had found scraps of paper hidden in the cracks between the wooden planks of the floor. On these scraps of paper some people had written the names of every station they passed on the train journey, and some had written the final destination: Auschwitz.

We had heard on the radio that Auschwitz was a place of death, but we also knew it was a work camp. Maybe Mum and I would be two of the lucky ones, put to work at Auschwitz instead of being murdered? I was young, strong, well-built for my size and in good physical condition compared to others because of my access to extra food from our fruit trees, and so maybe I could help my mother stay alive once we arrived. I had done so for four years, so surely, I could do it there too. It was a small chance but a chance I had to take because how could I allow my mother to

The Strength of Hope

be sent to Auschwitz while I continued to hide? I couldn't. I had lost my entire family and I wasn't going to lose her too.

'Please, Abram,' Mum insisted. 'I'm only a burden to you. I'll present myself and you go on hiding. It's your only hope.'

'No, I am coming with you,' I said firmly.

In that moment I truly believed I could help my mother. My father was gone and so it was up to me to stay with her and keep her safe. I could not let her go alone. I knew that if I lived, I would always have this moment on my conscience. So, on 25 August 1944, we packed a few bits of food and some clothes, and I helped my mother down the shaky rope ladder for the last time.

Out on the street, we joined a large group of people who were also walking to the Jewish Prison to present themselves for deportation, including some friends from the Bund, who looked as worried and defeated as I felt in that moment.

Soon after this we were loaded onto a train, along with hundreds of others, and told that we would be transferred to passenger trains at the next stop. Most of us knew by now that this was a lie, but our exhaustion made us indifferent.

I found out later that our train was the second last arrival at Auschwitz from Łódź ever, and that one week after we left, the Nazis abandoned the Łódź Ghetto, leaving those still in hiding to come out safely.

12

THE HORROR

The journey was long, miserable and uncomfortable. Dozens of us were squeezed inside a cattle car for three days and nights, with one bucket to use as a toilet, and another filled with water that we all had to share. That was all.

Everyone on our train was from the Łódź Ghetto. After five long years of constant hunger, fear and loss, most people were distressed and exhausted and had no idea what was about to happen or where they were going. Some of them may have believed they were being sent to a 'safe workplace' as per Biebow's speech, while others may have been less trusting and assumed they were going to a labour camp of some kind. In any case, I chose not to tell people in that carriage what I knew about Auschwitz, if in fact that was where we were headed, and how many Jews had been murdered there. What would it achieve other than panic and distress in what was already a highly stressful environment?

There were many familiar faces on the carriage, including my good friend, Heniek Wajnberg, from the Morning Star Club, but my only focus on that terrible journey was my mother. Her nerves were at breaking point and I tried everything I could to keep her calm as she clung to me with one hand and her small bag of belongings with the other.

'It will be okay, Mum, everything will be fine,' I whispered in her ear in the crowded carriage, echoing the words she had heard my father say so many times in the past. 'I will keep you safe.'

But any hope I had of protecting her vanished the moment the train stopped, and SS guards flung open the heavy doors of our car. There was a barrage of noise, panic and movement in our crowded carriage and the SS guards started screaming at us.

'RAUS!' they screamed.

'Everybody OUT! Men to one side! Women and children to the other! Take nothing with you!'

It was dawn on the 29 August 1944, and we had just arrived at Auschwitz-Birkenau.

Mum and I clung to each other in the carriage, waiting behind the others. We were jostled forward, and I helped Mum down off the train. The elderly and the young kids were having trouble getting down from the carriage. I saw the SS were hitting some of them with their clubs to hurry them along.

At 5am it was just barely light, and the cold winds were blowing down from the Carpathian Mountains. The scene on the ground before us was chaotic. Vicious, specially trained Alsatian dogs were straining at their leads and barking and SS guards, and prisoners in striped uniforms who were presumably working for the SS, were shouting at us in Yiddish.

'Women to the left, men to the right!' they yelled. 'Single file!'

People were crying and screaming as they moved or were pushed into lines, and in the distance I could see flames coming out of chimneys.

In that moment, I knew that I should never have brought my mother to this terrible place. Mum too knew that she was not going to survive once we were separated. It was obvious how frail and weak she was, and every shred of hope and bravery I possessed was extinguished then. Anyone could feel the evil in this place, it was all around us.

Everything happened so quickly. Mum squeezed my hand, urging me to look at her.

'Abram, you must do everything humanly possible to survive,' she said, speaking quickly and starting to cry. 'And when you do, wherever you are, you should tell the world what happened to your family and other Jews.'

Seeing the tears on my mother's face was devastating.

'I promise,' I whispered, holding back my own tears.

Mum's small hand was wrenched from mine and in seconds we were separated. She disappeared into the line of women being herded down the platform and I had one final glimpse of the back of her head before she was swallowed up by the crowd of crying, screaming women and children.

I had no time to process the fact that I had lost my mother. Within moments of our separation, I was pushed into a line of men. Suddenly, we were all being jostled towards the man who would decide my fate that morning.

The camp's physician, Dr Josef Mengele – also known as the Angel of Death – wore white gloves and held a conductor's baton in his hand, which he used to wave us left or right. Of course, none of us knew which the better side was, but I was waved to the right along with five men I knew from Łódź, including my friend Heniek.

We were directed towards a cinderblock building where, we were told, we would be taking a shower. Immediately suspicious, the six of us from Łódź made a pact. If the first of our group to be sent in didn't come out again, we would know they had been killed. If this happened, the rest of us left would not go quietly. We would cause a disturbance, do something, anything, to make the guards shoot us. We would die on our own terms. We were determined not to walk submissively to our deaths.

I was the first of our group to be sent in. I was terrified but gave my friends a nod to let them know that if I came out, I would give them a signal that all was okay. I just hoped this would be the case.

Many prisoners wearing striped uniforms were waiting inside for us. They all held truncheons in their hands, and randomly brought them down on anyone they wanted to for no reason as they shouted orders at us.

'Strip!' they shouted. 'Fast! Only keep your belts and shoes!'

We were directed to throw our clothes outside, on top of an already huge pile.

The next order came as we stood there shivering in the cold. 'To the barber! Move!'

With my belt and shoes in my arms, I was pushed to the side where every hair on my body and head was shaved off. Next, a prisoner smeared disinfectant all over my head and body. It burned like hell on my newly hairless body and my head that was covered in fresh cuts from the hack shaving job.

'Into the showers!' they shouted, pushing us all through a door and into a large concrete room. The door clanged shut behind us, and those few seconds of anticipation felt like an eternity. I had no idea what was about to happen. I stared up at the shower heads and, as I waited for the water to pour out, I thought about my mother and where she was right at that moment. Was she in a huge concrete room like this one, standing alongside dozens of other naked and terrified women? Had they shaved her head too? She must be so frightened. Thinking of my mother in a place like this was almost too much to bear.

Some of the men were quiet, like me, but others wept and wailed, crying out names of their loved ones and calling for their mothers. Then, hot water poured from the shower heads above us, and shouts of relief echoed around the room.

As our group was herded out of the shower block, naked and dripping wet, I turned to look over my friends waiting on the other side of the block. I could see Heniek craning his neck, desperately seeking me out among the newly shaved group of men. I knew I would be hard to spot since I was so much shorter than everyone else, and without the recognisable mop of blonde curls on top of my head. So, I stood on my toes and raised my hand up high so Heniek and the others could see that I was alive. I saw a smile of relief spread across Heniek's face and knew he had seen me. Now my friends could walk into the showers knowing they would be coming back out.

After leaving the shower block, we were herded into another

set of barracks where we had to jog past tables piled high with clothes. The prisoners standing behind these tables threw trousers, jackets and berets at each of us as we passed. No care was given to what size anyone was, of course, so when I went to put my clothes on, I discovered the jacket was so large on my tiny frame that I could wrap it around myself three times. The trousers were the same – far too long on my short legs. Luckily my six-foot-tall friend was given clothes much too small for him, so we did a swap. We were given no underwear or socks, but I was so grateful to have been allowed to keep my shoes that it didn't bother me.

My mother had ordered my shoes just before the war broke out in 1939. They were sturdy and had sheepskin inside and were to see me through the brutal Polish winter. Those shoes had served me well throughout the cold ghetto winters. I had been fortunate none of the guards noticed what good quality my shoes were. If they had, they would have taken them away and replaced them with wooden clogs.

Once our group had our clothes, we were loaded into the backs of trucks and transferred to the part of Auschwitz known as the 'Gypsy Camp' – so called because thousands of Sinti and Roma and their families had previously been held in this section. We had no knowledge of the gruesome reason why this section of the camp was unoccupied at the time but found out later that they had all been sent to the gas chambers just before our arrival.

Auschwitz was enormous. Around 40 square kilometres, it was made up of different sections including Auschwitz 1, Auschwitz 2 (Birkenau) and Auschwitz 3, which was called

Monowitz-Buna. The 'Gypsy Camp' was part of Auschwitz 2 (Birkenau) and known as 'the Quarantine'. This was because prisoners were regularly taken from our area to work in factories around the camp, replacing those who had died.

There were numerous blocks within the camp and Heniek, my other friends and I were all put in Block 4. Birkenau was huge and contained around thirty blocks with around 500 prisoners crammed into each one. Not many of these blocks had bunks and they only had tiny windows in the ceilings so a little light could filter in. Each block was assigned a *Blockführer* (Block leader) and under him were the *Funktionshäftling* (kapos). The kapo wore a green triangle, which signified that they had been criminals before arriving at Auschwitz. These were the same men, dressed in striped prisoner uniforms, who had shouted at us when we were getting off the train, and who struck out at us with their truncheons as we undressed for the showers. The kapos were usually mean, cruel bastards who used obscene Polish and Yiddish language, the likes of which I had never heard in my life. The kapo in charge of Block 4 was a Pole named Macek, and his crime before coming to Auschwitz was murder. In my opinion, kapos were the worst kind of humans. Some of them were bastard Jews who had turned against their people to save their own skin and receive rewards and treats from the Nazis. We all lined up in front of our new Blockführer, and he began to shout at us.

'Listen!' Macek yelled. 'We have instruments here that can see through your body, so if you have swallowed any valuables, you must declare them now!'

He waited for someone to step forward, but no one moved. 'If you are found with anything you will hang,' Macek continued. 'Only yesterday two people were found to be hiding jewellery.' He pointed to the ceiling above us and smirked. 'They were hanged from that beam.'

This was our welcome to Auschwitz.

13

AUSCHWITZ

Block 4 had a concrete floor and no beds. Five hundred of us were crammed in with no blankets, no pillows, and no room to move. It was impossible to lie down so the only way to fit us all in was if the first person sat with his back to the wall, then spread his legs so the next person could sit between them. I quickly figured out that if you were at the front, you could more easily be hit by Macek, so, as soon as we were inside, I ran to the back of the block and found a spot against the wall. Sure enough, Macek began circling us tapping a chair leg against the palm of his hand.

'Any noise and I will split your heads open!' he barked. 'If I hear one whisper in the night, I'll kill you.'

It should have been impossible for me to sleep that first night, crammed against so many other bodies with my back against a wall, and in shock from losing my mother. It all felt so surreal. Like a nightmare I couldn't wake from. But sheer exhaustion won out and I soon passed out, as did my 499 new roommates.

It was not a deep sleep because if anyone woke, they

instinctively tried to turn, momentarily forgetting where they were, waking those crammed up against him. The stirring and agitation spread through the block, eventually reaching the kapo who was sleeping near the entrance. Hearing the commotion, he jumped up, brandishing the chair leg and started hitting those closest to him.

My old sports instructor from the Morning Star Club was near the front and when the kapo brought that chair leg down on his head, it split open. None of us could get close enough to help him and when dawn broke, we could only watch helplessly as the kapos dragged him out, leaving a large puddle of blood on the floor behind him. I had no idea if my old instructor was dead or alive in that moment, but this incident only reinforced the fact that rushing to the far wall had been a good instinct.

At 5am a bell rang out across the camp.

'Roll call!' Macek shouted, that chair leg still firmly in his hand. 'OUTSIDE!'

Macek drove us all out of the block and into the cold, dawn air to line up in the space between our block and the next, where we then waited, unsupervised, for forty-five minutes. It was a long and uncomfortable wait. We had been given no food since arriving twenty-four hours earlier and were all hungry and exhausted. The icy wind was bitterly cold and cut through our light clothing. As we stood, waiting, we came up with a way to create our own 'human ovens'. Standing back-to-back, we rotated so that everyone had a turn at being in the middle of the 'oven'. This was the only way we could find to get warm, even if it was only for the briefest of moments.

The guards finally arrived to take roll call, which ended up taking far longer than it should have. Each time the guards counted incorrectly, they would start again. All the while, the kapos screamed profanities and abuse at us, using the foulest language I had ever heard. This was our very first roll call at Auschwitz and we would quickly come to dread them. They happened twice a day and each time the numbers needed to add up exactly. Even the dead had to be counted.

After morning roll call, we moved to another area to line up for our lukewarm 'coffee'. They called it coffee, but it looked and tasted nothing like any coffee I had ever tried – more like dirty water. But we were grateful to have something to put in our bellies at that point.

After this we were ordered to the toilets. The latrines at Auschwitz were in large barracks that had two long planks of wood down the middle. We were only permitted to visit the latrines once a day and there was no privacy or drainage. Once there, we were rushed in in groups, given a few seconds to relieve ourselves, then rushed back out again. There was barely time to pull down our trousers, let alone do anything else. We had no toilet paper so had to wipe ourselves with our hands, or not at all.

There was no water to wash with in the latrines block, so we were sent to a separate washing block where we were allowed very little time and given nothing to dry our bodies or faces with. We soon learned that it was up to the kapos if we were allowed drinking water during the day. When the weather turned stinking hot they would often deprive us out of spite, and so many of us chose to drink the water in the mornings instead of washing in it.

Even on the hottest days these bastards would not allow us even a sip of water.

After washing, we were left alone for a few hours. On that first morning in the camp, Heniek and I took the opportunity to walk around and check out the other blocks. When we witnessed a kapo beating a prisoner to death for accidentally stepping in his path, we realised we would need to keep our heads down while wandering. Kapos were always on the lookout for someone or something to relieve their boredom, which usually meant beating up or killing prisoners simply for their own amusement.

At any time of day, we could be subjected to humiliation and abuse by the kapos. Every one of us was a potential target for a sadistic kapo who was looking for some 'fun' to relieve the boredom. On a couple of occasions, the kapo and Blockführer chose a couple of hundred of us for 'work'. They had us pick up heavy stones and run from one end of the camp to the other for many hours. I was forced to do this several times and it was one of the many times I would silently thank my father for encouraging me to stay so fit, because anyone who fell behind was clubbed to death, shot or torn apart by the guard's vicious dogs. This would happen right in front of us all, and then we were the ones forced to carry the dead bodies back with us for the evening roll call.

At lunch time we were given what the guards called 'soup' but was just dirty water. We were given one large bowl between five of us, but no spoons, so we would each take a sip and then pass the bowl along to the next person. We would continue in this way until the soup was all gone. We were all out of our minds with hunger by then, so watched each other closely to make sure no one took more than their single sip.

The days began to pass and, as I became used to my new routine, I began to take more notice of our surroundings. I made a conscious effort to closely observe and then memorise everything I was seeing so that I could tell people what happened here, just like I promised my mother I would. I had no pen or paper to keep notes, and even if I had it would have been far too dangerous to write anything down. The punishment for keeping notes of any kind was death. People in the camp spoke of some Auschwitz prisoners, including the *Sonderkommandos* (prisoners forced to work in the gas chambers) who had made notes and hidden them away, but the Nazis were always on the lookout for anyone who was writing anything down. I would have to keep all the notes in my head, so I made sure to pay close attention to every detail of what was happening around me. If I didn't survive then so be it, but, if I did, I wanted my memories of Auschwitz-Birkenau to be clear.

The first thing I made a mental note of was how close the crematorium was to our camp – only 50 or 60 metres away. Huge wafts of smoke belched out of the chimneys and across the high barbed-wire fence that separated us, twenty-four hours a day. The smell of death choked the air.

We could always smell burning flesh in our part of the camp because the Nazis burned people on pyres if the crematorium was unable to cope with the load. It was shocking and incomprehensible. I had been aware that Jews were being murdered at Auschwitz but had no idea about the scale of the operation unit I saw and smelled it for myself. There was no possible way I would have believed it unless I was there to witness it for myself. Who could believe such a thing? It was unfathomable.

By then I had had to admit the truth to myself – that my poor frail mother had ended up in that inconceivable place. It was too shocking and heartbreaking to imagine. The very idea of my mother ending up in that place was a concept I could not bring myself to think about for too long, or I would lose the strength to carry on. My dear, beautiful, kind and caring mum, the woman who had spoilt and nurtured me, who had baked the most delicious honey cakes in all Łódź, the woman who gave me life, taught me kindness, tolerance and patience, was gone.

I had sworn to protect her and keep her safe, but now she was almost certainly dead. In the end, I couldn't save her. This was the worst realisation of all. What kind of son cannot protect his mother? Seventy-eight years later I still feel the pain I experienced in the moment I lost her. I was a son in mourning but was unable to mourn the way I wanted to, the way I should. I wanted time to reflect on the wonderful woman my mother was, but the only time I had to myself in Auschwitz was at night. Even then it was hard to focus on my thoughts when I was lying on a cold concrete floor squashed up against the smelly, bony bodies of other broken-hearted men. It felt wrong to think of my mother in the crematorium – a place full of so much fear and pain and death.

Who did I have to take care of now? As far as I knew at that point in time, no one in my family was alive. It had been over two years since we had heard from any of my sisters, and I was starting to lose hope that they were still living, especially after what had happened to my parents. So, if they were gone too, then there was no one in the world who I belonged to now. And if I had no family, then who was I?

Would I find peace again? Would I find people to love and belong to and be with again? I had to believe I would for without hope there is no life. But in those first few days at Auschwitz, I felt untethered and alone in the world. Dark thoughts ran through my mind ... *It is my fault she's dead. I shouldn't have let us leave our hiding place in Łódź. I could have kept her safe there. I should have talked her out of it.*

Unlike others in the camp with brothers, fathers and sons to look out for, I only had to worry about myself. Of course, I worried for my friends and wanted them to survive too, but it was not the same stress and worry you carry for your blood relatives. Trying to keep others, as well as yourself, safe was an extra burden and worry for those men who had loved ones in the camp with them.

The hunger and the fear were enough to drive people out of their minds. We would dream and talk about food so much that sometimes I could almost taste my mother's cholent and her sweet, delicious honey cakes. My family were not with me in person, but they were always in my heart and mind. I thought about my mother and father every day, and wondered about my sisters, but I also knew that to get through this I had to focus on my own survival.

Being a non-religious Jew, I didn't put my faith in God,

The Strength of Hope

only in myself. Auschwitz simply confirmed what I had believed all my life. There was no God. I respected the choices of those around me to pray and keep their faith in God in these horrific circumstances, but I never understood it.

'Where is God?' I would ask my friends. 'There is no God in this place.'

One day, I heard a story about a Nazi officer who approached a rabbi in the camp and began to mock him.

'You Jews and your God,' he laughed. 'If he's the almighty one then he should be able to help you, no? Well, you show me. You pray to your God and if he doesn't save you after five minutes, I will shoot you.'

The rabbi didn't say a word. Just looked straight into the Nazi's eyes for the full five minutes.

When time was up the Nazi laughed and said, 'The five minutes is over. Where is your God?'

'He helped me already.' The rabbi smiled.

'How?' The Nazi laughed. 'I'm going to shoot you now and you'll be dead.'

'He helped me because he made me what I am,' the rabbi said. 'Not what you are.'

This story made me very sad, and all I could hope was that his faith gave the rabbi comfort and solace at the end of his life, because the Nazi shot him dead.

I may not be religious, but I have always respected people like the rabbi who have such strong faith in God and religion. Everyone should be free to have their own beliefs without fear of persecution. We all belong to the same race. It doesn't matter the colour of your skin, the shape of your eyes, your ethnicity or religion. What hurts one human being also hurts another.

I constantly thought about Mum's final words to me, that I should do everything humanly possible to survive.

What did she mean by 'humanly'? I concluded that my mother wanted me to survive, but still wanted me to be a good human. She wanted me to hold on to the morals and values I had grown up with, in the midst of all this evil. She was saying that I should never, ever, become like *them* or do anything to dehumanise myself in this hell of a camp. And so, I made a vow to myself and to my mother; I would do everything 'humanly' possible to survive this hell.

14

AN UNLIKELY ALLY

Some people in our group had numbers tattooed on their arms within a day of their arrival, but I was never given one. Prisoners in our camp were used as replacements for workers in other camps when needed. Prisoners were only sent to the tattooist once they were chosen to replace someone under Auschwitz's jurisdiction.

Without numbers on our arms, my friends and I soon realised that no one could keep track of us, which meant we could change blocks within the 'Gypsy Camp'. We decided to start looking around for another block and leave number 4 and the sadistic Macek forever.

One morning, the six of us moved across to another block, only to discover that the kapo there was even more sadistic than Macek. He frequently threatened us with the crematoria saying we would be 'fried in the frying pan!' He also made us do daily 'exercises' for our health. Many of the prisoners in this block were so weak and malnourished that they could barely walk, but they were forced to do push ups in the mud along with the rest of us. My youth and fitness served me well here. I got through the exercises without stopping, but others who couldn't manage were severely beaten, sometimes even killed, depending on the kapo's mood that day. Many times in Auschwitz, I silently thanked my father for encouraging me to lead an active lifestyle as a young boy. I know that training and fitness saved my life many times over.

Another one of this kapo's main amusements was to make us line up outside, take off our belts and hold them across our hands while doing knee bends. If the belt slipped off, which it invariably did, we received a severe beating. I saw many prisoners beaten to death during this exercise and only managed to escape a beating myself because I cheated. I used my thumbs to hold my belt in a particular way to prevent it from falling off. Thankfully the kapo didn't look too closely at my grip, or it could have been the end for me too. Every second of holding that belt felt like an hour.

Having to endure this kind of inhumane treatment day after day made it easy to slip into despair. My friends and I saw it in the faces of those around us and fought hard against the impulse to do the same, as hard as it sometimes was. We knew that if we gave in to despair and lost hope, we were dead.

'Just hang in there,' Heniek and I would tell people. 'We must survive one day at a time. While there is life, there is hope.'

I didn't always believe this but saying these words to others helped me. Hearing them come out of my mouth reminded me of my father and the way he had given hope to so many in the ghetto in a similar way.

It was early one November morning when we were all taken to the showers. By that time, I had been in the 'Gypsy Camp' for over two months and hadn't showered once. On this morning, the camp was still dark when we were made to undress and walk, naked, to the shower blocks. It was so cold that there was frost on the ground. By the time we arrived at the shower block we were all frozen stiff. When we got inside, the hot water that sprayed our freezing cold bodies was extremely painful. There were no towels to dry ourselves with, and we were all forced to walk back to our block, still naked and now dripping wet, retrieve our clothes then head back outside for roll call. We were like blocks of ice as we stood there in our damp clothes. Many men developed terrible colds after this day. Some ended up with pneumonia and were subsequently sent to the gas chamber. Luck was on my side again that day. I didn't develop a sniffle, cough or sneeze from that morning, which was amazing. So many men were dying all around me by then. Every morning, Heniek and I would wake up to find more dead bodies around us or missing from roll call. So, we decided to go shopping for another block again.

There was one block that seemed to have far more people than other blocks. Block 12 had around 1500 people in it instead of the usual 500. Something strange was going on over there.

'We should investigate,' I told Heniek.

Heniek agreed and so after that morning's 'coffee', we went to check it out. We spent much of that day watching the German Blockführer in charge of Block 12. The first thing we noticed was that he wore a red triangle instead of a green one on his uniform, meaning he was a political prisoner, not a criminal. A good sign.

We also noticed that he made sure everyone in his block received an equal amount of food when it was being distributed. Also, he yelled at the prisoners, like other Blockführer and kapo but never hit them, which was very unusual.

It was clear why people were leaving their blocks to come here. This Blockführer was a good German, at least the best we had come across in over five years. Heniek and I wondered if we should try to engage with him. After watching him closely for a few more days, we decided to try our luck one morning. This was a huge risk. Any other Blockführer in the camp would undoubtedly have beaten us to death if we tried to speak to them but we felt sure this German was different.

We walked slowly towards him with friendly smiles on our faces.

'Hello,' I said, nervously.

We both held our breath as the man looked up at us. Amazingly, he smiled back.

'Hello.'

Gradually, and cautiously, we began to exchange a few words. We learned that his name was Wilhelm, and he was a political prisoner who had been in various camps for seven years. Wilhelm had been allocated a special room away from everyone in Block 12 and, after chatting for a while, he invited us to see it. We talked some more in his room. He told us that he was a social democrat and had taken many beatings over the years. So many, in fact, that half his buttock was missing. I might not have believed it except that he showed us the proof.

'We are social democrats too,' we told him.

'Then I will try to look after you,' Wilhelm said. 'I choose the kapos on my block, so they are not too bad. If you can keep your arms from being tattooed, I will be able to help you.'

'Thank you,' we said, stunned.

'I will never fight for the Nazis,' Wilhelm frowned. 'I would rather die in this camp.'

We couldn't believe our luck. Somehow, we had managed to find the only Blockführer in Auschwitz who was a human being. Heniek and I went back to tell the rest of our friends and the following morning, straight after roll call, we all moved to Block 12. It was good to be in a place where we could feel a little safer, but we weren't naive enough to think we could let our guard down completely. We also had to do everything to avoid getting that number on our arms.

Selections happened randomly at any time of the day or night. When they did, there was no way of knowing whether you were being selected for work duty or the gas chamber. During the selection process, we were made to line up in groups of five. I decided early on that if I stood at the back the guards might think I was trying to hide and choose me to teach me a lesson. Therefore, I always stood right at the front of the line and took the chance they would look straight over my head and beyond me. Now that we were in Block 12, I hoped that Wilhelm might also be able to help me if I was selected. This happened a few times. When I was selected, Wilhelm would place himself between the SS men and me. When the selection process was over, he would stay in front of me, giving me a chance to sneak back into the crowd and hide behind the other prisoners.

Wilhelm saved me on numerous occasions, and I owe him my life.

One day, at the end of 1944, Wilhelm disappeared for an entire day. We were all concerned that our protection was gone, but also worried for him. What had happened? Where had he gone? Did the Nazis find out about his kind ways and send him to the gas chambers? When he finally returned at the end of the day, with a huge smile on his face, we were relieved.

'Where were you?' we asked.

'They wanted me to join the army,' Wilhelm told us, 'but I told them, "I will never fight for you Nazis!"'

He was as surprised as us that they didn't beat or kill him then and there after such a bold statement.

Friendships with men like Heniek and Wilhelm kept me going at Auschwitz-Birkenau, both literally and mentally. This connection with others, and the sense that we were in this together, made me feel that I wasn't alone. That gave me hope and the strength to go on. There is nothing more important than human connection, as well as having hope to cling to, no matter how small. My friends and I would talk about 'when this is over' and try to keep each other's spirits up. We even talked about the possibility of one day having our own children and giving them a better life than the ones we had been handed. This hopeful kind of talk gave us something to focus on, and to look forward to during such misery, pain and despair. We looked after each other. We helped each other survive.

LESSON LEARNED

Some of the best people in your life can come from places and circumstances you least expect.

15

RIDING MY LUCK

Periodically, representatives from large German enterprises would come to Auschwitz to buy slave workers for their businesses. These men paid the SS a small fee of five marks per prisoner. The money was supposed to cover the cost of the upkeep of the prisoners but in fact went straight into the Nazis' coffers.

In November 1944, an engineer from one of these enterprises came to the camp. Once again, we were all taken outside and lined up, but this time the man asked, 'Who here is a metal worker?'

Instinctively, I went to move forward, having worked in a metal factory in Łódź, then stopped. Was this a trick or an opportunity? And was I willing to take a gamble that it was the latter, even if that meant risking my life? In a few short seconds, I decided to trust my luck. It had gotten me this far and this might be the only chance I had to get out of this place.

I stepped forward. The man turned his gaze on me.

'How many turns does a boring machine operate at per minute?' he asked.

This was a tricky question to answer. In Łódź, I had operated a middle-sized boring machine, but there were many different sizes and they all operated at different speeds. The machine I worked operated at about 900 turns per minute, but what if that wasn't the answer he was looking for?

I immediately regretted my decision to step forward, but he was staring, waiting for an answer. Right or wrong I had no choice but to give him a number.

'1200,' I said, bracing myself for whatever was to come next.

He stared for a moment longer, then turned away without asking me anything more. I wondered in that moment if he even knew the answer himself. Either way, it seemed that he had accepted mine, which was all that mattered.

'I will take him,' he told the guard.

So, without being able to say goodbye to Wilhelm or my friends, I was ordered towards a waiting truck. When I stepped up into the back of it, I looked around at the men already there and saw a childhood friend from Łódź, another Heniek, and we gave each other a short nod.

I had no idea where we were going. All I knew was that, after three long months, I was leaving Auschwitz-Birkenau death camp. It was amazing I had lasted one day, let alone ninety, in a place where 85 per cent of people were sent to their deaths by Doctor Josef Mengele on arrival, and thousands of prisoners died from starvation, beatings or hypothermia.

But I knew my survival had been sheer luck, nothing more.

Mengele could easily have sent me to the left when I got off that train with my mother. I might have dropped that belt and received a beating from the Blockführer bad enough to kill me. I might never have found Wilhelm – a man who would save me from selection multiple times. My survival up to this point had nothing to do with smarts or strength, as many people smarter and stronger than me had perished here. It was all down to luck, nothing more.

I sat in the back of the cattle truck, watching the hellish place grow smaller and smaller in the distance, and said a silent final goodbye to my mother.

Soon after, we were loaded from the truck onto cattle trains and travelled many days and nights, over 650 kilometres. It took a long time because there were Allied bombings and air raids occurring all over at that time. The bucket in the train car for us to use for a toilet was overflowing for the whole journey and we were given very minimal food. The guards who stood on the roof of our train with guns would just push small amounts of food through the cracks of the door every now and then. We arrived at a new camp on the outskirts of Braunschweig – a sub-camp of Neuengamme, which was an infamous place where prisoners were sent to be murdered or have medical experiments carried out on them. In Braunschweig, we had heard that some prisoners who were unwell had been sent there, and so of course my first thought was that the same was about to happen to us.

We were taken off the train and straight to barracks where we found bunks, straw mattresses and blankets. After our accommodations at Auschwitz, Heniek and I thought this was pure luxury. However, we soon discovered that the building was badly constructed. Moisture dripped from the roof throughout

The Strength of Hope

the night, so we all woke wet and freezing cold in our bunks the next morning.

Then began a new routine in a new camp. I much preferred it to my daily life at Auschwitz, although it was exhausting. Six mornings a week, our group walked 10 kilometres to a nearby truck manufacturing factory, where we worked all day. This was late December, so very cold, which was unfortunate for those who were given outdoor jobs. Luck was with me again as my job involved cleaning truck engines indoors. These trucks had been damaged and, before the engines could be repaired, they needed to be cleaned. I wondered why the German had requested a metal worker specifically for such a job but wasn't going to complain.

Our work was regularly interrupted by the consistent bombing of the nearby railway line and factories. After each bomb dropped, we were made to stop whatever work we were doing to go outside in the freezing conditions and clean up the rubble and mess. At the end of the day, we would all walk back to the camp at Braunschweig. We didn't know who was doing the bombing but hoped it was a sign that the Americans and British were getting closer. It was tiny skerricks of hope like this that kept us going, especially on those days when we had to endure the sadistic treatment of the kapos.

The kapos in charge at Braunschweig had been imported from other concentration camps. Most were Germans, apart from one who was a Roma, and the best of the lot. One of the German kapos had been a boxer before the war, and he was a brute. I wondered if he lashed out and punched people for no reason because he hadn't achieved the fame and success he desired in his boxing career. If the person he punched tried to stay upright, he would keep attacking until they finally went down, and we quickly worked out that this brute would only be satisfied with a one-punch knockout. Rather than trying to stay on our feet, we learned to fall straight to the ground as soon as he threw his first punch. Satisfied, the kapo would walk away and leave us alone.

The boxer was not the only brutal kapo at Braunschweig. Most of them were sadistic and cruel. Sunday was our only day off, but the kapos made us clean the entire camp on this day and wouldn't let us go to the toilet without official permission. One day, I was desperate to go but was refused permission. I held on as long as I could but, eventually, I couldn't wait any longer and snuck off to use the toilet.

There had been nobody around when I entered the latrine, but when I walked out, I found the kapos waiting for me. They dragged me to the infirmary, produced a pair of pliers and proceeded to pull out the nail of my right index finger. It was excruciating but I willed myself to stay silent, not wanting to give them the satisfaction of uttering so much as a tiny moan of pain. When they let me go back to the barracks, I was left with a badly bleeding finger. We had no antiseptic, and I knew of people who had ended up with infections that became gangrenous. When selections took place, these were the first people to be taken. Not wanting to risk an infection, I decided to use my own method of antiseptic. I'd heard one's own urine is a good make-do for antiseptic, so I peed on my finger, then found a scrap of paper to clean the wound. I had to keep looking over my shoulder the whole time to make sure no kapos could see what I was doing.

Parents and Sisters

My mother, Chaja Goldberg (top left), the best cook in all of Łódź. My final promise to her changed the path of my life.

My father, Herszl Goldberg (top right). He was my hero, and he taught me about the importance of a positive mindset.

My beloved sisters Frajda (left) and Estera (right). Both were killed by the Nazis.

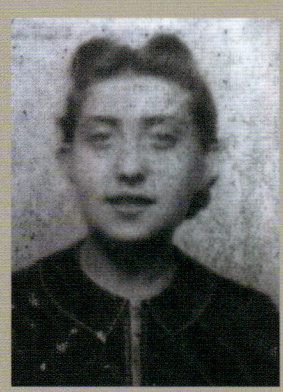

My eldest sister, Maryla, with her husband Moniek and son Danek. After I was separated from her for many years, my remaining sister and her family would eventually join Cesia and me in Melbourne.

During the War

When we returned to home from Poland, we discovered, to our horror, that barbed-wire fences were being built around the poorest section of Łódź. Our home was now part of a filthy ghetto, and we were prisoners. (United States Holocaust Memorial Museum, courtesy of Robert Abrams)

I encountered a lot of evil people during the Holocaust. In my opinion, Rumkowski (pictured here) was one of the worst. He turned on his fellow Jews to curry favour and protection from the Nazis. (United States Holocaust Memorial Museum, courtesy of Ruth Eldar)

The selection ramp at Auschwitz is the last place I ever saw my mother. I later learned that she was taken straight to a gas chamber and murdered. (United States Holocaust Memorial Museum, courtesy of Yad Vashem)

I will never forget walking into the Wöbbelin camp and seeing the skeletons of other human beings piled 6 feet high. It haunts me to this day. Initially we thought we had been left at Wöbbelin to die, but, instead, the moment I had been dreaming of for years had finally arrived: liberation. (United States Holocaust Memorial Museum, courtesy of R.J. Soldinger)

Liberation

Five Abrams – Abram Belzycki, Abram (Mumek) Morgentaler, Abram Biderman, Abram Goldberg and Abram Jakubowicz – in our SKIF uniforms. The SKIF was a big part of my life before and after the war, and a place where I made life-long friends.

Bund – 1945, Frankfurt, Germany. I am front left, and Mumek is front right. After I was liberated, one of the first things I did was seek out my fellow Bundists. I was one of the first Bund members to return to Łódź from the camps, and my friends in the Bund were there to welcome me with food and shelter.

I never lost the gymnastic skills I learned at the Morning Star Club. More than once, my physical fitness saved my life.

Abram, Abram (me) and Jack looking smart in Berlin in 1945. After what we had lived through, we were determined to make the most of our freedom.

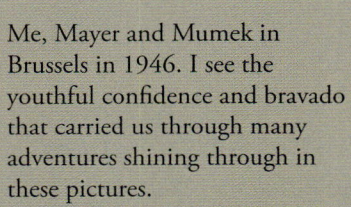

Me, Mayer and Mumek in Brussels in 1946. I see the youthful confidence and bravado that carried us through many adventures shining through in these pictures.

The Start of a Love Story

Post-liberation was a blissful time. After so much deprivation, it felt like the whole world was open to me. I was full of optimism for the future, and even the simplest of pleasures, such as playing ping-pong with a friend, felt wonderful. This was what I was doing five months into my stay in Belgium when I first saw the woman I would love for the rest of my life, Cesia.

When we met, Cesia was very shy and far from the social butterfly she would later become. Here we are during our courtship in Belgium. I knew she was the one for me but had to go slowly because I didn't want to scare her away! Bottom left, Cesia is wearing a bag I crafted especially for her.

Australia

Elka Eckstein, Cesia, Abram Tennenbaum (Cesia's cousin), me, Josl Eckstein and Dorka Dorenblatt (Szlajcher).

Even though the nightlife in Australia was much quieter than we were used to in Belgium, Cesia and I never regretted moving here for a minute. We believe that life is what you make of it, so we threw ourselves into Melbourne's cultural scene and spent every moment possible enjoying the safety and freedom our new life had to offer. Along the way we made many wonderful new friends, especially among Melbourne's growing Jewish community.

Dressed to impress in the 50s (top left); swinging in the 60s (top right); beehives and 70s fashions (bottom left); out on the town in the 80s (bottom right).

Family

Cesia, Charlie and me – 1954

Helen, me and Cesia, Melbourne – 1960

Cesia and Helen – 1962

Becoming parents to Charlie and Helen is the greatest joy Cesia and I have had in our lives. Our children signified a new beginning. We would never forget what happened to us during the Holocaust, but rebuilding our family went some way towards easing the pain of losing so many loved ones.

Friends

Cesia and I travelled to Canada in 1973 for an emotional reunion with Mumek (left). I had not seen my boyhood friend since 1947.

Mumek, Amelia (Mumek's wife) and Heniek (Mumek's brother). We visited them in Montreal many times over the years and shared a wonderful friendship. In 1996, when Mumek passed away, Cesia and I travelled to Auschwitz to help Amelia fulfil my old friend's final wish: that his ashes be spread at the site where his mother had been murdered.

Cesia and I both love to cook and have our friends and family over to eat. She will tell you she's a natural cook, but I promise I taught her all she knows!

Running Goldy's was an exciting and happy era for our family. The restaurant was situated in the centre of the theatre disctrict and became a favourite spot for the local performing arts fraternity. (*Journeys of Melbourne's Coffee Pioneers: Trailblazing Passions* by Sandra Makris)

There was a 16 year old girl living in Brussels
Who fell in love with a gymnast with muscles
Their eyes met at the same level
Who would have bet that she'd marry this 'devil'

With no money to spare
Their wedding was rather bare
With no wedding dress or crushing of glass
No chuppa or ribbon on cars.

Now it's 50 years later
Let's make the simcha even greater
High tea will be served from four-thirty to nine
Please come and join us for a glass of wine.

Tudor Court is the place to meet
To give this 'young' couple a wonderful treat
The date is Monday the 9th of June
And please call one of us soon.

Celebrating our 50th wedding anniversary, surrounded by loved ones, is a night Cesia and I will remember forever.

Daniel and Bettan wrote this poem about Cesia and me, which featured on the invitations.

Bono, pictured here sitting at the top left of the table with Nastassja on his lap, was like a brother to me. He was one of the most inspirational and courageous men I ever knew, and I was proud to have him as a life-long friend. Among his many achievements, Bono played a key role in establishing the Jewish Holocaust Museum in Melbourne.

Cesia and me with our grandchildren, Daniel, Daley and Nastassja, in 1997. Cesia's beaming smile says it all; we adore being grandparents.

Me, Cesia and Nicky – 2014. Cesia and I had many blissful years together after our children moved out of home, and before she went to live at Gary Smorgon House. We always found the joy in every day. Something as simple as playing with our dog, Nicky, would light up my wife's face with the beaming smile I have loved for so many years.

While on holiday, I was lucky to be invited to take part in a ceremony to commemorate the 1943 Warsaw Ghetto Uprising, at the Rapoport Monument in 2001. I lit the eternal flame, and it was an incredibly moving and emotional experience.

Educating the younger generations about the Holocaust helps me fulfil the promise I made to my mother, to bear witness to what had happened to us and help ensure it never happens again.

Fiona Harris has helped me to write my story, and over that time our families have become good friends. We have shared many happy occasions. Here, Fiona (seated to my right with her arm on my shoulder) and her husband, Mike (next to Fiona), join the Goldbergs for dinner.

The Goldbergs, 2022. From left to right: (standing) Dean, Paul, Bettan, Isabelle; (seated) Nastassja, Sienna, Helen, Cesia, Abram, Charlie, Daniel.

After 75 years together, the girl with the brown curls is still the most beautiful woman in the world to me.

I knew I would be punished again if they caught me disinfecting my own wound.

The kapos were stringent when it came to military precision in the camp. For example, each morning when we lined up for roll call, the tops of our shoes needed to be in line with each other and pointing straight ahead. One morning, just as a German kapo was approaching to carry out his inspection, I glanced down to make sure my feet were in the correct position. He stopped in front of me with a murderous look in his eyes. I knew from the way he lifted his boot and pushed his hips back, that he was about to kick me straight and hard in the genitals. Instinctively, my hands darted out to cover myself just as his steel-toe capped boot made contact, slamming into my arm, just above my right wrist. It left a nasty wound that would not stop bleeding afterwards. Again, I used my urine antiseptic treatment, and managed to avoid infection.

I still have the scar to this day.

16

LIGHT AT THE END OF THE TUNNEL

We stayed in Braunschweig for about a month before our group of 200 was marched to Watenstedt, around 20 kilometres away. It was January and snowing, so the ground was frozen. I wouldn't have lasted such a long walk if it weren't for my sturdy sheepskin-lined shoes. They kept my feet warm on those long, cold, wet marches. To this day, I am convinced my footwear is a big part of why I survived. By ordering those boots for me all those years ago, my darling mother had unknowingly saved my life.

I didn't know it at the time, but as I was marching across Germany, the Red Army were marching into the Łódź Ghetto to liberate everyone who was left there. In those final months of the war, the Nazis plan was to bring all prisoners from the east across to Germany. They knew the Red Army was getting closer, as were the Americans, but the camps in Germany were starting to get very crowded.

We arrived at one of these overcrowded camps in Watenstedt, where the guards immediately took our clothes away, saying they were going to disinfect them. We were left practically naked for two days until they gave us clothes to wear again, but they were not the clothes we had arrived in. I was just relieved they hadn't taken my shoes.

There was no space for us at the camp in Watenstedt, so we continued our journey through Germany, getting rejected from camp after camp and then moving on to another one where the SS guards hoped we would finally be taken off their hands. We travelled for many days and nights, sometimes marching and sometimes on trains. Finally, we arrived at Ravensbrück, a women's camp, but not many women were left there. It mainly held people like us, prisoners from other camps, including Yugoslavs and Poles. Our group was kept separate from all of them, as well as from the few women who remained in the camp.

Heniek and I, along with some others, were taken out to clean up an area near Ravensbrück that had been bombed. As we cleaned, I found parcels of food from the Red Cross that had been intended for the Jews. Each parcel was around 2–4 kilograms and filled with chocolate, Pall Mall cigarettes, milk, magazines, cheese, biscuits, and tinned butter. The Germans never delivered these parcels to us of course, but my friend and I managed to steal a bit of chocolate and cigarettes out of some of the parcels when our supervisor's back was turned.

A few days later, Heniek and I were walking around the camp when he started shouting and running towards the barbed-wire fence that separated us from the women. Despite her emaciated appearance, my friend had recognised a woman on the other side as his mother. They gripped each other's hands through the fence and shed many tears. It was a joyous and incredible reunion for the mother and son, but short-lived as we were forced to move on two weeks later. This time we were squeezed into cargo train carriages like sardines, although the Germans gave out food parcels as we boarded, one between two people. I immediately exchanged my cigarettes for bread.

In the short time we had been at Ravensbrück, many men from our group had died, too weak and emaciated from hunger to go on. If the Germans had delivered those food parcels a bit earlier, these men might have lived, but now it was too late. By the time we were given the food parcels on that train journey, some people's hunger was so immense that their bodies were unable to cope with rich foods like butter and cheese. A man Heniek and I had become friendly with was one of these unfortunate souls. The poor man tried to have some food on the train, but it had been so long since he'd eaten that he couldn't swallow. Many people died in this way because the food was simply too fatty and rich for their starved bodies. I spent the journey rationing out my bread.

Our destination this time was a camp 100 kilometres or so outside of Berlin called Wöbbelin. At that point, we had been travelling in an enclosed cattle truck for so long that I had lost all sense of what part of the country, or even which country, we were in. It wasn't until after the war that I learned where these places were.

The moment we arrived the Wöbbelin guards took our parcels away, but this was less disturbing than the sight that greeted us as we stumbled out, eager to stretch our sore, stiff limbs.

The Strength of Hope

Thousands of skeletal corpses piled 5 or 6 feet high covered the Wöbbelin camp. As we walked into the camp and got closer, we realised that some of the skeletons on these piles were still alive. It was a gruesome and eerie sight that haunts me to this day.

We soon learned that this wasn't a camp for Jews, but for slave labour prisoners from various occupied countries. The Germans had built Wöbbelin with the intention of keeping American and British Jews there, but it was full of Poles, Russians, French, Yugoslavs and many others when we arrived. The camp was half-finished and had an abandoned feel to it. There were no floors, doors or windows on many of the barracks and our, now smaller, group was moved into one of the new blocks with no windows. We stayed there for about a week until we were once again loaded onto trains at midnight on 1 May. I was relieved to be leaving a place full of so much horror and death.

On this next journey, we were herded into open cars instead of enclosed ones. The fresh air was a welcome change, but as the train approached a dense forest, it began to slow and eventually stopped.

'EVERYBODY OUT!' The SS guards shouted. 'YOU ARE ALL GOING INTO THE FOREST TO COLLECT BLANKETS!'

Of course, my first thought was that this was a trick. Surely the SS would wait until we were deep in the forest and then slaughter us with their machine guns. What else were they going to do? It defied all logic that these soldiers would want us to have blankets to keep warm. No. They must have run out of places to send us, and so their only solution was to dispose of us.

I had no intention of walking into a trap and to my death.

Heniek and I quickly made a plan. We would walk into the forest, then sneak away from our group and hide in the thick brush until the gunfire had ceased. We would only make our escape once we heard the train move away again. Our other friend was far too weak and ill to join us. He could no longer swallow, and his stomach had shrunk so much that even if he had been able to eat, he wouldn't have been able to keep it down. Heniek and I didn't want to leave him behind, but he insisted on staying with the group. We took our place behind the others and marched into the forest.

When the guards' backs were turned, Heniek and I slipped away from the group and hid in the dense forest. We waited for what felt like an eternity, but may only have been an hour or two, for the sound of gunshots and screams, but the forest stayed quiet.

Eventually we heard footsteps and ducked our heads down behind the bushes. When we peeked out again, we were amazed to see our group heading back through the forest. And what were they carrying? Blankets! We couldn't believe it! How was this possible?

After a hushed conversation, Heniek and I decided to rejoin our group. It was probably a safer option than staying on the run where an SS guard could shoot us on sight at any moment. We slipped back into the line with our fellow prisoners and marched back to the waiting train. We were now the only ones in the group without blankets to keep us warm.

We were at least right in assuming the SS guards had run out of places to take us because as soon as we had all boarded, they ordered the train to turn around and head back to Wöbbelin. When we arrived there, we were told to go inside one of the newly built blocks and 'NOT COME OUT!'

This block was different to the one we'd been in before because it did have windows, albeit half-finished ones. We stayed in there overnight, and the next morning we woke to the sound of a rumbling overhead and fighting in the distance. We rushed to the half-finished windows to look out. The first thing we noticed was that there were no SS guards stationed outside our block. This was highly unusual and, feeling very confused, we began whispering and murmuring among ourselves.

Had the SS really left us here unguarded? What if it was a trick?

We had heard stories of other camps where this had happened – guards pretended to leave and then, when the prisoners ventured outside, they opened fire, killing them all. We had learned by now not to trust the Nazis. We decided it was safest to stay put for the time being.

Over the next couple of hours, we heard canons, the rumbling of tanks and artillery fire. We assumed that all this commotion meant the Americans and British were getting closer, but if that was true then what did that mean for us? What would the Nazis do with us now? Part of me desperately wanted to believe that this was the sound of the Allies advancing, but another part knew that if this were true, the Nazis would almost certainly kill us now. So, in this moment of great hope – the greatest hope I had held in my heart for five years – there was also great fear. *What reason would the Nazis have for keeping us alive now?*

We all waited in excruciating anticipation for whatever was to come. Would there be the sound of gunfire? Dive bombers? Would we hear screams of terror as the Nazis methodically executed every prisoner left in the camp?

We waited in silence for a while longer and, after hearing nothing for quite some time, a small group of us finally decided to risk leaving the block to scope out our surroundings. This was a dangerous move, especially if the Nazis were still close by and waiting for us to emerge, but a voice deep within me told me to take the chance. It was the same voice that had told me to step forward when that industrialist at Auschwitz had asked for a metal worker all those months ago.

Taking a deep breath, I, alongside Heniek and some other prisoners, walked outside. There, we were met with a sight I had dreamed about for so many years: American tanks.

17

LIBERATION

On that momentous day, Heniek and I stood and stared in amazement at the tanks, and American soldiers walking through the death camp. More amazing to us was the fact that there was not a single Nazi in sight. It took a few moments for the reality of the situation to sink in. It had finally happened. The Americans were here, and we were free of the Nazis.

We had been liberated.

Heniek put his arm around my shoulders, and we stared at one another in silence for a few moments, too shocked to speak. The feelings surging through us were overwhelming and indescribable. After five long painful years it was finally over.

At the age of twenty I had suffered more pain and loss than any human should have to endure. I had lost everyone in the world that I loved. And for what? What had been the point of it all? Why had so many people, including my entire family, needed to die and endure so much pain, humiliation, and suffering? They hadn't. It had all been for nothing. None of what we had lived through over the past six years made the slightest bit of sense. And the fact that I had survived, that I was still here for this incredible moment of liberation, also made no sense. It was a difficult reality to fathom as I stood in my clothes, now little more than rags, staring at our saviours that cold morning in May.

We then watched as these brave, strong soldiers, who had come to save us, broke down in tears. Their shock, grief and anger were immense, and no wonder. The sight that met them upon walking into Wöbbelin was horrific. Thousands of skeletal corpses were piled around the camp, and, against all odds, some of those seeming corpses were still breathing and wandering slowly towards them. The expressions on the soldiers' faces said it all. They were stunned and traumatised by what they had found here.

Slowly and carefully, the Americans led those of us still mobile over to a makeshift medical area where doctors checked us over. I was in okay health, considering, but weighed just 29 kilograms. The doctors and soldiers were all very kind.

When the medical checks were completed, the Americans gathered us together and addressed us as a group.

'You are now liberated,' they told us. 'You are free to go and do whatever you like.'

Some of the Yugoslavs and Russians headed straight into town, presumably to have revenge on the German prisoners there, revenge they had been fantasising about for so long. But Heniek and I couldn't bring ourselves to do the same, as much as we might have wanted to. If we tortured and killed the Germans, it made us no better than them. Despite the hardships and abuse I had suffered at the hands of the Nazis over the past six years,

I just couldn't bring myself to kill anyone in cold blood.

My mother's words still rang in my ears – her request that I do everything 'humanly' possible to survive. Mum would not have wanted me to hurt anyone. That was not good human behaviour. My father would not have wanted this either. His philosophy, in line with the Bund's, was to rebuild our lives as Jewish people, to establish families and maintain our Jewish and human perspective on the world, not to take someone else's life.

Of course, I wanted revenge but not by becoming a murderer. The revenge I wanted was bigger than personal revenge. I wanted to see the people who had committed these heinous crimes against humanity on trial in a courtroom, where people could bear witness to what they had done. For me, the sentencing was not as important as for the Nazis to admit their crimes in front of the whole world. Even then, I knew that there would never be any real justice. There was no punishment that could equal the atrocious crimes the Nazis committed. I would never forgive them for taking so many lives purely because people were a different ethnicity to them. I didn't have the right to forgive for my family, or for the six million others who were killed at their hands.

After thanking the American soldiers, although mere words of thank you could never be enough, we left them to further investigate the horrors at Wöbbelin. Heniek and I, along with some others from our group, then headed to Ludwigslust, not for revenge, but to celebrate our new freedom.

When we arrived there, we found an empty building where the SS had been living before abandoning the town. The apartments inside had luxurious rooms with huge bathrooms, cupboards full of food and the softest beds we had ever seen or lain on. We ate a little, took our first baths in years and lay down on these exquisite beds for some much-needed sleep. But sleep would not come. Our minds and bodies were unable to adjust to this new freedom, or to this kind of luxury. In the end, we all lay on the carpeted floor (still such a luxury!) and immediately fell into a deep sleep.

The next morning, Heniek and I set out to explore the rest of the buildings in town. Among many extravagant and luxury items we found cellars stacked full of wine, whiskey and champagne. We took the French champagne back to our new room, opened it and drank straight from the bottle, passing it back and forth until it was all gone. The sweet liquid fizzed in my mouth and tasted so sweet and delicious that I was in heaven. The only alcohol I had ever tasted before then was when I took sneaky sips of my mother's cherry wine before the war. But French champagne was a whole new taste sensation and like nothing I had ever experienced.

It tasted so good that Heniek and I went back for another bottle … then another. I have no idea how much we ended up drinking, but I do know that when we were done, we slept for twenty-four hours straight. When I finally woke from my champagne-induced slumber, there was just one thought in my mind.

Getting home to Łódź.

18

HEADING HOME

'Home' is a word most people associate with loved ones, family and friends. The phrase 'coming home' makes most think of people they love, waiting to greet them with hugs and kisses. But on the long journey back to Poland, I had to mentally steel myself for the fact that there would be no mother, father, sisters, or relatives waiting for me there.

Of course, I held on to a small glimmer of hope that my sisters were still alive, but after so long with no news I knew it was unlikely. It would be better for my mental state to just accept that my entire family was gone, rather than go on believing they were alive. It was too distressing.

I hoped I would maybe find some old friends back in Łódź, friends I hadn't seen since the liquidation of the ghetto or since leaving Auschwitz. But my main mission was to get home and retrieve the boxes Bono and I had buried. Those boxes contained important items, including our radio, personal diaries, photographs, reports Bono had taken from radio broadcasts, posters we had taken off the ghetto walls and my Polish and

Yiddish diaries. All of it was evidence of life in the ghetto and, more importantly, precious mementos of my family. I had to see if the boxes were still there or had been looted after liquidation.

Bono and I had agreed that whoever survived should return to Łódź to find them, so this was the first thing on my mind when I woke in Ludwigslust that morning. I didn't know if Bono had survived the war, so I needed to fulfil the promise I made to my friend.

I knew the journey back to Łódź would not be easy since the railway lines and stations between Germany and Poland had all been bombed. Also, I discovered that the only trains that were still functioning were very slow and had to keep stopping as the tracks were under repair. But none of this was enough to deter Heniek, myself and a few others from our mission to get back to Poland.

Our little group set off from Ludwigslust on foot. We walked along the tracks, hoping to come across a working train at some point. A lot of the time there were no trains in operation, so we walked or hitchhiked a lot of the way. Sometimes we did come across working trains, but they were always very crowded. However, we soon found a way to get ourselves on these trains despite the lack of space.

When there was no room in any of the cabins or corridors, we would simply climb up onto the roof and travel that way. Unfortunately, the tops of these trains were convex-shaped, which made it difficult to hold on as the train sped down the tracks, particularly because we were all so weak and exhausted. We knew if we fell asleep, we would roll off and almost certainly die. So, we came up with a solution. By this point we'd found some strong military belts discarded on the ground and used these to tie ourselves to the steel bar that ran along the length of the carriage roof. This proved to be a very good decision since all of us fell asleep on top of the train and woke to find the train rumbling along the tracks, with us dangling off the side by our belts.

Our journey back to Poland took around twenty days, and a couple of weeks after that we finally arrived back in Łódź.

We met and talked to a lot of people on our journey and heard that the Bund was re-establishing itself in Łódź. Therefore, my first order of business when I finally arrived in my hometown in the beginning of June 1945 was to find my fellow Bundists, even before going to look for the boxes. I was among the first Bundists to return from the camps in Germany and so received a very warm welcome. Many people offered me food and a place to stay, some of whom were old friends from the Bund, including a young man named Jacob Lewin. Jacob was three years younger than me and had been in SKIF too. He had also been a gymnast at the Morning Star Club, but with the younger group. It was good to see so many familiar faces and know they had survived as well.

I learned the fate of other friends and neighbours, many of whom had either died in the ghetto or not been heard from since they were taken to Auschwitz. I also learned that when the last train left the Łódź Ghetto on 31 August, Rumkowski and his whole family had been on board. Apparently, Rumkowski had ended up in the gas chamber soon after his arrival at Auschwitz.

Of course, I tried to find out any news of my sisters, but no one had heard from them or knew anything of their whereabouts.

After our warm welcome at the Bund headquarters, Heniek and Jacob came with me to look for the boxes. We went straight to the tree to dig up the box with the radio in it, but it was gone. Someone had been looting, looking for valuables, and must have thought they'd hit the jackpot when they found a locked metal box. Imagine their disappointment when they discovered only a small radio and documents that were of no value to them. I can only assume they'd thrown it away. This was very upsetting, but we just had to hope that the looters had not found our second box, buried near the latrines.

The three of us whooped with delight as we dug down and saw the lid of the metal box poking out of the dirt. I opened it and took out some of my personal documents, including precious photos of my parents and sisters, and left the rest there for Bono to find. I had no idea at that point if he was still alive, but if he was, I wanted him to have the joy and satisfaction of finding something waiting for him in Łódź should he return. Now what to do?

My friends and I were alive, young, and back in our hometown. For five years we had lived in fear on these streets, forced to comply with the harshest of regulations, but now? Now the Nazis were gone, and Łódź belonged to us again. Obviously, we had to celebrate.

My friends and I drank a lot of alcohol that night. Late at night, we ended up walking arm in arm down Zgierska Street, swaying and singing at the tops of our voices. Four young friends, free and not so steady on our feet, holding on to each other and laughing in a place where we would have been shot on sight for doing such a thing not so long ago.

A couple of Poles walked past us and noticed that one of my friends had a small bottle of vodka sticking out of his pocket.

'Ha!' he laughed. 'Before the war, it was always the Poles who were drunk on the streets! But now it is the Jews!'

'Ooh!' my friend called back to him, pointing to the vodka in his pocket. 'I know you're hoping there is still some vodka in this bottle for you!'

We all laughed, including the Poles, and then the four of us carried on swaying down the street in the warm summer air.

It was a wonderful feeling.

19

SEARCHING FOR SURVIVORS

Apart from enjoying fun drunken nights with my friends, there was really nothing left for me in Łódź. I had no emotional connection to my town anymore and just being there was a painful reminder of everyone and everything I had lost. So, when an opportunity to leave Łódź and travel through Europe presented itself, I jumped at it.

After the war, all Jewish political parties were still active in Germany, so the Bund were looking for volunteers to go from camp to camp, searching for friends and fellow Bundists. They were keen for us all to amalgamate and organise ourselves into groups again. Despite all we had been through, we were proud Jewish people and knew that we had to keep fighting for our rights. It wasn't over yet.

The destruction of the Jews had not been a surprise to those of us in the Bund. We had never had any illusions about how many Germans perceived us and had seen evidence of it for many years before the war. But now, our goal was clear. We had to rebuild. This was the most important thing. Hitler would never be victorious or have his wish of erasing the Jewish people from the world. Therefore, I, along with my friends Jack Lewin and Abram Jakobowicz, volunteered to head back to Germany to search for our people.

We set off from Łódź in July 1945, hitchhiking and jumping trains once more, finally arriving in Berlin three weeks later. At that time, Berlin was divided into four zones: American, British, French and Russian. We wanted to get into the American or British zone, but as we had come from Poland we were automatically placed into the Russian zone. These different zones all had border controls in place, so we were told we'd have to wait another three or four days before we could cross the border into the American zone.

We settled in to wait in a big empty hall that was housing many other Bund members and their friends. We talked and sang songs together but waiting around was something none of us were particularly good at. An older person who was rugged up in the corner of the building was Jacob Clemenski, who would go on to become a noted resistance fighter. We were young (Jack was only eighteen) and we had just survived a war, so we became bored very quickly. On our second night there, Jack and I decided to head out into the city, or what remained of it, not in the habit of sitting around and doing nothing. Abram decided to stay back at our lodgings.

I wanted to get myself a watch, so Jack and I found a local German watchmaker. While we were there a Russian soldier came into the shop carrying a huge grandfather clock.

'I cannot carry this clock back with me,' he told the

watchmaker in Russian, 'so I want you to use the parts from it to make me a wristwatch. You can keep the other parts.'

It was clear that the German watchmaker didn't understand a word of what this Russian was saying, but we did and struggled to stop ourselves breaking into fits of laughter at this ridiculous request. We didn't want the Russian to know we understood and were laughing at him. We quickly left but I'm certain the Russian didn't end up getting his grandfather wristwatch.

Venturing back out onto the streets, Jack and I noticed a section of bombed-out ruins that had been cordoned off. Russians were conducting black market searches in this section, looking for anything of worth that they could sell. We walked over to them and struck up a conversation with a Russian soldier who, we guessed from his Asian features, was from Manchuria. He was very friendly and happy to talk to us, and after a brief chat with our new friend, we said goodbye and headed out into the city again. There was a show playing in one of the big theatres, so we decided to check it out. Neither of us had enough money to buy tickets so we snuck in through a back window and made our way up to one of the more lavish sections of the theatre, like a box, but even nicer; the kind of seats royalty would have sat in before the war.

We were feeling very happy with ourselves as we waited for the show to begin when Jack nudged me.

'Look,' he said, pointing down to the front row below us. 'There's the Manchurian soldier we talked to this morning.'

I scoffed. 'Just because that soldier is Asian doesn't mean it's the same guy!'

The Strength of Hope

But Jack was adamant. 'It's him,' he said. 'I'm going down to talk to him.'

'Well, I'm staying here,' I said, watching Jack get up and walk out of the box. *It won't be the guy,* I thought smugly. *He's going to make a total fool of himself.*

The show started and Jack still hadn't returned. I leaned over the padded rail and tried to search for him below, but the theatre was dark so I couldn't make out anyone in the audience from up in my royalty box. After another twenty minutes I decided Jack must have been right about it being our friend after all, so decided to go and join him and our Russian soldier in the front row.

However, when I got down to the stalls and began making my way along the front row towards Jack, the expression on his face told me something was wrong. Very wrong. Even in the darkness I could see that my friend was pale and frightened. I sat down next to him and he leaned over to whisper, 'It's not the same soldier!'

He pointed at something, but I couldn't see what it was. I would soon find out.

The show was still going when all the lights in the theatre suddenly came on and there was a noise behind us. I turned in my seat to see that the audience was full of Russian soldiers, and walking up the aisle were more, and they were all carrying machine guns.

The soldiers walked directly to the front row and stared down at us.

'You're under arrest,' one of them said in Russian.

Jack and I were very confused at this point, but probably

not as frightened as we should have been. After all we had been through, having soldiers and machine guns in our faces was a familiar sight. The soldiers pulled us up and out of our seats and, with guns at our backs, marched us to a nearby jail. They took us inside and down some stairs to a small, dark dungeon where a big group of glum-looking Nazis were also being held.

I couldn't believe it. After finally escaping the Nazis here we were locked in a dungeon with them! I didn't feel comfortable being in the same room as them, but I wasn't scared of them either. Not anymore. These Nazis didn't have weapons and they weren't nearly as intimidating without them. Still, we couldn't even bring ourselves to look in their direction, let alone engage with them. They had just as little interest in talking to us. The only thing we knew for sure was that these ten or so Nazis were feeling very sorry for themselves, but Jack and I certainly felt no sympathy for them or their situation. We were more preoccupied with our own survival than the fact that we were in a dungeon with two Nazis. Our only thoughts were, 'how are we going to get out of here?' and 'will we ever get out of here?'

The Russians gave us no explanation as to why we'd been arrested, or what they wanted with us. They just locked us into the cell and went back upstairs, leaving us with our silent cellmates. Jack and I spent the night whispering to each other and trying to plan for how to get out of the unexpected mess we'd found ourselves in.

The next morning, two soldiers came back. They unlocked the door, then pointed at me, ordering me to come with them. I glanced at Jack, who was completely terrified, and gave him

The Strength of Hope

a nod. I was the older of the two of us so felt it was my job to stay calm and reassure him that everything would be okay, even though I wasn't entirely confident this was the case.

The soldiers marched me upstairs, took me to a tiny grey room with a small metal table and two chairs, and gestured for me to sit down. A man, who I soon realised was a Russian interrogator, came into the room and sat opposite me with a stern expression on his face.

He began to ask me questions about who we were and what we were doing in Germany. I understood Russian because it is similar to Polish, and I had always had a good ear for language, but I didn't want him to know that, so I answered him in Polish.

'I don't understand what you're saying,' I said. 'I only speak Polish and Yiddish.'

After a few more minutes of this back and forth they finally brought in an interpreter.

We had all heard about the Soviet Union's interrogation techniques over the years, even before the war, so I had an idea of what was coming.

'You had better tell us the truth,' the Polish interpreter said. 'We know better than you!'

'If you know better than me, then what are you asking me?' I responded. 'I'm Jewish and have just been liberated from a concentration camp where I was a prisoner.'

None of what I was telling them seemed to make any difference or help my cause. The interrogation lasted for a couple more hours before they finally took me back to the dungeon where a nervous Jack was waiting.

As he pushed me into the dungeon, the soldier snapped, 'Tomorrow morning you will be transported to Siberia with the Nazis!'

He grabbed Jack and pulled him out of the dungeon, slamming the heavy iron door behind him.

Jack got the same interrogation as me and gave them the same information. The only difference was that he had been liberated by the Russians from Auschwitz on 27 January. Also, Jack had a number tattooed on his arm so was able to give them proof that he had been in a concentration camp. Even still, when the soldiers brought him back to the dungeon, they said that he would be heading for Siberia the following morning as well.

Neither of us got much sleep that night. It was incredible to us that we had escaped death by the Nazis, and been liberated from the camps, only to end up in a prison under Russian interrogation and potentially being sent to Siberia. Over and over that night we asked each other, *how could this be happening?*

The next morning, the soldiers opened the door of our cell and we braced ourselves for the impending journey to Siberia. But instead of looking at us, they shouted at the Nazis and marched them out instead, slamming the door and leaving Jack and I alone. We stared at each other. What the hell was going on? A little while later the soldiers returned for us.

'OUT!' they shouted, aiming their machine guns at us.

Jack and I got up and marched up the stairs and out the back of the prison, the soldiers with their guns at our backs. We could see a truck parked in the distance, on the other side of a gated fence, and glanced at each other. That must be the truck

The Strength of Hope

to take us to Siberia. What choice did we have but to get on it? There was no way we would be able to escape with armed Russian soldiers at our backs. But as we reached the fence, one of the soldiers stepped in front of us, opened the gate, and turned back to us with a snarl on his face.

'Run!' he snapped.

We stared at him, too shocked to move.

'Run!' he said again, pointing at the street beyond the open gate.

Jack and I glanced at each other. We knew they might shoot us but if they'd wanted to kill us, they could have done that back in the dungeon.

The two of us took off, running as fast as our legs could carry us.

Jack and I had been in the Russian prison for over twenty-four hours, so our friend, Abram, was elated to see us arriving back safe and sound. When we told him and a few others our story, they were amazed and understandably nervous. The experience made the three of us even more determined to get out of the Russian zone as quickly as possible.

We watched the border for the whole day and noticed that American trucks regularly entered the Russian zone, presumably to deliver supplies. Later that afternoon we approached a driver of one of these trucks and told him we wanted to enter the American zone. This American must have seen the desperation in our faces and felt sorry for us because he agreed. The three of us soon found ourselves in the back of a truck covered with a tarpaulin. Luckily the truck wasn't searched and we soon crossed the border into the American zone.

We thanked our American driver and headed straight to the station to catch a train to the first Displaced Persons (DP) camp on our itinerary. This camp was Polish but situated in a British section of Germany, which had been divided up between America, France and Britain.

We arrived to a friendly welcome and were immediately offered food, shelter and drinks, including bimber – a homemade vodka produced by the Poles in this camp. I had never before drunk vodka but didn't want to offend them by saying no. I took a small sip and almost gagged – it tasted horrible, but I tried to look like I was enjoying it. After that, I kept my lips tightly together and only pretended to drink from the cup. Jack and Abram did the same. Gradually, everyone around us got so drunk that they all started passing out. That's when the three of us tipped our bimber back into the barrel.

We only stayed a few days at this camp because we could find no friends or Bund members there. We set off again, travelling deeper into Germany, and eventually arrived in Hanover. We asked around and found a house for Jews who had survived the war where I met some old Łódź friends, including twin brothers, Beniek and Heniek Dunkel. They had both been members of the Morning Star Club, and their families and mine had known each other for many years. It was an emotional reunion, especially when they told me that one of our old sports instructors was here in Hanover. He had suffered a stroke soon after liberation and was in a nearby hospital.

Of course, we went to visit, and found him in a large room,

surrounded by Germans. He was lying in bed, unable to move and barely able to speak. It was terrible to see him this way. When I approached the bed, he gestured for me to lean down.

'Abram, look at what has happened to me,' he whispered in my ear.

I squeezed his hand and sat by his side, trying to give him some small comfort. But it was very sad. To have survived the whole of the war only to have a stroke so soon after liberation seemed very tragic and unfair.

From Hanover, we travelled to another DP camp in Bergen. During the war this area had been the site of a concentration camp called Bergen-Belsen and had been discovered completely by chance by a British SAS officer and his driver after liberation. When the British and Canadian forces finally entered the camp, they found 13,000 unburied bodies. They took all the remaining survivors to hospital and then burned the camp to the ground to minimise the spread of typhus, which was rampant. When we arrived, there was nothing left of the original camp.

The Bund was very active here in Bergen, heavily engaged in political, social and cultural activities. They had even started organising political meetings, social groups and theatre performances. Jack and I met up with a few more people we knew at this DP camp, including Henia and Hawa Rosenfarb, and their mother, who had miraculously survived Auschwitz. Another familiar face was Lilka Nutkewicz, who was a few years older than me and had been a youth leader at SKIF.

A great moment was meeting up with my good friend from Łódź, Mumek, and his brother, another Heniek. It was wonderful to see Mumek alive and well, and we had much to catch up on. He had been at Auschwitz too, and he too had lost his mother there when they arrived on 23 August, but our paths had never crossed in the death camp.

Soon, Mumek and I began spending a lot of time together at the Bergen DP camp, and not long after this a man named Majer Nirenberg approached us. He had also been in the Łódź Ghetto, along with his brother who was a Bund leader, and I recognised him instantly. Majer had come from Belgium because the Bund leaders there had asked him to find one or two people to get three individuals out of Łódź and bring them back to Belgium. He had heard Mumek and I were together in Bergen, and thought we would be good candidates for the job.

Of course, we accepted the mission.

LESSON LEARNED

Think twice before talking to strangers in dark cinemas.

20

A MISSION WITH MUMEK

Remembering the troubles we had recently encountered in the Russian zone, I was reticent to travel back to Łódź via Berlin. So, I suggested to Mumek that we take a different route, travelling from Bergen to Feldafing, a city near Munich. After that, we could travel through Austria and Czechoslovakia and then into Poland. This route would take much longer than if we went via Berlin but would hopefully be easier and safer.

If we had had access to a map, we would have seen exactly how long this journey was going to take and might have risked going back through Berlin after all. It was a VERY long detour indeed and would take much longer than I anticipated.

We were given very little money for the journey but knew we would be able to board trains without buying tickets, and that our food and lodging costs would be minimal. Neither of us were big eaters and knew we could sleep on the side of the road if we had to.

Mumek and I began our journey by boarding a train to Feldafing. We heard there was a Bund leader there who had been a friend of my father in Łódź. I hadn't seen him since being deported but hoped he would remember me. Luckily for us he did and gave us both food and shelter for the night. Mumek and I registered with the city councils of every town we visited, so we could receive food rations. Sometimes we were cheeky and asked for more than they gave us. If they objected, we would thump the desk and exclaim that we had been prisoners.

'After depriving us of so much for so long, the least you could do now is give us extra rations!'

They always did.

We continued our journey by train but never paid because we had no money. If any train conductors asked to see our tickets, we told them that we were Jewish and wanted to go to Poland. If they insisted, our youthful aggression would come out again and we'd tell them to leave us alone or they 'would be sorry'. I may have been a small man, but they could see that I was strong. Mumek and I obviously looked like two men who would not be pushed around so they usually ended up leaving us alone to carry on with our unpaid journey.

We proceeded through Austria to Czechoslovakia, where we encountered our first real obstacle. The Russians controlled the border at Czechoslovakia and came through the carriages to check everyone's papers. Of course, we didn't possess any documents of identification, so the border guards took us off the train to question us. Mumek and I explained that we were on our way home to Poland and didn't have documents because we had lost them all in the war. Their only response was that without documents we would not be able to travel into Czechoslovakia.

They took us to a small building on the border and told us they would be back for us later. I had told Mumek about my experiences with the Russians in Berlin, and neither of us was keen to have a similar experience here. As soon as the border guards left us alone, we took a quick look around and realised the windows were not only open, but big enough for us to climb through. The drop to the ground was only little more than a metre, so we jumped out and ran as fast as we could. Those Russians must have been very surprised to find an empty room when they came back!

When we finally arrived in Prague, the people were kind and generous and did all they could to help us find Jewish people to stay with. We ended up finding some Jews, but only stayed a few days to look around before continuing our journey to Poland.

At the Polish border, we told the guards we were returning from the camps, and they let us through with no problems. It had now been almost four months since our liberation. With more access to food and water, I had regained a little weight and was no longer wearing rags. In fact, Mumek and I considered ourselves to be quite sharp dressers in our leather jackets and dark pants. So, I was feeling good as Mumek and I walked through the front entrance of the Bund premises in Łódź.

Straight away, I spotted a familiar tall physique on the other side of the room. The man's hair was much shorter, and patchy in places, and he was much skinnier than when I'd last seen him but there was no doubt in my mind who this man was.

'Bono!'

He turned and smiled when he saw me. We hugged – not

an easy thing for a six-foot-one and a five-foot-nothing man to do – but hug we did. I was so happy to see him. We sat down to talk, and he told me what had happened to him since we last met.

Bono's mother died just before the liquidation of the ghetto, and Bono himself had been ordered to stay, along with 800 other workers, because of his work as a locksmith. But Bono refused to abandon his Aunty Klara, so presented himself alongside her for deportation. Both of them were sent to Auschwitz, where, just like my dear Mum, Aunt Klara was murdered upon arrival. From there, Bono was sent to two other camps, Mauthausen and then Güsen, where he was liberated in 1945. He'd been very sick and spent the following few months in a Vienna hospital but was feeling much better now, and his hair was starting to grow back. It pained me to hear about his mother and Aunt Klara, and, of course, I was very sorry to hear that he'd been so ill.

I told him my story, and that I had only found one of our buried boxes still there. Bono too had made this discovery and was disappointed about the radio but happy that at least one box remained. Seeing my friend again was the highlight of my trip back to Łódz and, a few weeks later, Bono gave me a photograph of himself when I was leaving, which I still have to this day. Written in Yiddish on the back are the words *'To my friend in pain and in happiness'*. It was November 1945 and I have cherished this photo and note for all these years.

After my emotional and happy reunion with Bono, Mumek and I spent a week meeting up with various people and friends who were also returning to Łódź. We also helped at the Bund organisation. Our priority was to organise the people on Majer's list and bring them back to Belgium, which was an easy task to complete. We found them in Łódź immediately, including Majer Nirenberg's sister, and all three were happy to arrange to go back with us.

One of their friends was a woman, Wlatka Pelta, who worked as a courier on the Polish side of Warsaw. She wanted to go west too, and we agreed that one more person in our travelling group would not be a problem.

The Bund gave Mumek and I instructions to memorise and told us to deliver these instructions to a DP camp at Sulzheim, near Frankfurt. The Zionists oversaw the camp there, and the Bund was illegal, which is why we could not write the instructions down. A week after Mumek and I arrived back in Łódź, we said goodbye to our friends and set off for Belgium with our little travelling group. We had planned to retrace our steps back through Czechoslovakia, but when we arrived at the border the Russian guards refused to let us through again. So, we travelled all the way back to Łódź to make a new plan and decided to take the more direct route through Berlin.

However, when we reached the Polish–East German border, more problems awaited us. The Polish border guards confronted us, demanding to see our documents, but of course we didn't have any. We were all feeling very stressed by this point, and had no choice but to go back to Łódź and get help from the Bund.

They told us we might have better luck crossing the border at a place in western Poland called Kostrzyn, so we set off again in that direction. When we arrived there, we found that the town had been bombed very badly and that the border guards were using a badly patched-up building as their headquarters. Once again, we were told that we could not cross into Germany because we did not have official documentation, and they took Mumek and me into their bombed-out ruins to interrogate us.

'We have official instructions,' we told them. 'We are on a mission to Germany to deliver them.'

'Then why don't you have any documentation?' they asked.

'The orders came through at very short notice,' we explained. 'It happened very quickly, and we were told to leave immediately. There was no time to obtain documentation.'

We could see that the guards were starting to believe us and might even think we were more important and senior than we were, perhaps even delegates from the Communist Party. So, we took the opportunity to bluff them.

'If you want, you can call your superiors, and they will tell you who we are!' we said boldly.

Hearing our confident tones, and with us acting cocky as hell in our leather jackets, the Polish officers began to worry that they might get in trouble for detaining such important people. One of them was visibly trembling.

'The train has already left for the day,' one of them said, much friendlier now. 'But there will be another tomorrow. In the meantime, we can give all of you accommodation in the officers' quarters for the night.'

Mumek and I could barely contain our glee but waited until we were well out of earshot before we told the others what happened. Mumek and I were feeling very smug, and we all had a good laugh. But our smugness would not last long. The next day we were put on the train to Berlin only to be greeted at the border by Russian guards who told us we couldn't enter with no papers.

Still feeling confident after our experience in Kostrzyn, Mumek and I insisted on seeing the commanding officer of the guard. They took us to see him, and he looked us up and down, from head to toe before saying in Yiddish, 'Are you Jews?'

We couldn't believe it! The commanding officer of the Russian guard spoke perfect Yiddish. Luck was on our side this time. Unlike the story we had given the Polish guards at Kostrzyn, we told the truth this time, explaining in Yiddish that we had instructions to deliver to the DP camps. He nodded and said there was a train going to that area in one hour's time. He would make sure we were on it. One hour later, true to his word, the commanding officer himself escorted our group onto the train, even finding us a cabin.

We travelled into the Russian zone of Berlin but knew better than to strike up conversations with any random Russian soldiers while we were there. We stayed with friends in a deserted house, and over the next few days, we were very cautious, and knew we must be careful when approaching the American truck drivers entering the Russian zone. We talked to one of the drivers, just as Jack, Abram and I had last time, telling him we were Jewish and wanted to pass into the American zone. Once again, the Americans agreed to help us and came up with a signal for when we should board the truck, not a moment before. They told us to move as far forward in the back of the truck as we could once inside. When we received their signal, we did what they told us

The Strength of Hope

and shortly afterwards, one of the Americans climbed into the back and covered us with a tarpaulin.

At the border, the guards glanced inside the truck, and, seeing nothing, waved us through. At last, we were back in West Germany.

I have a document from Belgium that lists the details of the people from the Bund who were smuggled into Belgium from Germany just after the war. It has their names, dates and places of birth, and the names of the DP camps they came from, all in Yiddish. I am on that list, which gives my correct birth date: 5 October 1924. However, a document I brought from Germany when I came to Belgium gave my birth year as 1928. This was because I had had no documentation to show my age, since everything had been taken away from us, so I said I was born in 1928; I looked young enough to get away with it, which was very handy when travelling through Germany, from DP camp to DP camp. The younger we were, the more food rations we could demand from the city councils of the places we passed through.

First stop was the DP camp at Bergen so we could deliver our four companions. We were given a warm welcome and many people there wanted us to stay for a while, but Mumek and I had to leave right away to deliver the instructions to our Bund connection at Sulzheim.

The man's name was Sewek Tigel and when we asked where we could find him, we were directed to a flat near the camp. A woman wearing a red dressing gown and holding a telephone to her ear answered the door.

'Hello,' I said. 'Is this the home of Sewek Tigel?'

'Yes,' she replied. 'I'm his wife. I'll get him for you.'

Sewek came to the door and when we told him who we were and who had sent us we all went inside to talk. We gave Sewek the information we had memorised, and everything went smoothly. Mumek and I ended up having several meetings with other Bund members over the next few days, although we always had to be very discreet as the Bund was still illegal in Sulzheim.

We left Sulzheim after a few days and returned to Bergen where we found out that the Bund was organising to smuggle Bundists over to Belgium and the two of us were high on the list. But Mumek and I made it clear that we wanted no part of it. We had so much experience at crossing borders by ourselves by then that we were too proud to be part of an operation where *other* people would be responsible for getting us over the border. More importantly, the money the Bund would have to pay the people-smugglers could be better used for others who needed assistance getting across.

So, Mumek and I headed back to the border and bunkered down for a day or so to observe how things there were operating. We checked the train schedule and watched the railways, and before long a freight train pulled in and was stopped for inspection. We could see that the train had no passengers, only one engineer and one fireman who were both up front in the driver's compartment. Mumek and I looked at each another, both with the same idea in our heads.

When the train was given the all-clear by the border guards and started to pull away from the station, Mumek and I made our move. We jumped up and – careful to stay out of the border guard's sight – ran alongside the train. When we reached the front of the train we jumped up and into the engine cabin, giving the engineer and the fireman a hell of a shock.

'Hello,' I said. 'I'm Abram and this is Mumek, and we want to go to Belgium.'

The two of them stared back at us, stunned.

'We can't do this,' the engineer finally said, frowning and shaking his head. 'You can't just—'

'Listen,' Mumek said, taking a step towards them. 'We've just been liberated from the camps and won't be happy if you don't take us, if you know what I mean.'

It may have been wrong for us to threaten people in this way, but we were so young, cocky and sure of ourselves then. After all we'd been through over the past six years we felt as though we had nothing to lose.

I gave them my friendliest smile. 'If you could slow down a bit when you get 100 metres past the border we'll jump off, thanks,' I said.

What could they say? We were already on board, and I don't think either of them wanted to try and throw two young, headstrong Jews off their train. They agreed to take us, and so, as promised, soon after crossing the border the engineer slowed the train down. We thanked them, wished them well and jumped off the train, rolling down a small grassy embankment into a field.

We had been given the address of a Bundist who lived in a small town a few kilometres past the border, so we walked to his house after jumping from the train. It was close to midnight by the time we knocked on his door and the man himself opened it, initially annoyed at being disturbed so late at night. But when we told him who we were and where we had come from, he immediately invited us in.

After a deep sleep in a comfortable bed, Mumek and I woke the next morning to discuss plans with our kind host. He said he would arrange our train tickets to Brussels that day.

'I won't be coming with you,' he told us. 'So, because you are travelling without documents, you must board the train and then immediately pretend to be asleep until you arrive in Brussels.'

We were old hands at the whole 'travelling without documents' caper by now, so didn't really need this advice. But we kept our mouths shut out of respect for our fellow Bundist and thanked him for his help.

The train trip went smoothly, with both of us pretending to sleep for the entire journey. We arrived, unchallenged, in Brussels later that day. We had the address of the Bund headquarters – 12 Rue de Camions – which was a short distance from Brussels train station, and we headed straight there. We found many familiar faces there and people we knew who had already been smuggled across the border.

Mumek and I were happy and relieved to have completed yet another successful journey, and to finally be safe in Belgium.

LESSON LEARNED

Sometimes you must take a risk or lose a chance.

21

BELGIUM

Mumek and I were foreigners and therefore not allowed to work in Belgium. To stay in the city, we needed to apply for a permit, which would have to be renewed every three months. In the meantime, the Bund organised accommodation for us with a Bundist couple, named Szmul and Rywka Litmanowicz, who had two daughters younger than us. We stayed with the Litmanowicz family for a few months, until we moved again to stay at another friend's flat.

Mumek and I spent a lot of time at the Bund premises. A lot of members would hang out there because it had a restaurant and a recreation room with various games and a ping-pong table. I was looking forward to playing the game I had loved in my childhood. Mumek and I had no money, so ate at the Bund restaurant a lot in those first few weeks. The meals were quite substantial, an entrée, soup and then meat for the main course, followed by a compote. They also came with a Belgian beer.

One day, the restaurant manager must have noticed how voraciously Mumek and I were tucking into our meals because when we finished he asked if we were still hungry. When we answered with an emphatic, 'Yes!' he told us we could have the same meal again, starting at the entree. I didn't think we'd be able to fit it all in, but we did! We were young, active and hungry, and our attitude was to live, and eat, to the fullest.

I had been a witness to so much suffering, and experienced so much loss and pain, that it was sometimes surreal to find myself living a 'normal' life. How do you ever put a past like ours behind you? It was not easy. Always at night there were bad dreams. Nightmares where I was being hunted and chased. Always this terrible fear. Hiding, climbing, running ... endless running. But during the day I stayed positive and clung to the tiny pieces of hope I had left. Hopes for Maryla's survival, that my sister had somehow managed to survive in Russia and that I would see her again one day. Also, I knew that I had to fulfil the promise I made to my mother, and the first step towards that was to not just enjoy my new life in Belgium, but to speak out by staying politically active in the Bund.

It was good to have a place where we survivors could meet and talk about our shared experiences. As sympathetic as people who hadn't had our kinds of experiences were, and as kind as the non-Jews in Belgium were to us, it was difficult for them to truly understand. The Bund premises was a place where we were surrounded by people who we could share our trauma and stories of loss with and know that they could relate. That was so important. I hoped that wherever I ended up in my life I would always have somewhere where I would feel just as supported and understood.

I was still an active member of the Bund and at our meetings we discussed many of the political events going on in Belgium. Even though it was strictly prohibited for us to do so, Mumek and I joined the mass rallies, marches and protests that were organised by the Belgian Socialist Party. We felt it was important to support the people of Brussels, even though it was illegal for us to do this and we knew we could be deported if caught.

Not only were we politically active, but we were culturally active too. The Bund established a successful Yiddish theatre group in Brussels. Most of the actors had been participants in Yiddish theatre before the war, and the plays were all in Yiddish and written by famous Jewish writers. Mumek and I loved going to see these plays that weren't just political, but that also represented real life. We became good friends with all the actors and staff at the theatre company.

By now it was March 1946 and Mumek and I had been in Belgium for five months. After all the adventures I had had since liberation, I was feeling full of excitement and optimism about my life and what the future might hold. Although I would never forget the past six years and all that had happened, I would not let it make me a negative and unhappy person. I was determined to settle here in beautiful Belgium for a while and enjoy the simple pleasures in life, like going out with friends, eating good food and playing ping-pong with Mumek. This is exactly what I was doing at the Bund premises one morning when two young women walked through the lobby.

They were petite and pretty and looked so alike that I guessed they must be sisters, but it was the smaller of the two who caught my eye.

22

CESIA PART 1

My name is Cesia Goldberg (nee Amatensztejn), and I was born on 9 May 1929, in a village just outside of Łódź called Piotrkow. My family moved to Łódź when I was very young, and lived on Żydowska Street, which ran off Zgierska, the road Abie lived on before the war. But of course, I didn't know him then.

I had one older brother, Abram, born in 1922, and a sister, Hela, who was born in 1925. My mum was so beautiful, and my dad was a good, kind man. They met in Vienna and loved each other very much. I remember we lived on the first floor of a building that had a balcony, and when my mum would go out, my dad would stand on the balcony just so he could watch her walk away. Theirs was a true love story. My parents were not politically aware or active, not like Abie's family. But they were clever, loving and kind people.

Before the war, my dad had a job making slippers from beautiful soft leather. We were not poor but not rich either. Just somewhere in the middle. We were traditionally religious Jews, but modern, not orthodox. We would always light the candles on Shabbat and go to synagogue for Yom Kippur.

I was very good at maths and languages in school, but I didn't play sport. I loved being in class. I remember one night before the war I was lying in bed and heard my parents talking about me.

'This little one,' my father was saying, 'She will grow up to be something.'

I felt so excited about my future when I heard that. Who knew what I might become? There were so many possibilities for a young girl like me who was so loved and had such a supportive family.

I was ten years old when the Nazis marched into my hometown of Łódź. At that young age I didn't really understand war or what 'occupied' meant. All I knew was that from that moment on, my young, carefree life was over. There was no more school, no more being allowed out on the streets on my own and my big brother suddenly left home to go to Russia.

When they first built the ghetto, our family had to share our small flat with another family. It was very squashy, but we were okay.

It was all very scary and confusing, although I felt mostly safe at home with my mum, dad and big sister, Hela. But I have never known such hunger as when I was in the ghetto. It is impossible to imagine. We were given watery soup once a day and one loaf of black bread that we had to divide between the four of us, and that had to last us a whole week. It was very hard not to eat it all at once, but we knew that we had to make it last and save it until the last moment. I nibbled a little bit of my piece each day.

Living in the ghetto was very hard for my parents. They were so worried about my sister and me. I had to start work when I was eleven. I got a job in a factory that made boots for soldiers, using a sewing machine but also sewing by hand. It was hard work, and I was very tired at night.

I dream a lot, sometimes even now, about those days in the ghetto. Even now, I'm emotional. Even now, I'm holding myself back not to cry. I still feel so much pain when I talk about it. But I want to tell everybody, to let the world know.

The Strength of Hope

When the Nazis said all children in Łódź must be handed over, my parents were very scared for me. Even though I was twelve I looked much younger so they wanted to hide me during the searches.

Our neighbour was a baker who had a young grandchild, only a few months old, who he had to hide too, and he agreed to hide me with the baby, and the baby's mum and dad, in his oven. There was a separate part above the main oven that was big enough to fit the three of us and the baby. When we heard the Nazis coming, we all climbed in the top part of the oven to hide and wait for them to pass. But the Nazis fired a gun in the air near us and it woke the baby and she started to cry. The baby's mother panicked. She knew her baby would be taken away and killed if they heard her, so she stuffed a rag in the baby's mouth to keep her quiet. When the Nazis had gone, the mother quickly took out the rag, sure her baby would have suffocated, but the baby was still alive. She was so happy, but then two years later the mum, dad and baby were all sent to Auschwitz and murdered there. It is hard to believe even now.

Hela was put on the list for deportation from the ghetto in 1944, so the four of us went into hiding. I was fourteen and very scared, but I knew my parents would do everything they could to keep my sister and me safe for as long as possible. I remember my dad sitting on my bed and crying as he talked to me and my sister.

'You know, children,' he said, 'if we don't survive, I want you to contact my sister in Vienna. She has many of our photos and precious possessions.'

The Nazis told us that if we presented ourselves that we would be sent to Germany and that we would have a good time there. So, on the 24 August, my mother, father, sister, cousins, aunties, and uncles all presented ourselves at the Jewish prison for deportation. I didn't know what would happen when we got there but at least I was with my parents. I held tightly to my mum's hand as we walked and hoped that there would be a better life for us in Germany than in the ghetto.

The train ride was horrible. We were all squashed in on top of each other and it was boiling hot and almost impossible to get any air. I was so small that my mum tried to lift me up so I could breathe. There was so much yelling and pushing when we got out of the train and someone was shouting, 'RAUS! RAUS! MEN TO ONE SIDE, WOMEN TO THE OTHER!'

My dad, uncles and boy cousin, Berek, were shoved to one side, away from us, and the rest of us stood in a queue – my mother, aunties, cousins, sister and me. My sister was in front of me and she turned to me. 'Stand on your tiptoes!' she whispered. 'There are no other children here!' So, I went up on my toes as Mengele walked along the line to look at us. When he got to me, he said, 'She's a child!' The German guard standing next to him looked down at the little buds that had started to grow on my chest. 'But she will work,' he said. My mother was sent straight to the gas chamber, but my sister and I were not. It is a miracle. Abie would say there are no miracles, but I disagree. This was a miracle.

Hela and I were in Auschwitz for a couple of weeks before an industrialist woman came to buy us and take us to Germany for slave labour. When I was taken from the camp, they hit me so hard on my arm that I had three black markings on there for weeks afterwards.

Hela and I were sent to Hamburg where we were made to pick up stones and rubble from bombed-out areas. One morning, there were twenty of us working with a red-cheeked German soldier standing at the end of our row supervising. He took a packet out of his pocket and unwrapped it and made sure all of us could see it was bread before he called his dog over. We were frightened to look up, but he knew we all saw him throw the bread to the dog to eat.

The soldier knew we were all starving. It was so cruel.

The last camp I was in was Bergen-Belsen. It was a death camp and there were so many dead people you can't imagine. The Germans didn't want the British to see all the corpses – they wanted to hide the bodies and destroy all evidence of Bergen-Belsen. We had to carry many bodies to a huge place so they could destroy them. I don't know what happens after death, but I will not go to Hell because I have been there already. I saw Hell before my eyes.

After the war, I didn't believe in God. I thought, 'How could a baby just born in the Łódź ghetto be thrown down from the second or third floor into an open truck?' This is something Abie saw. How could that happen? What had a baby done wrong in life? So many terrible things happened. But slowly, with my age, I changed my mind about God.

I was very sick when the British arrived to liberate us and so they put me in the hospital.

When I was better, Hela, me and our cousins Pola and Sala went to a DP camp in Germany in July 1945, and saw our cousin Berek there. Pola and Sala were so happy to see their brother alive, and Hela and I were happy and excited because we knew he had been with our father and assumed Dad must have survived too.

Berek told us that my father had survived Auschwitz but got sick with typhoid when they sent him to Germany, near Dachau, then to Kaufering to dig holes. Berek looked after Dad as much as he could but then he got sick too. When he was better, he asked what had happened to his uncle, my father, and they told him he had died and was buried in a mass grave. Hela and I were devastated and cried for many days afterwards.

Someone in the DP camp said to Hela and me, 'Over there is a Polish camp and there are some Jews there.' We went to see if any more of our friends or relatives were there and saw a friend, Bluma. She was married to a man named Motek, and we met him and his brother, Herszel. Hela and Herszel started to spend time together in the camp and soon fell in love. They married a couple of months later.

Herszel was a Bundist and arranged for the three of us to go first to Vienna and then to Belgium. We went to find our aunty in Vienna, like our father said we should, and after asking around we found her and her husband. It was very emotional to see them again and we cried together over the tragic loss of my parents and her brother. They gave me beautiful photos of my mum and dad, which I have to this day. These photos are very precious to me.

The three of us then travelled to Belgium. I was seventeen and very shy then. I looked young too, even younger than I was. When I went to the pictures with my friend, they wouldn't let me see the adult movie because they thought I was underage.

One day, my sister asked me to come with her to the Bundist club to see Herszel. The first thing I saw when I walked inside was a handsome young man playing ping-pong. Who is that? I wondered.

23

THE SMALL GIRL WITH THE DARK CURLS

The pretty young woman who walked into the club that morning was tiny, smaller than the average woman. Her dark hair was pinned back at the front and long curls, slightly windswept, bobbed around her shoulders. She had a scarf wrapped around her neck and was wearing a camel-coloured coat and a green dress with tiny white flowers all over it, and had a black leather handbag over one arm. I was glad I'd decided to put on a clean white shirt that morning, even if the sleeves were rolled up for my game with Mumek. I was also glad my blond hair had grown back. I wore it short at the back and sides and now had a quiff of longer hair on top.

As the two young women walked past, the small girl with the dark curls looked towards the games area and saw me staring. I smiled and she ducked her head shyly and looked away. But before she did, I glimpsed a small smile. I was so distracted that I let Mumek's ball fly straight past me.

'My point!' Mumek cried.

But I didn't care. The only thing on my mind now was

getting some more information on who this cute girl was. I put down my paddle and went to find out.

'Abram!' a bewildered Mumek called after me. 'Where are you going?'

Ignoring my friend, I headed over to the restaurant where the two girls had just sat down.

'Hello,' I said, approaching their table. 'I'm Abram. Have you just arrived in Belgium?'

'Yes,' the older girl said, smiling at me. 'I'm Hela, and this is my younger sister, Cesia.'

Cesia! Now I knew her name.

Cesia smiled up at me shyly but didn't say a word.

'Would you like to join us?' Hela asked, gesturing to the empty chair at the table.

'Thank you.'

Cesia stayed quiet as Hela and I chatted, but smiled and nodded as her sister told me how the two of them came to be in Belgium, occasionally glancing at me from under those dark lashes.

Hela was twenty-one, the same age as me, and Cesia was seventeen. The most astonishing part was learning that they too were from Łódź. I had never seen this small girl in the ghetto during the war, and even if I had I wouldn't have given her a second glance. She was only a child then, ten when the war started, and I was fifteen, but things were different now. Now, I was a confident twenty-one-year-old who was determined to win the affection of this pretty young adult.

We soon discovered that our paths had almost crossed the

year before when Cesia and Hela had been staying in Hanover at the same time as me. While there, the two sisters had met up with our mutual friends, Beniek and Heniek Dunkel, but we must have just missed each other. How lucky it was that I had decided to play ping-pong with Mumek that morning at the exact time when Cesia had walked through the door! Had I not, we would have missed our chance again and may never have met at all.

Cesia occasionally contributed to the conversation as the three of us sat talking, but not much. Much later, she told me that she could see immediately that I was a kind, gentle (and handsome!) man, but more than that, that we were two people who understood each other. So many in the world would never be able to relate to, or comprehend, what we'd been through in the Łódź Ghetto and afterwards, but we could. It was comforting for both of us to find someone with whom we shared a common language. Hela's husband, Herszel, was a Bundist, so it was he who had organised for the three of them to be smuggled out of Germany and into Belgium. As we sat talking, I said a silent thank you to Herszel for bringing this beautiful girl into Brussels and into my life.

Over the following days, Hela and Cesia spent more and more time at the Bund premises, becoming part of our growing group of friends. Cesia and I gradually began sharing more of our personal experiences from the past six years with each other. I learned that her family was very different to mine in that they were not politically active at all. Cesia had never met anyone like me who had had access to an illegal radio, or who was part of an underground movement that hid documents and attended secret meetings. And I was glad to hear that, unlike me, she had only had to endure a couple of days at Auschwitz before she and her sister were chosen for work duty and sent to Hamburg to clean out the ruins of bombed-out houses.

But in other ways our experiences were very similar. We had both lost parents in the gas chambers. Cesia's mother was sent there moments after they arrived at Auschwitz, just as my mother had been. We had both lost many friends and relatives in the ghetto and at the death camps, we had both starved in the ghetto and we had both been exposed to horrific events that we were far too young to see. Also, we had both grown up feeling very small compared with everyone around us. Cesia was just four foot eight, only two inches shorter than me. It was a rare thing for me to be around a person I didn't have to crick my neck looking up at all the time. Before long, Cesia and I struck up a friendship. Not long after that, I found myself falling head-over-heels in love with the small girl with the dark curls.

We started going out together, but never alone, always with others around us. There was a big group of us, all young, all Jewish and all members of the Bund who had survived the war. Ours was a communal life. We all had a thirst for fun, music and laughter, and Brussels was our playground. Every night we went out dancing, eating and drinking in cafes and restaurants, seeing theatre and cabaret shows and walking the streets of our beautiful new city until the early hours of the morning. Cesia and I drank it all in, enjoying every moment, as we took our time getting to know each other. Cesia was still incredibly shy, so it took a while for our romance to bloom. These days my wife is an ebullient, talkative, social, confident woman who is surrounded by adoring friends and family. Everyone who knows Cesia laughs fondly at the way she never stops talking and laughing. But seventeen-year-old Cesia was a very different person. She was so quiet that I sometimes had to lean over to hear what she was saying, but I was prepared to wait. I knew this girl was worth it.

I'm almost certain that I fell in love with Cesia the moment I saw her, but it took longer for her to feel the same way. If we were out walking alone, Cesia would let me hold her hand, but as soon as we got near our friends, she would pull her hand away, uncomfortable with public displays of affection. Of course, I also understood that this young woman was probably still suffering some post-traumatic stress from everything she had been through. She had seen so many horrors, lost many loved ones and was understandably wary of the world around her and those in it. Cesia was mentally and emotionally scarred, like so many of us, and she had been so young when the war started. To endure the kind of ordeals, suffering and anguish we experienced daily in the ghetto was enough to traumatise a young girl on its own, without losing her parents in such a terrible way as well. I needed to be gentle, mindful and patient with this shy, quiet young woman.

I knew early on that I wanted Cesia to be a big part of my future. I could already see that beneath that shy exterior, this beautiful woman possessed a zest for life, which suited me very well. I knew that I wanted to marry and raise a family with her. Most importantly, I knew that my mother would have adored her. So, yes, I could very easily see my future with Cesia but didn't want to scare her away by sharing these dreams with her. I would find out later that she was thinking the same thing, but of course I had no idea at the time.

Eventually, Cesia began to trust me and open up a little and, a few weeks after we met, I finally convinced her to come with me to the cinema. Alone. The two of us never went anywhere alone, so I was very happy when she accepted my invitation.

The cinema went dark as we took our seats. I looked over at Cesia and saw a tiny smile tugging at the corner of her mouth as she stared up at the screen, waiting for the film to start. I studied her in the half-light; she was wearing pink lipstick with a hint of blush on her pale cheeks and her freshly washed dark curls sat on the shoulders of her blue dress. She was so beautiful. I felt as if my heart was about to burst.

An urge came over me. I leaned over and, in Yiddish, whispered in her ear, 'Cesia, I love you.'

She glanced at me, eyes wide, startled by this unexpected declaration of love. As the film in front of us started, we kept our eyes on each other and I waited nervously for her response. But she stayed silent.

Maybe it had been too soon? Maybe I should have waited? What had I been thinking? Now she would never agree to be alone with me again!

Then she smiled and, as the music and opening credits of the film began, Cesia reached out, took my hand and squeezed it. Happiness washed over me. She may not have given me a verbal response but she didn't have to. There in that crowded Brussels cinema, that squeeze told me all I needed to know. Cesia turned back to face the screen but kept my hand in hers.

From that night on it was official. Cesia and Abram were a couple.

A few days later, she let me kiss her for the first time. I was twenty-one years old and had never kissed a girl before. But after kissing Cesia, I knew I never wanted to kiss another.

To this day, I never have.

24

A GRAND AFFAIR

Some might say Cesia and I were too young to know what true love was but, at seventeen and twenty-one, we already felt as though we had lived two lifetimes. The things we had seen and experienced made us feel older than our years, and we knew, better than most, that life is too short and precious to waste any time. This moment, here and now, was all that mattered. If you found someone who made you feel the way we did, you had to take the opportunity when it was there. Cesia and I both knew all too well that everything in your life could change in a single moment.

As our romance blossomed in 1946, Cesia and I continued to stay busy and involved in the various Bund activities on offer. The Bund organised two holiday camps each year, one in summer and one in winter. The summer camp was near the sea, while the winter camp was inland, close to the mountains. Cesia and I attended our first holiday camp together, along with a large group of friends, and all of us in the Bund became very close. Throughout 1946, I went on many of these camps, sometimes with Cesia, sometimes not, and had the time of my life. We were with friends in the great outdoors, enjoying the freedom that still felt so new to us, and living our lives. It was the greatest joy and some of the happiest times of my life, including the day on one of these camps when I received a letter from someone I had almost given up all hope of ever hearing from again.

My sister, Maryla.

She had finally managed to leave Russia and returned to Łódź where she met someone who recognised her. The man told her I had survived and was living in Brussels. She was ecstatic to hear this and wrote to the Bund headquarters on Rue de Camions straight away to tell me she had survived and was back in Poland.

The joy I felt upon receiving this letter was indescribable. To know for certain that a member of my family was alive after all this time was amazing. Tears welled in my eyes as I read my sister's letter. Cesia was delighted for me too, of course. My happiness was hers as well. I was desperate to see Maryla immediately, but this was not possible. As Mumek and I had learned, it was not an easy task to cross borders at that time. My sister and I would have to wait a little longer for our long-awaited reunion. However, I wrote back to her that very day, telling her how happy I was to hear from her, and that I would do all I could to get back and see her as soon as possible.

Towards the end of 1946, I started an illegal apprenticeship in handbag making. I was not legally permitted to do an apprenticeship of any kind but knew I had to find a trade and learn a skill for the future. Once I became good enough at my work, I applied for a job in a factory that made crocodile and snakeskin handbags. I got the job and soon became very proficient in the art of handbag making. A few months after starting I was made foreman.

Meanwhile, Cesia started attending classes at a vocational training centre run by ORT – also known as the Organisation for Rehabilitation through Training – an organisation formed to teach young Jewish people a trade, and that had been around since 1880. To this day, it still exists in some countries. Part of her course involved working in a tailoring factory, where Cesia learned how to hand stitch and use a sewing machine. The factory was owned by the Litmanowicz family – the same people who had taken Mumek and I in when we first arrived in Belgium. After this, Cesia worked at another tailoring factory owned by the Wajsman family. Jumo Wajsman had been in the Łódź Ghetto too, but we first met in Belgium. Jumo was also a Bundist and we became very close friends with him and his wife, Ruzka. Jumo had been very lucky and avoided being sent to Auschwitz, but Ruzka was subjected to Josef Mengele's barbaric experiments there. Both Jumo and Ruzka would also resettle in Australia, where Ruzka eventually died due to complications caused by those experiments.

Cesia and I moved in together at the start of 1947. Under Belgium law, Cesia was still considered underage, but we were able to do it because we had her sister Hela's approval. Normally the two of us would have rented a room in a house, which perhaps would have a kitchen, but we knew if we did, we wouldn't have been able to have friends over. Luckily, there was a space available on the second floor of a building not far from the Bund headquarters.

The building had a fur shop on the ground floor, the fur factory on the first floor, and our flat was above that on the second floor. We had a small living room, a kitchen, and a bedroom that was just big enough to fit a bed in. There was no shower, and the toilet was on the floor below, but we didn't mind. We were so happy to have our own place. The best part about this place was having the whole building to ourselves on Sundays, when the shop and factory were closed, and we would have parties, sometimes up to twenty-five people crowded into our tiny room.

Our new home had an interesting history. Cesia and I were the third couple to live in that room, the first being Dorka Dorenblatt and Nunek Szlajcher, who had moved into the single room together, married soon after and moved out. The second couple were Majer (Kopel) Ceprow and Roza Nitka who moved in, married soon after and moved out. When they found out about these other two couples, our friends quickly dubbed our new place the 'Lover's Nest'.

Cesia and I worked hard at our respective jobs every day, then we came home to prepare dinner, ate and then headed out with our friends. We never went out alone. It was always with a large group or another couple.

It was a warm early June night in 1947, when I took Cesia's hand and got down on one knee in the 'Lover's Nest'.

'Will you marry me?' I asked a stunned Cesia.

'Yes,' she laughed.

I couldn't believe my luck. The pretty girl with the dark curls had agreed to be my wife!

It is not an easy thing to get married when you have no

identification or official documentation, so I immediately wrote to Maryla to ask if she could find mine and Cesia's birth certificates in Poland. She was soon able to track mine down but had no luck finding Cesia's. Cesia was sure she had been born in Łódź, but there was no record there of her birth, and it wasn't until much later that we would discover Cesia was in fact born in Pratków.

Without Cesia's documentation, we were told we could only marry if we had Hela's official approval as she was Cesia's legal guardian, which we did. Cesia was eighteen and I was twenty-two when we went down to Belgium's town hall, the Grand Plaz, for a civil ceremony on 10 June 1947. I used the last of that week's money to buy Cesia a wedding present – a lovely gold chain that she still has now.

Cesia and I were one of a few couples getting married at the Grand Plaz that day. The couple before us were in their mid-thirties, pregnant and seemed slightly miserable about the whole situation. At the end of their ceremony, the female celebrant called us forward and when she looked down at us, a huge smile broke across her face. I guess we must have been quite the contrast from her previous couple: two very small, very young people, bursting with excitement at the prospect of beginning their lives together.

It was a simple ceremony but in a stunning setting. The Grand Plaz was magnificent and around 300 years old at that point. Cesia and I both took the day off work for our wedding. We couldn't afford a party afterwards, and certainly not a honeymoon, so went straight back to work the next day and got on with our new lives as husband and wife.

LESSON LEARNED

Life is beautiful, and you must live it every day. Despite any problems, the sun will rise each morning.

25

REUNITING WITH MY SISTER

Two weeks after our wedding, I left my new bride in Brussels and travelled to Poland to meet Maryla. The opportunity to travel had come up through a soccer team I was associated with in Belgium. I was one of the team's officials, and they were scheduled to travel to Wrocław for a match. I was required to go along and saw it as the perfect opportunity to go and see Maryla.

My sister had managed to obtain my birth certificate and send it to me by then, so I was able to apply for and receive my Polish passport. We had still had no luck finding Cesia's birth certificate so she couldn't come along. Even if she could have, we weren't able to afford travel for both of us at that time.

I had managed to save $100 to give to Maryla, which I hid in my shoe. Hela's husband was a shoemaker in Brussels and put the money in the heel of my shoe before I left just in case there were issues with foreign currency at the border. I also wanted to bring my sister a gift and wondered what I could give her. Eventually, I decided to take her bananas. Unlike in Poland, fruit

The Strength of Hope

was plentiful in Brussels so I filled a small briefcase with as many bananas as I could fit inside.

I hadn't seen Maryla for seven years, not since the start of the war in 1939, so I was excited, but also nervous. Would we feel like complete strangers to each other? Would it be awkward? Was she as nervous as I was? I would just have to wait and see, because first I needed to perform my duties in Wrocław for the soccer team.

The city of Wrocław had been badly damaged in the war, and it was terrible to see, but the local Bundists invited us to a special evening they had organised just for us, which cheered us greatly. I felt honoured when I was asked to say a few words, and over the course of the evening I met a lovely couple named Hania and Guter. I offered Hania and one of her friends a banana from my briefcase and they were delighted and confused. They had never seen a banana before and had no idea how to eat it, with the skin on or off, and we had a good laugh.

Once my official duties in Wrocław were over, I arranged my travel to Łódź. I found out I could fly to Łódź in a couple of hours, and for almost the same money as a train. I had never been on a plane before so decided to fly. The aeroplane was a four-seater, and carried only the pilot, me and two other passengers. I wasn't frightened at the time but looking back now I probably should have been. It was such a small aircraft and not in the greatest condition. I think it is a miracle that we arrived in one piece and would never get on a rickety plane like that now.

When our small plane landed at Łódź's tiny airport, my brother-in-law, Mendel, was there to meet me. He explained that Maryla would have come to meet me too but was seven months pregnant and not up to the journey. I knew from my correspondence with Maryla over the past few months that her first husband had been drafted into the Russian army at the start of the war and never heard from since. Their son, Danek, was now six years old, and she had recently married Mendel. She met her new husband when she started work as a teacher at the Jewish Orphanage in Helenówek, where Mendel Zelmanowicz was a guard. The orphanage had been set up for those children who lost parents during the war. Maryla and Mendel married soon after meeting and were now expecting their first child together.

I was full of excited anticipation as Mendel and I travelled back to Helenówek, and when we finally arrived at the orphanage it was a very emotional reunion. Even though she looked much older than when I'd last seen her, I recognised her immediately. She looked healthy and happy, and we fell into each other's arms, hugging and crying for a long time.

Danek was a nice, polite boy, and excited to meet his Uncle Abram for the first time. He was even more excited when I bought him his first ever ice cream a few days later.

I stayed in Łódź with Maryla, Mendel and Danek for three weeks. During that time my sister and I talked a lot. We had a lot to catch up on, and so many stories and experiences to share, and I was fascinated to hear my sister's story.

When she and Jacob had first left Łódź to go to the east, they were unaware of the Molotov–Ribbentrop Pact – a non-aggression pact between Nazi Germany and the Soviet Union that included an agreement that neither would aid an enemy of the other – which meant the Russians would not let them enter. After several attempts, and after bribing a Russian guard with a watch and their wedding rings, Maryla and Jacob crossed into the Soviet Union. Danek was born in Orsha (in today's Belarus) on 4 Nov 1940. In June 1941, Jacob was taken into the Red Army, and was never seen or heard from again. Stalin never trusted Jewish communists, so Maryla and Danek were sent to a *kolkhoz* (collective farm) in Kazakhstan, where they received a letter in 1943 informing them that Jacob was missing in action.

Maryla did not want to talk too much about her life in Kazakhstan, except to say that it was very cold and that there was constant hunger. She was first working in the field and with animals, but because of ill health and shortage of teachers, she began teaching. During that time, Maryla nursed Danek through typhus, dysentery and tuberculosis, which killed many of the exiled children. It took her and Danek five long, difficult months to get from the exile in Kazakhstan back to Łódź. The journey involved a constant search for food and being too scared to speak until she knew if the people around her spoke Russian or Polish. Using the wrong language meant the difference between getting food or getting hurt.

Finally, back in Poland, Maryla started to look for all of us and this is when she heard that I was in Belgium. This happy discovery brought an abrupt end to her joining the ranks of the communist elites.

After the war, the Soviet Union imposed a communist government on a Catholic Poland. True believers were hard to find in Poland after the war and the government was struggling to find enough believers to lead the population into the promised paradise of communism. Maryla was an active member of the Communist Party and was offered various positions in their hierarchy. However, she was soon called to the party secretariat and informed that it was forbidden for party members to correspond with anyone in the decadent capitalist West. When, she refused, because of me, she was thrown out of the party.

We talked about our parents and sisters, Frajda and Estera, too. I told Maryla about the postcard we received from Estera in 1942 saying she was safe and being well cared for. Of course, we both knew by now that she and Frajda must already have been dead by then. Postcards like those, received by families all over Poland, were part of the Nazis plan to keep us calm while they murdered members of our family. Although it was wonderful to see Maryla again, our meeting was also tinged with a heavy sadness because we had to accept that we were the only Goldberg family survivors.

I also met up with many friends while I was back in Łódź, including Bono. It was good to see him, and he was happy to hear about my marriage and the life Cesia and I were building in Belgium.

Finally, it was time to return to Brussels – this time by train – but I promised Maryla that we would meet again soon. She was eager to meet Cesia and I was looking forward to meeting my new niece or nephew when they arrived in the world too. This baby would be the first Goldberg to be born after the war, and the first new member who would keep our family line going. What a joyous occasion it would be.

Back in Brussels, Cesia and I continued to squeeze the good things out of our everyday lives, but there was always a deep sadness within me. I had been a witness to so much suffering, and experienced so much loss and heartbreak, that it was impossible to put those memories behind me. Yes, I was living a 'normal' life in Belgium, but what could be normal after so much trauma and pain?

I had nightmares, always about running and hiding. Fear was at the centre of every nightmare. Sometimes I would see my parents, sometimes my sisters, sometimes babies being thrown from windows, but always I would wake feeling the same panic and sense of loss. I hadn't forgotten the promise I made to my mum that terrible morning at Auschwitz. I knew I owed it to her, my family, friends and the six million Jewish people murdered to tell the world what happened and help rebuild. Part of that plan involved starting my own family with Cesia one day, but that was a little way off. We were both still very young and had to build a secure life for ourselves first.

Cesia and I noticed that a lot of our friends were starting to leave Europe for lands across the seas. It was understandable. Europe held such sad and traumatic memories for so many of us that being there was a constant reminder of what we had endured and lost. Mumek's brother, Heniek Morgentaler, arrived in Brussels in 1946. He had started studying medicine in Germany and wanted to continue his studies in Brussels. Eventually, he moved to Canada, finishing his medical degree there. Mumek followed him there shortly afterwards. I was sad to say goodbye to the friend I had enjoyed so many adventures with, but we promised to stay in touch and knew we would see each other again.

By 1948, Cesia and I began to talk about where we wanted to start our new life together. We knew we couldn't stay in Brussels forever because at that time, a foreigner could never become a Belgian citizen. There was also the constant worry that a third World War was going to break out. The Cold War had begun, the blockade of Berlin was in progress and the threat of war between the West and the Soviet Union was very real. If there was another war, we wanted to be as far from Europe as possible. Belgium had been good to us. We were illegal refugees who had had such wonderful times in this beautiful country. Most importantly, Belgium had brought my true love into my life. But many other friends were starting to leave for Canada too, just like Mumek and his brother. Many were also heading to America and England, as well as another country that felt so far away to us that it might just as well have been on another planet – Australia.

Australia appealed to us for many reasons, not least because it was a democratic country and far away from Europe and all its troubles, but also because many friends had gone there. Cesia and I felt that going to Australia would be a continuation of our community and Jewish lives, and the Bund had headquarters there too. We had also heard Australia was a place where music and culture was embraced almost as much as sport. My boss at the handbag factory had applied for a permit to enable me to work legally in 1947, but it was taking a very long time to come through, so in 1948 Cesia and I put in our application to travel to Australia. In December 1949, a nice Belgian policeman delivered a letter to our home.

'I'm sorry,' he said. 'Your Belgium work permit for the handbag trade has been rejected. But you can apply again for work in a different trade if you want to avoid deportation.'

'Thank you,' I told him. 'But we've just had our permit to leave Belgium for Australia approved.'

It was official. We were off to the land of Oz.

26

TOWARDS A NEW LIFE IN AUSTRALIA

Cesia and I had our permits to go to Australia, but it wasn't as simple as hopping on a ship and leaving. There were a lot of bureaucratic procedures to go through first and there was no Australian Embassy in Belgium, so we had to do everything through the British Embassy. We both had to pass a medical examination and many people were rejected because they had tuberculosis, although some managed to convince someone to go in their place so they could pass the medical. Both Cesia and I passed our medical, but another hurdle we faced was the quota stipulating that no more than 25 per cent of refugees on any ship could be Jewish. Australia was to become home to a high proportion of Holocaust survivors.

After a short wait, the embassy advised us that we had been approved for a ship to Melbourne, which we would need to board in Italy. In January 1951, Cesia and I, along with a small group of friends who were leaving on the same ship, bid an emotional farewell to our friends in Belgium and boarded a train to Italy. Cesia and I were two of around one hundred refugees on the train, and it was very crowded. There were no sleepers, but the view from the train windows was so stunning that none of us minded. We travelled through Belgium, Luxembourg and Switzerland's beautiful mountains and thoroughly enjoyed the whole journey.

Our small group disembarked in Naples, where we were then divided up to stay in separate hotels. Cesia and I were put in the same hotel as our friends, Dorka and Nunek Szlajcher, and their two-year-old daughter, Marie. We requested one large room for all five of us so we could stay together and save money.

Not long after we had settled into our hotel room, we were told by our contact from JDC – the Jewish humanitarian organisation that was helping us and thousands of others after the Holocaust – that our ship needed repairs so we would not be leaving as soon as we'd hoped.

'How long will the repairs take?' we asked.

'They could take up to a month,' the man told us.

We were very upset to hear this. We were eager to get to the other side of the world and start our new lives and had no idea what we would do in Naples for a whole month.

Nunek and I left our wives in the hotel with Marie and headed down to the docks to find out exactly what kind of repairs the ship needed. But when we arrived, we discovered that the ship was anchored about a kilometre offshore, so there was no chance of asking anyone on board any questions. But Nunek and I were young, daring and not easily deterred by small setbacks. Neither of us were good swimmers, but we hired a small wooden boat and rowed right out to the ship. Of course, we realised immediately that we couldn't see anything from our tiny boat as it bobbed alongside the gigantic ship, and obviously we weren't allowed on board.

Annoyed and frustrated, the two of us went back to see someone at the JDC offices.

'We have wives and a two-year-old with us,' we said, thumping the man's desk. 'We need to leave Naples on the next ship!'

Our thumping must have worked, because the five of us were put on a list to leave on the next ship, *The Sorrento*, in two weeks' time. We found out much later from friends that *The Sorrento* was bigger, better equipped and cleaner than the one we were meant to sail on. Those in our group who waited a month for the repairs told us in Australia that their ship was terribly old and in such bad condition that it may as well have been built in the Middle Ages. Hearing this, Nunek and I were glad we had made a fuss and got ourselves on *The Sorrento*. There were Bundist passengers from Sweden, Belgium and Paris on board, around twenty-five people in all. Out of the 1500 passengers on board, 200 of us were Jewish.

Somehow my good health stayed with me again on *The Sorrento*. High winds and rough seas made the journey anything but smooth sailing and everyone around me got very seasick, but I was fine. Even the ship's crew were unwell. Passengers were vomiting anywhere and everywhere on the ship, and the terrible smell made people's already queasy stomachs feel much worse.

Cesia became sick on day one and someone told her the best thing to do was to lie down. So she lay on the bed in our cabin

The Strength of Hope

and stayed there all day. I checked on her every now and then to see how she was but could see she was not getting any better. If anything, she was getting worse.

'Why don't you come onto the deck?' I said finally. 'A lot of people are sick, so you won't be the only one. The fresh air might help.'

Although waves were crashing onto the deck and it was not easy to stay dry, or still, up there, I hoped it would be better for Cesia than lying on a bed all day. Eventually, she agreed to come. Soon after leaving the cabin, Cesia was sick again, but that was the last time she was ill for the rest of the journey. It made me wonder if lying down had made it worse and that if she hadn't listened to that person, she might not have been sick at all.

Poor Dorka was sick for the entire journey. She headed straight to her cabin as soon as she boarded and stayed there the whole time we were at sea. So many people on the ship were sick for the entire journey that sometimes I would be the only one in the dining room at mealtimes. Most people couldn't bear even the smell of food so there I was, sitting in a vast empty dining room with more food in front of me than I had ever seen, let alone would be capable of eating, in my life. I don't know how I was so lucky, but I did not get sick even one time during four weeks on the seas.

At one stage, Cesia and I were up on the deck when Nunek walked past carrying Marie in his arms. He looked terrible, very pale, and like he was about to throw up.

'Nunek,' I said. 'Give Marie to me, quick!'

My friend practically threw his daughter at me before he ran for the side of the ship to throw up.

The ship travelled through the Suez Canal, then across to Colombo, where we were allowed to disembark. The five of us went on a rickshaw tour of the city, and a guide took us to see many beautiful sites.

The Sorrento finally docked in Fremantle, Western Australia, after four long weeks. When we disembarked it was a Sunday in 1951 and we couldn't believe how quiet it was. Everything was closed. There was almost no one on the streets and nothing to see. We managed to find one fruit shop that was open and bought some fruit to take back on the ship. The journey from Fremantle to Melbourne was very rough, but most people were used to it by now, including Cesia. She wasn't sick once on the final leg of our journey.

On 15 March 1951, we spotted land from the deck of the ship. All we could see in the distance was trees and greenery, no tall buildings in sight. Cesia and I stood on the deck, arms around each other, feeling an overwhelming sense of joy and relief as we docked at Station Pier in Port Melbourne. We had made it to the other side of the world.

Our new lives could finally begin.

Below us on the docks, thousands of people were waiting for their loved ones; it was quite a sight. Everyone was jostling for position, desperate for a first glimpse of their family, friends and relatives. Streamers flew through the air, handkerchiefs waved and people were shouting, crying and laughing. Cesia and I leaned over the rail, desperately searching the crowd for Cesia's sister, Hela, and her husband, Herszel, in among the sea of faces.

They had been living in Melbourne since September 1950 and were so excited to welcome us there.

Finally, once our belongings and documents were all checked and approved – it takes a long time to process 1500 passengers – we walked down the gangplank, stepped off the ship and onto the pier. The first thing that struck us was the heat. We had never experienced anything like it. It was so hot. The weather in Australia was obviously going to take some getting used to.

Hela and Herszel were part of a welcoming party of around 200 or so Jewish friends who had come to greet our small group, including our old friends, Roza and Majer (Kopel) Ceprow from the 'Lovers Nest' in Brussels and my old buddy from the Russian dungeon, Jack Lewin. But Cesia only had eyes for her sister, Hela. The two sisters threw their arms around each other, laughing and crying with happiness. Hela and Herszel had brought their now five-year-old son, George, with them too and we were overjoyed to see them all.

They took us back to their place in Fitzroy so we could freshen up and catch up on the last few years. We had a wonderful night together and it made me so happy to see Cesia reunited with her sister. It made me think of Maryla and our plan to have her join us in Melbourne as soon as we could organise it for her and her family.

The following day, Cesia and I went to the Bund premises in Carlton. We became members straight away, and it wasn't long before we were attending meetings and events with old friends from Europe including Dorka, Nunek, Majer (Kopel) and Roza who had all lived at our old 'Lovers' Nest' in Belgium.

We were also introduced to many new people. Just as we had in Belgium, Cesia and I immediately felt blessed to be part of such a wonderful and supportive community, all the way on the other side of the world.

Everyone was eager to introduce us to our new city. My old friend Bono was in Melbourne too, having immigrated in 1950. Bono was still a bachelor and working as a knitter but would soon go on to work in the travel business and eventually establish Jetset Tours (originally Astronaut Travel) with Isi Leibler and Lionel Landman. After arriving in Australia, Bono had immediately become active in both Jewish, and non-Jewish, life and soon became a vice-president of the Kadimah Jewish Cultural Centre and National Library, president of the Bund and delegate to the World Conference of Yiddish Literature and Culture. It was clear that my old friend's values and passions had not changed since our days working for the underground in the ghetto.

Not long after our arrival in Melbourne, Cesia and I were invited to a religious Seder – a Jewish ritual and ceremonial dinner in commemoration of the Jews' exodus from Egypt, held on the first night of Passover. During the ceremony, someone reads from the Haggadah (book), which tells the story of Passover, and it is very long. Cesia and I had never in our lives had to sit through a religious Seder, and we both struggled to stay awake. It took so long, and our stomachs were rumbling loudly from hunger by the time it finished. It was the first and last religious Seder we ever attended.

I had just £5 in my pocket when Cesia and I arrived in Melbourne but was eager to explore my new town for a couple of weeks before starting work. Hela and Herszel's balcony overlooked the Fitzroy football ground, and it was here that I witnessed my first game of Australian Rules Football. I had never heard of this sport and was mesmerised as I watched the players run around on the grass, jumping high in the air, kicking an oval-shaped ball instead of a round one. And such long kicks! Sometimes the ball travelled 50 metres through the air and straight through two huge white sticks at the other end of the ground. For someone like me, who had only ever known football to mean soccer, Aussie Rules was fascinating, and I loved it instantly.

Melbourne felt like paradise to us. Unlike Europe, with all its political upheavals, post-war ruins and sad memories, Melbourne was a calm oasis. You could almost believe there had never been a world war at all. And although I was many miles away, I never wanted to forget what had happened. I was determined to keep my promise to my mother and knew that one day I would.

Although our new city was flat like Belgium, it was much quieter. Back in 1951, the streets of Melbourne were deserted after 6pm, which was a great shock to us. So much of our lives in Europe had revolved around the nightlife there. We were used to working from 7am until 6pm, then going out until at least 2am most nights. Brussels had been alive and bustling twenty-four hours a day, but now we found ourselves in a city where everything shut after dark. This was very strange to us, especially on weekends when everything shut at 2pm on Saturdays, and nothing at all opened on Sundays.

On Saturday evenings, the women would all dress up in

their dresses, hats, gloves and handbags, the men would put on their monkey suits, and they would all head out to the cinema or theatre. But as soon as the show finished, they would head home, and the streets would be quiet once again. No one that we knew went out in Melbourne the way we had in Europe, but Cesia and I were not complaining. This was our new life, and we were committed to it. We felt safe here. For the first time in my life, I felt like I didn't have to look over my shoulder anymore. We knew that in time, things would change, and, of course, eventually they did.

We decided not to have children until we had saved enough money. We were still so young, and our priority was getting work and eventually our own business. That was always our goal.

A family could wait until we were more established and could give our children a good life.

27

FROM PRESSURE TO PRESSER

When my permit to work in the handbag trade had been rejected in Belgium, I decided to learn to press clothes instead. Herszel had begun pressing when the shoe repair business was not so good, and he taught me the basics before going to Australia.

When we got to Melbourne, news spread quickly among the Jewish community that a presser had arrived, and a man named Golombek came to see me within a day of our arrival. He was the boss of a tailoring factory that made trench coats and he needed a presser.

'You can start tomorrow if you want the job,' he told me.

But I said I couldn't start for a couple of weeks because I needed to rest. In fact, I wanted time to explore my new town, but didn't tell him that. Golombek was determined though and came to see me at Hela's flat many times over the next two weeks, always asking when I could start work. Eventually, I felt like I had explored enough of my new city for now and told him I was ready to begin work. We started wage negotiations, and Golombek said he would pay me £13 per week, but I told him that should be a starting wage.

'I am very fast,' I told him. 'I do my job very well, so why don't you try me out and see what I can do? Then we can negotiate again.'

He agreed and I set about proving myself.

The factory was in the city, in William Street. It was very dark and stuffy inside, with rats running around. I was not impressed with my working environment, but I thought if they paid me enough money I would do the work. There was no pressing machine, so everything was done by hand. I soon realised that I had much more experience than the other people working there. My trial period lasted a couple of days and in that time I showed Golombek that I was indeed very good and very fast. The negotiations began again, and I told him I wanted £20 per week. On top of that, they should also pay my tax.

Golombek was very surprised at my bold demands.

'Take it or leave it,' I said before he could argue.

After ten days, Golombek came back to my house and said he had thought about my terms and would accept them. I am certain he must have tried out other pressers in those ten days and realised they weren't as good or as fast as me, so he came back to offer me the job.

Not long after I started work, we relocated to a much nicer, larger factory in Little Bourke Street. Golombek decided he needed to modernise, so he installed a pressing machine. He positioned the new machine right near a huge window that collected the hot afternoon sun. To operate that steaming, heat-generating presser right next to blazing heat coming through the window on hot summer days was not very pleasant.

Our factory was busy, so Golombek asked me to do overtime. I said I would but that he would need to pay me overtime rates. He told me that would be too expensive, so I did some quick mental calculations and said, 'What if you pay me 'piece work'?'

He thought this was a great idea, and assumed he would save money this way, so agreed. Unfortunately for him, my work was so fast that I ended up making more money than I would have if I was being paid overtime rates.

After a couple of weeks, Golombek came to me. 'I want to change the deal back to paying you overtime rates,' he said.

But I shook my head. 'No, you agreed to pay me piece work, so that is what you must do.'

I have always been a man of my word and so expect the same from others.

Cesia and I didn't know a word of English when we arrived in Australia. I spoke French, Polish, Yiddish, German and understood Russian, and Cesia spoke Polish, German, and Yiddish. We both had an ear for languages, but it still took us a long time to get the hang of this new language. Most of the people we were mixing with at that time spoke Yiddish or Polish, like us, so it was only when we were out in shops or meeting new people that we had a problem understanding what people were saying.

Sometimes it could be very hard, especially when we were grocery shopping and couldn't ask questions about where certain foods were, or what they were. There were many kinds of food and drink in Melbourne that we had never seen or tasted before. When we went to the milk bar to buy bread and milk in those early days, we held out the money to the shopkeepers in the palms of our hands so they could take the right amount.

We couldn't go to school to learn English because we couldn't afford it. We had to go to work to make money. Cesia got a job sewing jackets for children on her machine at home, and all day long she would listen to the radio as she sewed. This is how she gradually learned English.

In our first few months in Australia, I learned many things about managing finances, including the difference between borrowing money versus having cash to pay. I was taught a valuable lesson when we got a loan to buy our refrigerator. By the time we had paid it off I discovered that I had paid almost as much in hire purchase interest as the retail cost of the fridge. That was when I decided to adopt a philosophy that I continue to follow to this day: when I have money I will buy. I did not want to make someone else rich through paying interest.

Theatre was always something Cesia and I enjoyed; we started going to theatre productions at the University of Melbourne theatre hall with our Jewish friends. We often knew the general plot of the play, so could usually follow the story without understanding what the actors were saying, but it was also a good way for us to get familiar with this new language. We had a very rich Yiddish cultural life too and saw many Yiddish plays and movies with friends like Bono and others from the Bund.

Some Jewish people we knew regretted coming to Australia.

They said it was like a cemetery and complained that their new city was too quiet or dull. But Cesia and I never regretted coming here for a single second. We knew we were safe and that we would never have to look over our shoulders again, and that was one of the many upsides to living in a quiet town.

Cesia and I knew that our new life would have its challenges in the beginning, and that there would be a lot of adjustments to be made. This is to be expected when you are starting out with a spoon, a pot and nothing else. But pots and pans are not things that should make a difference to a life. Melbourne was our home now and we wanted to make the best of it. Our success here would all come down to us, our ability and hard work.

At every Jewish celebration, gathering or event Cesia and I attended in our first few years in Melbourne, there would always come a point when a few of us would end up discussing the Shoah in some way. A lot of survivors in our community didn't want to talk about what happened. There were also a lot of people in the Jewish community who didn't want to hear our stories, because it was too hard for them to hear, but that never stopped me from telling mine. Even if somebody told me they didn't want to listen, I still wanted to talk, just as I promised my mother I would, but would try to do so without anger or bitterness. With so much loss, hardship and pain, everyone in our community was traumatised to some degree.

The most important thing to me was that we, as a people, did everything we could to keep these stories alive in our minds. That we kept reminding ourselves and others what is possible when people are brainwashed into murdering others for no reason other than that they are different. I never wanted to let people forget what happened to the Jewish people, even while I was lucky enough to be living a full and happy new life on the other side of the world.

Creating and extending our own family was a priority for Cesia and me. We came to Melbourne looking for peace, love and contentment, because after all we had endured, we knew that this was what life was all about. We could never forget the past, but we also knew we had to focus on building a future.

In 1951, a few months after moving to Melbourne, Cesia and I found a room to rent on Elgin Street in Carlton. It was a very small room, and we didn't have much, but we appreciated every little thing we did have. I also wanted to keep myself fit, so I joined the Maccabi Sports Club. They had a soccer team, which I didn't play with, but attended a lot of their matches. I was working such long hours by then that I didn't have a lot of spare time for sports, but I did take up ping-pong again. Four of us formed a team, and I was happy to be playing the game I had loved so much as a child again. But then something else happened, which made me far happier than any ping-pong championship could.

Cesia became pregnant with our first child.

28

FAMILY LIFE

Throughout Cesia's pregnancy I found myself reflecting a lot on the past. The knowledge that I was to be a father was bringing up a lot of memories of my own parents and childhood. One thing I knew was that I wanted to be the kind of father that my own dad had been – a man who spread hope and positivity, and who taught his children to stand up for themselves and showed them what true bravery is. Of course, my experiences in the war had also taught me that bravery comes in many different forms.

As a kid, I thought bravery simply meant getting my back up against a wall and lashing out at the bigger, meaner kids, just like Dad told me. A few years later, I would learn that there is also a quiet, strong type of bravery. The kind of bravery that thousands of people in the ghetto displayed when they kept going and held onto their will to survive under such horrendous conditions. That kind of unbreakable inner strength was incredibly brave. There were also those whose bravery was much more recognisable and visible. The kind of bravery displayed by women like Roza Robota.

Roza was a prisoner at Auschwitz at the same time as I was, and was part of the underground movement in the camp. It was Roza's job to sort through the belongings of the newly arrived prisoners after they had been stripped of all their possessions and catalogue them in the block known as 'Kanada', so named because Canada was a free country and had a plentiful supply of whatever you might need in life.

Roza worked in close proximity to the Sonderkommandos, who were Jewish prisoners forced to perform a variety of duties in the gas chambers and crematoriums. Sonderkommandos were different to the kapos in that they had not been criminals before the war and did not derive any pleasure from the duties they were forced to carry out.

Every now and then, the Sonderkommandos were replaced with new prisoners because the Nazis didn't want them revealing the sordid and horrific details of what went on in the gas chambers. Therefore, when the time came for the Sonderkommandos to finish their allotted time working in the crematorium, they were all gassed.

The Sonderkommandos knew that this was to be their fate, and so Roza and some of the other workers began planning an uprising.

Because of the nature of her job, Roza had some degree of freedom to move around the camp, and so was able to contact people who worked in the camp's factories. Over time, she managed to contact three Jewish girls who worked in the munitions factory and enlist their help to smuggle small amounts of explosives to her. The girls did this by sewing the dynamite into the hems of their dresses, taking it out of the factory and transferring it to Roza via members of the underground. Another method they used to get dynamite there was by utilising the workmen who cleaned the chimneys and repaired the crematorium's roof. The workmen had to carry in buckets of tar to line the roof and had constructed false bottoms in the buckets, which allowed them to bring dynamite into the buildings.

It took a few months but eventually they had accumulated a sizeable quantity of explosives. Roza knew that time was running out and that they needed to act immediately. The camp was not expecting as many new transports and so she knew the Sonderkommandos would be murdered any day.

The uprising began on 7 October 1944. Crematorium number four was destroyed by explosives and during the fighting that ensued, a few SS were killed. There had been a particularly cruel SS officer who had beaten the Sonderkommandos repeatedly and so during the uprising, the prisoners picked him up and threw him into an oven, burning him alive.

Sirens sounded all over the camp and all of us were immediately locked into our blocks. We had no idea at the time what was going on.

We found out later that the prisoners had very few weapons to fight with, so a few had chosen to run. Somehow, they managed to get away from the camp, and even to swim across the river. They hid in a barn where the SS soon found and killed them.

The SS went on a mission to find out how the Sonderkommandos obtained the explosives, and the munitions factory was the obvious place to begin their search. The three girls who had been involved with smuggling the dynamite in the hems of their dresses were taken, tortured and hanged. Roza Robota was also taken away and tortured, which was a huge concern for the underground movement. If Roza revealed the names of people involved in the movement it would put all their lives, and their operations, at risk. Some in the underground were able to get access to the dungeon where Roza was being held and she told them about the torture she was being subjected to. She also assured them that she hadn't given them a single name or piece of information, despite the pain and suffering she was enduring.

Not a single member of the underground was discovered by the SS because this incredibly brave woman stayed silent during relentless torture and beatings. Roza was hanged on 6 January 1945, just three weeks before the liberation of Auschwitz.

Almost seven years later, with the war over, safe in Melbourne and waiting for my first child to be born, I thought a lot about brave women like Roza. I also thought a lot about my own brave parents. Would my experiences in the Shoah make me a good father? Would they be detrimental to my role as a parent? I hoped with all my heart that they would not. I wanted to give my child the best life I possibly could, and all the love in the world, but I also wanted to teach them about the importance of gratitude and perspective.

My child would be fortunate to grow up in a country like Australia, and would hopefully never experience the kind of trauma, loss and pain that their parents had endured. However, this didn't mean that our child shouldn't know about their family's past and the history of their people. I was not going to shield my child from the terrible truth of what had happened during the Holocaust. I believe it is better to know the truth in life, regardless of how confronting or upsetting it may be.

When the American soldiers from the 82nd Airborne Division and the 8th Infantry entered Wöbbelin on 2 May 1945, they were horrified by what they found there, and their first instinct was to show the people in the nearby town of Ludwigslust the shocking truth

After liberating those of us left in the camp, these American soldiers went to Ludwigslust and made the people there march right past Wöbbelin so they could see for themselves the atrocities that had occurred so close to their homes. They wanted these German people to see what Hitler had done in their name. The townspeople were appalled at the catastrophic and inhumane conditions of the camp, and the thousands of corpses. When the *Burgermeister* (mayor) of Ludwigslust and his wife and daughter learned the full story of what had been going on in Wöbbelin, they committed suicide, unable to live with the guilt and shame of their ignorance.

Later, under American supervision, the people of Ludwigslust buried 200 bodies and held a burial service and erected a monument in honour of all of the victims.

The chaplain's burial address from that service is reproduced below because it is important to remember that the actions of the Nazis didn't happen in isolation from the rest of the German population.

Abram Goldberg

The Chaplain's Burial Address:

We are assembled here today before God and in the sight of man to give a proper and reverent burial to the victims of atrocities committed by armed forces in the name and by the order of the German Government. These 200 bodies were found by the American Army in a concentration camp 4 miles north of the city of Ludwigslust.

The crimes here committed in the name of the German people and by their acquiescence were minor compared to those to be found in concentration camps elsewhere in Germany. Here there were no gas chambers, no crematories; these men of Holland, Russia, Poland, Czechoslovakia and France were simply allowed to starve to death. Within 4 miles of your comfortable homes, 4000 men were forced to live like animals, deprived even of the food you would give to your dogs. In three weeks, 1000 of these men were starved to death; 800 of them were buried in pits in the nearby woods. The 200 who lie before us in these graves were found 4 and 5 feet high in one building and lying with the sick and dying in other buildings.

The world has long been horrified at the crimes of the German nation; these crimes were never clearly brought to light until the armies of the United Nations overran Germany. This is not war as conducted by the international rules of warfare. This is murder such as is not even known among savages.

Though you claim no knowledge of these acts you are still individually and collectively responsible for these atrocities, for they were committed by a government elected to office by yourselves in 1933 and continued in office by your indifference to organised brutality. It should be the firm resolve of the German people that never again should any leader or party bring them to such moral degradation as is exhibited here.

It is the custom of the United States Army through its Chaplain's Corps to ensure a proper and decent burial to any deceased person whether he is civilian or soldier, friend or foe, according to religious preference. The Supreme Commander of the Allied Forces has ordered that all atrocity victims be buried in a public place, and that the cemetery be given the same perpetual care that is given to all military cemeteries. Crosses will be placed at the heads of the graves; a stone monument will be set up in memory of these deceased. Protestant, Catholic and Jewish prayers will be said by Chaplains Wood, Hannan and Wall of the 82nd Airborne Division for these victims as we lay them to rest and commit them into the hands of our Heavenly Father in the hopes that the world will not again be faced with such barbarity.
– Major George B. Woods, Chaplain, US Army

I had promised my mother that I would spend my life telling people the truth about what happened to us in the ghetto and at Auschwitz and I would start with my own child. I also wanted to tell them how important it is to have hope, and how luck can sometimes play a big part in life too.

There were many different reasons for my survival, including good health, access to extra food, friendship, good shoes, but above all else it was pure luck. Many others had the same opportunities as me, the same access to food and information, but did not survive.

It would have taken just one unlucky moment and I wouldn't be here now. I could have passed the wrong guard in the wrong mood at the wrong moment. Sutter could have found our radio that day and I could have been sent to Chelmno. Mengele could have sent me left instead of right. I could simply have been in the wrong place at the wrong time. There were so many moments when I managed to escape death. My survival was largely down to luck, nothing more.

Although, holding on to a little hope helped me too.

My body, mind and spirit were all pushed to their limits over those five years, but through it all I had tried to emulate my father and his positivity. Positivity alone was never enough to save me from a Nazi's gun or truncheon, but it kept me going in those times when I needed something to focus on. I've always believed it is better to have hope and be positive than to be negative and complain. What for? What good does it do? At the time, I had to believe there was life beyond the war, beyond the ghetto, beyond Auschwitz, otherwise, what was the point of living at all?

This was the same message of hope I wanted to share with the world, and with my child. I knew that, when they were older, I would tell them the truth about what had happened to their family and people. The promise I made to my mother didn't just apply to the wider community. It had to start in our own home.

I would never forget.

29

I AM A FATHER

Our baby boy arrived on 15 June 1952. We named him Chaim, after Cesia's father, but from day one he was our 'Charlie'. It's difficult to put into words the love and elation Cesia and I felt the first time we held Charlie in our arms. We simply couldn't believe that the two of us had created this tiny creature. That he belonged to us and no one else. Charlie signified a new beginning and was a reset of sorts for both of us. Our family of two had grown to three and our beautiful baby boy would be the first of many steps towards helping to heal the pain of us losing so many other loved ones in our lives.

Motherhood had an enormous and positive impact on Cesia. Soon after giving birth, my once shy, quiet wife started to come out of her shell. I started arriving home from work to find not only her sister Hela sitting at our kitchen table, but other new mums too. After having Charlie, Cesia met and started spending time with more women in our community, and as her confidence with the English language grew, so too did her circle of friends. It was wonderful to see my wife becoming more social and gregarious.

In 1953, the Kadimah in Carlton held its first exhibition to mark the tenth anniversary of the Warsaw Ghetto Uprising. The exhibition included hundreds of reproductions of original photos and documents, material objects and books. It was the first time Melbourne Holocaust survivors had seen an exhibition like this where so many artefacts were all in the one place – a physical representation that was transmitted to Jews and non-Jews alike.

The Kadimah exhibition documented Jewish pre-war life, the formation of the Warsaw Ghetto and the labour and extermination camps, including Auschwitz and Treblinka.

Although it was harrowing to see those images on display – images that brought painful memories back into sharp focus – it was gratifying to see that people in our community were doing what they could to remind the world of what had happened to us.

It was difficult for me to get involved with these kinds of committees and projects at that time. I was working long hours at the factory and taking on more overtime, determined to provide a good life for my wife and child. Not only was I juggling work and family life, but I was trying to stay active too. The ping-pong team I was part of had started out in the lowest division, but as we played week after week, we began to win and eventually moved up to the highest one. Before long, I realised that I was working so much, and doing so much overtime, that I wasn't always able to get home to see Cesia and Charlie before heading off to my ping-pong commitments. The games started at 8pm and I didn't have a car so had to travel by bus to and from the game. Something had to give and so eventually I decided that I had to give up my place on the ping-pong team to focus on my family and making good money at the factory.

In 1956, five years after arriving in Melbourne, Cesia and I were finally able to afford our first home. 51 Lingwell Road, Auburn, was a semi-detached house, and Cesia's uncle bought the adjoining property a few years later. Buying our first home had taken a lot of hard work and savings, but it was all worth it. We now owned our own little corner of this beautiful city we had fallen in love with.

This was a happy time in our lives. Hela, Herszel and George lived across the road and I was in the process of making plans to bring Maryla and her family out from Poland. Maryla had given birth to her second son, Herszel, and they were having a hard time. Maryla's husband, Mendel, was a physical labourer and Maryla's health was not great, so it was not an easy life for them in post-war Poland. Knowing how hard it was for my sister over in Poland only reinforced my belief that we had done the right thing by coming to this wonderful country. We were so very lucky to live here and hearing stories from Poland only made me feel more grateful and more determined to make the most of our blessed life here in Melbourne.

We sent regular parcels and money to Maryla and Mendel to try and make things less difficult, but I wanted to get them all to Australia so they could have the same happy and safe existence as us. After the Hungarian revolution of 1956, it was easier for Maryla and her family to leave Poland. Prior to that, Jews had only been allowed to travel to Israel, but after the revolution Poland relaxed their restrictions and Maryla and Mendel were able to travel to Germany. Once there we arranged their tickets to Melbourne.

My sister and her family arrived in Melbourne on Christmas Day in 1957. It was a very happy and emotional reunion for both of us. Cesia and I insisted that the four of them move in with us in Auburn until they got on their feet financially. I helped Mendel get a job at Smorgons Meat Processing factory in Footscray and I got Danek a job at a knitting factory. They ended up living with us for a year, until they were able to afford their own place around the corner.

I passed my driver's license test in the late 1950s and soon after that we paid cash for our first ever car. Our new Holden FB was mauve and white, and I loved it on sight. I also loved the feeling of freedom that driving gave me. Suddenly, Cesia and I were able to explore even more of our beautiful new city.

Cesia got her license a couple of years after me, and she was so small that we had to put cushions both behind and under her, on the seat. We also had to have the pedals built up, so she could reach them. Even then, she was still very small and hard to see in the driver's seat. Sometimes people would see our Holden driving down the road and think it was an autonomous vehicle because Cesia wasn't visible in the driver's seat or behind the wheel.

Two years to the day after Maryla and her family arrived in Melbourne, Cesia gave birth to our second child. Chaja (Helen) Goldberg was born on the 25 December 1959 and was named after my mother. Helen was an adorable baby girl and I instantly fell head over heels in love with her. Charlie now had a little sister and our family of three had grown to four. We felt very blessed.

Our children embodied the message of hope I had clung to throughout my years in the ghetto and camps. Back then, I had dared to dream that I might survive and have a family of my own one day. I had held on to the hope that I might be able to create new life after so much death and sadness. Now, here were two life-affirming results of that hope. It was both overwhelming and cathartic in the best possible way.

The happy occasions of our children's births were tinged with sadness for Cesia and me as well. We both felt a great sadness that our parents would never meet their beautiful grandchildren, and that Charlie and Helen would never know their grandparents.

One day, when Cesia picked Charlie up from kindergarten, she noticed him watching the other kids around him as they walked out of the kinder holding their grandparents' hands.

'Mum?' he said, looking up at her with a puzzled expression. 'Where are my grandparents?'

Cesia burst into tears and had no idea what to say. After all, what do you tell a four-year-old in that moment? He was far too young to know all the details at that time but deserved to know the truth about his grandparents one day, when he could fully comprehend it.

Cesia and I had already spoken about how and when we would begin the conversation with our children about our experiences during the war. It was always a concern that our psychological trauma and pain might cause psychological wounds in our own children, but I wanted to keep the promise I made to my mother and to myself. While they were little, however, we would keep the details very vague.

When Charlie got home from kindergarten that day, Cesia told me what he had asked her, so I sat him down to talk.

'Listen, Charlie,' I said. 'Your grandparents were killed by bad people. That is all you need to know for now. When you are older, I will tell you more.'

When they were old enough to comprehend, Cesia and I began to tell our children the stories of what had happened to their grandparents, their extended family and the Jewish people. Little by little, Cesia and I gave Helen and Charlie pieces of information about our past until they were old enough to hear the whole story woven together into one narrative. Our children didn't just hear these stories from us either. They were both growing up in a community where they were reading and learning stories from others in their lives too. The older they got, the more Charlie and Helen wanted to know, and so they continued to educate themselves on the Holocaust and the horrors inflicted on their people. To this day, I believe we did the right thing by telling them. To merely remember is not enough.

I believe that talking about our experiences is better than repressing them. I believe that if we don't let these stories out, the emotions they cause will fester, and potentially emerge in destructive ways. It is not easy to always talk about my experiences during the Holocaust, and I am especially on the verge of tears when I talk about losing my mother and father, because everything is still so vivid for me. It is all there, right in front of my eyes when I describe what happened. There are some images that will never leave me. But I know how important it is that I tell my story to younger generations.

Many of our friends in the Jewish community talked to their kids about what happened to them during the Holocaust like we did, but there were some with a different attitude.

'Why should we tell them?' they would say. 'It will traumatise them. How will it help?'

Whenever people said this to me, I would try to persuade them otherwise.

'Don't you believe your children should know?' I would ask. 'And not only them, but the people around you? One day your kids will grow up and find out from movies, books and other people in their community about the Holocaust. It is unavoidable. They will start to ask you questions because they won't know anything about their family or their people's story.'

I was able to convince some people, but there were others who refused to ever share any of their experiences with their children or grandchildren. Of course, I understood that this could be a defence mechanism for some people. That it might have been too difficult for them to recount those stories without reliving the trauma of it all again, and that was fair enough. I had many friends who had come to Australia at the same time as us who were still suffering from frequent nightmares, or who couldn't talk about what happened to them without crying.

So many of our friends had lost parents, brothers, sisters, uncles, aunties and cousins, and lived with a storm in their heart every day, just as I did. That pain and sense of great loss was always with us and never went away. We all struggled in our own ways, so of course I understood why some people couldn't talk about their experiences. But tragically, some of these people then passed away and it was their adult kids and grandkids who would ask us to tell them about their family's story because 'they didn't tell us anything'.

In 1960, my old friend, Bono was appointed convener of an organising committee for another exhibition on the Warsaw Ghetto. This one was much bigger than the one in 1953 and was a great success. Over six thousand people visited the exhibition, and it was to be the beginning of a long-term mission for Bono, along with a few others, to find a way to create a permanent centre in Melbourne that would keep the memory of the Holocaust alive for both Jews and non-Jews.

30

EAT, DRINK & BE MERRY

From the moment we first arrived in Melbourne back in 1951, Cesia and I were instantly surrounded by so many wonderful family and friends, and our lives have continued to be enriched by the time we've spent with them over the years.

My friendship with Bono stayed solid, and he was a regular visitor to our home once we came to Melbourne. Although Bono remained a bachelor for his entire life, and never had any children, he loved spending time with other people's families. I have a wonderful photo of him sitting on the floor of our lounge room playing with Helen and Charlie when they were young, and the look of delight on my friend's face still makes me smile.

Hela and Herszel's daughter, Shirley, was born in the same year as Charlie, so our children were all very close and spent a lot of time together. We all helped each other out with babysitting too. If I was working and Hela and Herszel had plans, Cesia babysat the four kids, and if Cesia was busy, I was the babysitter. The children would beg me to walk up and down the stairs on my hands when I babysat, and I was always happy to oblige.

Cesia and I had some wonderful holidays with our friends during this time too. The Goldbergs were one of five families who went away to Aspendale Beach every summer when the kids were young, and it was always a fun and relaxing time. One year, Cesia and I had a wedding to attend during our annual holiday, so we left Charlie and Helen with our friends and travelled back to the city for the wedding. We planned to stay at home overnight, then head back to the beach the following day.

But Cesia and I were not tired at all after the wedding so we decided to drive back to Aspendale to rejoin our friends and children instead of staying in the city. But when we arrived back at our holiday house, we found all the doors and windows shut and locked. Assuming we wouldn't be back until the morning, our friends had all gone to bed and locked everything up. Standing outside in the dark, I looked up at the house and could see one tiny window three metres above the ground.

'Abie,' Cesia said. 'What are you thinking?'

'I think I can fit through there,' I told her. 'Wait her and I'll let you in.'

I was in my early fifties by this stage, so Cesia was greatly amused when I stripped down to my undies right there on the lawn. I grabbed on to the drainpipe on the outside wall and climbed up to the window. Carefully, I took the glass out of the window and slid my body through it, just fitting. One of the benefits of having a small frame!

Once inside, I opened the front door to let in a giggling Cesia. By now it was 2am and everyone was asleep. We were so quiet that we didn't wake any of our friends, so imagine the looks of surprise on their faces the next morning when Cesia and I came downstairs to join them for breakfast!

Cesia and I loved being around people, which is why the idea of owning and running a restaurant first occurred to us. From back in our Belgium days, we had always enjoyed the hustle and bustle of restaurants and cafes, and the many different people you meet in those places from all walks of life. So, eight years after I first started working at Golombek's factory, just after Helen was first born, Cesia and I started talking about buying a restaurant or cafe business.

The idea of making and serving food to people greatly appealed to both of us. Since the war, I had never been one to care too much about eating food, but Cesia was an excellent cook, and I knew we could run a successful restaurant business together. I loved the idea of working in a busy and lively environment, full of people and chatter, especially after all the years I had spent doing such solitary work in factories.

In 1960, we started to look at what was on offer in Melbourne and eventually bought a small Jewish delicatessen called Little Vienna on Chapel Street in Windsor. Soon after this we sold our place in Auburn and moved our little family into the small flat behind the shop.

We made a good living from the delicatessen, but it was hard work. Cesia and I not only ran the shop, but also had to make all the deliveries using our own car and go out to all the wholesalers. As busy as it was, we enjoyed our time there, and ended up owning Little Vienna for about seven years. After the first couple of years of owning the business, we moved to a flat around the corner that was only a five-minute walk to Little Vienna. Both kids were in school by this point, at Windsor Primary which was just around the corner. There was very little traffic around in those days, so the kids could walk across our street and straight through the back gate of their school.

During our Little Vienna period, Cesia and I continued our involvement with Bund activities, as well as at the Kadimah in Lygon Street, Carlton. Kadimah is Hebrew for 'Forward' and the organisation regularly put on cultural evenings and events, as well as Yiddish theatre. The theatre was called the David Herman Theatre Group and was named after an active member of Yiddish theatre from many years ago. We also became involved in the Yiddish Sunday School where Charlie went, and regularly attended committee meetings. Cesia and I were also on the committee of Sholem Aleichem school – a secular Yiddish Kindergarten that Helen attended. There were twenty-one of us on the committee in 1967, both men and women. At that time, the men were involved in organising the school and the women arranged entertainment for the children and organised fundraising.

Cesia and I felt it was crucial to keep the Yiddish culture alive for our kids and grandkids. Yiddish is at the heart of the Jewish culture. Yiddish has been the vibrant language of many generations of Jews, both religious and secular, for thousands of years. It was the language of most Jews in the ghettos and camps during the Shoah and we knew that if we lost Yiddish from our community then we were also losing our spiritual identity as a people.

For many years we helped with fundraisers, hosting many in our home, to raise money for a Yiddish Sunday School. We eventually succeeded and the Sunday School operated out of one of the small buildings on the grounds of the Sholem Aleichem Primary School.

It wasn't just the Jewish culture and community that was important to us. As our English improved and we got to know more non-Jewish people, we bought ourselves a yearly subscription to the Melbourne Theatre Company. By now we could understand what the actors were saying, which was a huge improvement from when we had first arrived. We also subscribed to the Victorian Philharmonic Orchestra and saw them when they played in the Melbourne Town Hall and attended the ballet when we had time. It was a busy, but happy, time in our lives.

We sold Little Vienna after seven years and became co-owners at Cafe Scheherazade in St Kilda. Five years later, we sold our place in Windsor and bought a large upstairs flat in Elsternwick. (This flat is still in the family today and is where my daughter and her husband now live. We bought the flat below it and this is where I live now.)

After five years at Cafe Scheherazade, Cesia and I wanted to set up a place that was completely ours again. I knew that I wanted to find a restaurant in the heart of the city this time, where all the action was. I was remembering our wonderful nights in the bustling cafes and clubs of Brussels and was keen to replicate a similar kind of environment.

We began looking around for a business to buy but there

wasn't much on offer in the city in 1972. Cesia wanted to find a restaurant that was established and well run, but to buy something like that we would need to borrow an enormous sum of money, which I was not prepared to do. We eventually found a little French cafe at 212 Little Collins Street, Melbourne. It was situated behind and opposite the Melbourne Town Hall and run by two Jewish women. Cesia was not impressed when she first saw it, which I could understand, as it was very run down and didn't look at all appealing on the outside. But I explained to Cesia that a restaurant in a good position was much more important than the aesthetics. I could see the potential with this place; both the Regent and the Athenaeum Theatres were in Collins Street, and concerts were held in the town hall, so there would be a lot of people around the area. We had a lot of friends in the city too who I was sure would support us with their custom.

I also assured Cesia that we could spend less on a rundown place and use our experience to revitalise and build up the business, rather than paying out a large amount of money at the outset. We would throw out the menu, which was not good, and Cesia could create a delicious and appealing new one. My wife was such a good cook and had excellent taste when it came to food. Even if she wouldn't be doing the cooking herself, she would make sure the food we served was very good.

Cesia still wasn't convinced, so we spent a couple of days sitting in one of the cafes opposite, at different times of the morning and afternoon, watching the business. As we sat there, drinking endless cups of coffee, we took note of how many customers went in and out, as well as how many people walked past the cafe. After a couple of days, Cesia agreed there was enough business in the area for us to take a chance, so we jumped in and bought it. We knew we'd have to try and keep the customers already loyal to the cafe, as well as new ones, by treating them well and giving them good service.

Cesia and I set about cleaning and furnishing our new place, which we decided to call Goldy's – an abbreviation of Goldberg – and put in a good quality espresso machine. Cesia created a tasty, wholesome menu after doing research on cafes and restaurants in the city and making sure none of them were serving the kinds of meals we had on offer at Goldy's. Our menu would include dishes like gefilte fish, cabbage rolls, Cesia's famous veal schnitzel and cholent on weekends, as well as Cesia's delicious lemon cheesecake, sponge cake and honey cakes – the same kind that my dear mum used to make.

We decided that Cesia's job would be to supervise the kitchen, while I oversaw the running of the restaurant and looked after the books. I planned to do all the prep before the cooks came in at 6am and look after the coffee machine and register. Cesia would take any calls that came into the restaurant. Once we had given our new business a facelift and all the plans were in place, we hired a fantastic cook, and were ready to go.

We were nervous in the lead-up to that opening Saturday night. Would anyone come? Would our gamble pay off? Would people like the food on the menu? But all our worries went out the window when Goldy's opened its doors that week and every table in the restaurant was soon full. Many of our friends came along, and our sisters and their families, as well as a lot of people we didn't know. We had done very little advertising in the weeks leading up to the opening, but word of mouth had spread through the Jewish community and the city.

By this time, Charlie was twenty-two, and worked at Goldy's too. Helen was only fourteen, so while she went to school in the mornings, Charlie and I headed into Goldy's. Cesia came to the restaurant at around 10am each day, and if Charlie or I tried to call her at home before that time, the phone was always engaged. In fact, my wife spent most of every morning on the phone chatting to her many friends, and at one point, our biggest bill listed 1200 outgoing calls in three months. My wife spent her days and nights talking and socialising with our customers at Goldy's, who all adored her. She made everyone who came into the restaurant feel at home, which is one of the main reasons people kept coming back – that and the food, of course! Our regular customers started calling Cesia 'Goldy', and it stuck.

One day, one of our regulars was chatting to Cesia and as he was leaving said, 'Goldy, your smile is worth a million.'

'Give me a million and I will give you my smile!' Cesia responded.

Goldy's began to flourish, and after a year or so it was a great success. The musicians from the symphony orchestra came in for meals, as well as all the theatre performers. Even the TV star and comedian Paul Hogan came into Goldy's for our omelettes. We had actors from the Melbourne Theatre Company (MTC), as well as from other theatres around the

The Strength of Hope

city. This was before the MTC moved across the river to the Sumner Theatre, which didn't exist at that time.

We were always very busy on Saturdays because that was when the theatre crowd would come in before and after the matinee, and before and after the night performances. Sometimes our Saturday supper trade would go through until 2am on Sunday morning.

Cesia and I considered all people to be equal, so we never took bookings for the restaurant. We didn't want anyone taking priority over anyone else, no matter who they were. So, getting a table at Goldy's became a game for the Saturday supper crowd. As soon as the curtain went down at the opera, theatre or symphony, there was a mad dash to get in line at Goldy's.

Goldy's became a favourite spot for the performing arts fraternity, and as Cesia and I got to know so many people in the arts community, we started getting some wonderful perks. For example, we were subscribers of the Melbourne Symphony Orchestra in the Town Hall, but these concerts started at 8pm and that was right when we closed the restaurant. When the people from the Town Hall heard our dilemma, they came up with an idea. They would leave the back door of the Town Hall open for us, so we could get to the show on time. As soon as the dinner rush at Goldy's was over, Cesia and I hurried down the back lane behind Goldy's to the Town Hall, entered through the open back door, and went straight to the front row seats they had saved for us. We felt very special and grateful to these kind people.

It was an exciting and happy era for us, and we loved our customers and being a part of the whole Melbourne restaurant scene. But it was also very hard work. On any given day we had to be waiters, chefs, coffeemakers or dishwashers. Sometimes we needed to be all of the above in just one day.

Cesia and I became good friends with a lot of our regular customers at Goldy's over the years. These were some who were genuinely interested in our lives, both during and after the war, and would listen in horror and amazement when we told them about our experiences of the Holocaust. When they asked me if I hated the Germans, they were always surprised when I said that I didn't.

'I don't hate anyone,' I would tell them. 'Hatred is a terrible thing that destroys lives. I saw that for myself and so I will never hate. I cannot forgive the Nazis, but I don't hate.'

I told them that I was more interested in spreading positivity and giving hope to everyone I met, especially those who might feel like life was difficult and there was no point going on. I wanted them to know that I had held on to hope for many years, in the most hopeless of situations, and it had served me well. I was now living the life I had dreamed of in the camps.

'That doesn't mean that I don't still think about the terrible things that happened or feel the pain, even all these years later,' I would say. 'In fact, there has never been a single day since we arrived in Australia that Cesia and I haven't thought about what happened to us and our people. But there is always reason to get up in the morning. If you look hard enough, you can find hope and positivity in every situation.'

My customers would smile at me or sometimes shake their heads, not believing what they were hearing, but I kept telling people that life is beautiful and that we should appreciate every moment that we are alive. That was very important to me.

We owned Goldy's for eleven years, and by the end of that time I'd had enough. I've always known when it was time to walk away from one thing and start something new, and it was the same with Goldy's. We had a two-year lease with the council, who were the owners of the building. I wanted to negotiate for a longer lease because I was looking to sell the restaurant eventually, and a longer lease would be more attractive, but this proved to be a difficult process which dragged on for a year.

My children were pursuing their own careers and lives by that time, so they didn't want to take over Goldy's. It also needed significant renovations by then, so we decided to put it on the market and see what would happen. Some of our customers were interested, but they were not comfortable with the approaching lease expiry – there was only one year left on the lease by that point. I continued my discussions with the council, feeling sure we would be given an extended lease, but ultimately, they dragged it out.

Cesia and I agreed that if we didn't get a buyer by the end of the lease, we would close the doors and walk away. Soon after, someone expressed an interest in buying Goldy's. I didn't want to lose the deal so I told him, 'How about you pay me half the money for the sale, and the other half can stay with the solicitors until the lease is renewed.' It was a win–win for me and the buyer so he agreed. We were the ones taking the risk, but it was a better option than closing the doors and walking away with nothing. Luckily for us it all ended up working out. So ended another chapter of our lives.

LESSON LEARNED

Goodwill is valuable. It arises because of what you do and how you treat others.

31

STRENGTHENING COMMUNITY

Cesia and I knew that we wanted to travel overseas, but neither of us was ready to go back to Europe. It was still too soon for us, and the memories associated with that place remained too painful.

So, in 1973 we made plans to visit my old friend, Mumek, his wife, Amelia, and Mumek's brother, Heniek, in Montreal. It was a wonderful reunion as we had not seen each other since the two brothers left Belgium in 1947. We talked about old times, relived many happy memories, and some sad ones to. There was a lot of laughter between the five of us and Cesia and I ended up staying with Mumek and Amelia for a couple of weeks, before they both accompanied us to New York for another couple of weeks.

All up we spent a month with Mumek and Amelia in Montreal and New York, and, when we finally had to say goodbye to them, we promised we would be back to visit again soon.

True to our promise, in 1979 we put a note on the door of Goldy's that read: *'Closed for six weeks. What do you think? Don't we deserve a holiday?'* and went back to Montreal to see Mumek again. We also visited my old friend from Łódź, Jack Lewin, in Los Angeles.

Since our adventures travelling through Europe together all those years ago, Jack and his wife, Regina, had relocated to Melbourne in 1950, a few months before me, and had a daughter. Jack was working as a furrier then, but also pursuing an acting career part-time and doing plays at the David Herman Theatre. They stayed in Australia for ten years before moving to LA, and once there, Jack did a few small acting parts in TV shows and movies on the side. I hadn't seen Jack since he left Melbourne almost twenty years earlier, so it was wonderful to reminisce with him about our exciting and dangerous adventures as young men. His family loved hearing the stories of the two young, headstrong Polish Jews who made their way across Europe by jumping trains, were thrown in a dungeon with Nazis and narrowly escaped deportation to Siberia.

The next time we went to America was in 1983 for a Holocaust Survivor's conference in Washington. We also visited New York, San Francisco, and LA while we were there. We had a wonderful time overall but the morning we were due to fly to Washington for the Survivor's conference, something upsetting happened.

We were staying at the Sheraton Hotel in San Francisco and had become friendly with an Australian family during our stay. On the morning of our departure, we packed our bags and headed downstairs to say goodbye to them. Checkout wasn't until 10am and it was only around 9am, so we had plenty of time. When we returned to the room around thirty minutes later, we discovered that it had already been cleaned. We immediately suspected that something was wrong, as it was unusual for a hotel room to be cleaned before checkout. That was when we noticed that Cesia's handbag, which contained her jewellery, along with our passports and tickets to Washington, was missing. Cesia was in a terrible state as I called the manager and asked him to come to our room immediately.

'Who is the cleaner?' I asked him as soon as he arrived. 'I want you to call the police, please.'

The manager was very apologetic and called the police right away. They came to take our statements and said they would do all they could to find the thief. Unfortunately, this was a Sunday, and the Australian consulate was closed, so we could get no help from there. Finally, later that day, we managed to contact the Australian ambassador, who advised us that we'd have to buy new tickets to Washington. He promised that on our arrival he would provide us with the necessary documentation. I also rang Charlie to see if he could do anything from his end in Australia.

The two of us felt very vulnerable, stranded in a foreign country with no passports, tickets or I.D. Cesia was particularly upset because she had never possessed any jewellery at all before the war, and the rings, earrings and bracelets she had accumulated over the years, most given to her by me, were incredibly precious to her. At least she still had her gold chain from our wedding, which she was wearing on her neck that morning. The hotel was very good to us. They put us up in a very grand room and made a big fuss of us, treating us like royalty to make up for what had happened on their premises. They questioned the cleaner, who told them that the telephone rang while she was in the room. This turned out to be our friend's daughter who was supposed to be picking us up in San Francisco. She was calling to confirm our pickup time. The cleaner said that as the phone was ringing, a man had walked into the room saying it was his room and he was expecting a telephone call. The cleaner left and this man took Cesia's bag on his way out.

At around 4pm that day, we received a telephone call telling us that the bag, with our passports, ID and tickets, had been found in a hotel toilet at Fisherman's Wharf. The thief had apparently tried to flush everything down the toilet after taking out the jewellery – but had failed. Back at the hotel, the staff took our sodden paperwork out of the wet bag and dried it all out for us. Although somewhat water damaged, they were still okay to use for our travel.

We got on a flight to Washington early that evening and made it to our hotel at around midnight. It had been a very long and stressful day, so the two of us quickly passed out from exhaustion.

But there were more surprises to come on this trip. The next morning Cesia and I were sitting in the lobby, waiting to head out to the conference when a thickset, bald man with a long grey beard walked straight up to me.

'Excuse me, Sir,' he said, 'but do you know where I could get a taxi?'

I thought this man must be a bit of an idiot to not know to ask the hotel concierge for a taxi. But, not wishing to be rude, I pointed to the front desk and told him that he could order a taxi from the people there.

The man slapped me gently on the shoulder and laughed. 'You don't recognise me!'

I shook my head. 'No!'

He started speaking Yiddish, and that's when I realised he was someone I knew in the ghetto and from the Bund. But I hadn't seen him since then and would never have recognised him.

'You were slim last time I saw you,' I laughed. 'You had all your hair and no grey beard!'

We had a good a laugh, and he told me he had moved to Argentina after the war. He was in Washington for the conference too and had instantly recognised me in the lobby because of my small size.

The conference was a sobering affair, but Cesia and I were glad we had made the trip. The saddest sight that day was the crowds of people carrying signs around their necks, giving their names and asking if anyone knew anything about those family members that they hadn't heard from in years.

Our visit to the Holocaust Centre in Washington had been a moving and emotional experience. On the plane home from America, I thought about how meaningful it had been for those of us who survived to come together in Washington. These kinds of gatherings were so important and necessary. Although I had kept the promise I made to my mum by talking about what had happened to people in my community, it felt like we survivors could be doing more to get our stories into the public consciousness. The conference had reinforced my belief that there should be an official centre to house our memories and stories. This was something that I knew my good friend Bono, and others, had been working on back in Melbourne for many years now.

Whatever plans were being put into place, and however long it took, I knew that I wanted to be a part of this new centre and help in any way I could.

32

JEWISH HOLOCAUST CENTRE

By the late 1970s, the idea of establishing a Jewish Holocaust Museum in Melbourne was gaining momentum. The driving force behind this project was Aron Sokolowicz.

Aron was an Auschwitz survivor and a man of great passion. He lost his wife and four-year-old son at Treblinka and spent two years in the death camp before being transported to Ebensee where he was liberated on 18 January 1945. He and his family emigrated to Australia in 1957, where he became active in Jewish organisations and soon became president of the Federation of Polish Jews. He also organised yearly exhibitions of photographs at the Beth Weizmann Jewish Community Centre to accompany the Warsaw Ghetto commemorations.

Like so many of us, Aron had a fervent wish that the Holocaust not be forgotten. Over the years, he collected photographs and other memorabilia and it was these artefacts that became part of the temporary Holocaust exhibitions that had been held in Melbourne. The success of these exhibitions only intensified Aron's determination to establish a permanent

Holocaust Museum in Melbourne, as a memorial to the six million Jews who were murdered.

'This Memorial will help soothe our spirits,' he said, 'and give us a place to honour and commemorate our near and dear ones who have no graves of their own.'

Aron's enthusiasm attracted the attention of my good friend, Bono. I was so excited when Bono first told me about Aron's vision and the plans they were making together. The construction of a Holocaust centre had always been dear to my friend's heart, and he felt that a place like this was especially pertinent in a country and city that per capita had one of the world's largest populations of Holocaust survivors. I was busy with my young family and working to make a living throughout this period and didn't have the time to get involved with the planning of the centre but was always interested to hear Bono's updates when I saw him.

Of course, I knew that there had been robust and animated discussions going on for years among the Jewish community about the need for such a centre. There were differing opinions on why such a place would be necessary, and what purpose it would serve, but I had always believed it was exactly what our community needed and hoped it would come to fruition.

In 1980, the Kadimah Jewish Cultural Centre and National Library hosted another successful Holocaust exhibition in Gertrude Street, Fitzroy. This one included survivor testimonies, which marked a change in the exhibitions that had gone before. A small group of key people, including Bono and Aron, provided artefacts for the exhibition, and Bono had been interviewed for the audiovisual material that accompanied it. Five months later, discussions were held within the Victorian Jewish Board of Deputies' Jewish Heritage Committee about a proposed Holocaust Centre in Melbourne.

The enthusiasm shown at this meeting was infectious and started attracting people's attention, as well as practical and financial assistance. One of the major contributors was Mina Fink, who together with her husband, Leo, was deeply committed to remembering the Holocaust and assisting newcomers in Australia. She donated $50,000 in memory of her husband to move the project ahead.

When a potential site became available in 1983, Mina's donation enabled the Kadimah to acquire the building in Selwyn Street, Elsternwick. The building was situated between the Kadimah and the Sholem Aleichem College. The Kadimah had relocated from Carlton to Elsternwick in the early 1960s. The advantages of the close relationship between the Kadimah and the proposed centre were clear, and it was leased at $1 per annum.

Many over the years doubted that the Holocaust Centre would happen. Many also queried why it was necessary forty years after the war. But to me, the answer was simple: we, the eyewitnesses, the survivors of the Holocaust, will not be here forever and we need to leave a lasting, ongoing message for future generations. Bono also said that with such a museum, Jews and non-Jews alike would be able to study the annihilation of the Jews and others – as well as the heroism displayed by prisoners in the ghettos and concentration camps. He believed the preserving of historical artefacts and eyewitness accounts would help to fight disinformation spread by those who might seek to deny the truth of the Holocaust.

Once the site for the Museum had been confirmed, a governing body was formed, overseen by co-presidents Aron and Bono. Fundraising efforts brought in money from government grants and private donations, and it was wonderful to see so many Melburnians contribute.

Then finally, it happened. On 4 March 1984, the Jewish Holocaust Museum and Research Centre became a reality. We all packed ourselves into the car park between the Kadimah and the new centre for the opening ceremony. It was an incredibly moving occasion, and messages of congratulations and well-wishes for the future flooded in from around Australia and overseas, including a message from the president of Israel which read: *It is the duty of Jewish people to remind the world of the atrocities of the Holocaust.*

I felt so proud as I watched Bono speak to the huge assembled crowd.

'There will now be available a body of incontrovertible evidence in Australia that describes the destruction of European Jewry!' he announced.

As the Holocaust Centre was officially opened, there was non-stop applause, tears, cheers, loud and silent prayers, and a deep sense of satisfaction for all of us there that day.

We were ahead of the game in Australia. It wouldn't be until the early to mid-90s that the UK would establish any museums or exhibitions devoted to the Holocaust, and although the Los

Angeles Holocaust Museum began in 1961 it wouldn't find a permanent home until 2010.

Finally, here in Melbourne was a place where all survivors could come together to remember those we had lost; to grieve, talk, cry, laugh and remember together. More importantly, it was a place where we could educate others on what had happened so they would never forget. It was established, not only as a memorial to those we had lost, but also as a learning institution to teach future generations about tolerance, and the terrible consequences of racism and bigotry.

I knew that volunteering my time at the centre would be the perfect way to fulfil my promise to my mother. Every day, I would have the opportunity to talk to many different people, from all walks of life, about what happened during the Holocaust, so it would never be forgotten. So, in 1984, I became a volunteer museum guide at the Holocaust Centre and I have been there ever since.

What made our centre so unique was that it was we, the survivors, who were providing living history as we communicated to visitors. We were talking to people, not through the prism of hate, but with the message that love, tolerance and greater harmony should be the objective for all of us in this world. After all, our mission was not only to inform visitors about the evils of mankind, but also to honour acts of bravery and kindness that saved lives.

In the beginning, all museum guides were survivors, or children of survivors, and we did everything ourselves to save money. We cleaned, helped create the exhibitions, took visitors

The Strength of Hope

around, organised talks and much more. Except for a paid secretary, the centre was run completely by volunteers six days a week. These days there is a large staff including volunteers, administers, librarians and archivists.

We started having regular 'L'Chaims' in the kitchen every Monday at morning teatime. We kept an unlabelled bottle in the fridge, one that looked like an innocuous bottle of water, but was in fact filled with Polish vodka and lemon. Each Monday, we would bring it out, pour ourselves shots and drink to life and our survival.

The very first meetings of the centre were all in Yiddish, and up until the beginning of the 21st century, all minutes from the meetings were taken in Yiddish. All captions and writings about the items on display – that included some of the documents Bono and I buried in the ghetto – as well as the memorial plaques, were in both Yiddish and English. We volunteers communicated with each other in Yiddish too. Yiddish has played a key role at the centre since day one. It was important that the language of the millions of Eastern European Jews who perished in the Holocaust was part of the fabric of the centre.

English began to take over when the younger volunteers, who knew little, if any, Yiddish, started coming in, but that didn't mean that Yiddish was ignored. Yiddish is how we help preserve the uniqueness of the centre, a centre that Yiddish-speaking Jews established, and we owe it to the millions who perished to keep it alive.

I became a member of the executive board in 1989 and was made treasurer in the 90s – a position I held for fifteen years. The

Kadimah also started their 'Wednesday Club', which was a way for survivors and senior citizens to get together and stay socially active and stimulated every week. There were talks given by all kinds of speakers, as well as performances, music and food. Lots of food.

When I started volunteering at the Holocaust Centre, Cesia went to volunteer at the Kadimah next door. She ended up becoming head coordinator of the Wednesday Club for many years and absolutely loved it. Every week, she and the other volunteers made lunch for the Wednesday Club patrons, who all sat at long tables, happily talking and catching up with one another. In the beginning, a lot of the people who went to Wednesday Club only spoke Yiddish, but more non-Yiddish speaking Jews soon came along too.

Cesia had a book with a list of many people's names who she wanted to approach and would tick them off after she succeeded in getting them involved in the club. She was the only one who could understand her writing, because Cesia wrote names phonetically. For instance, she spelt Brian, as Brajon.

Part of Cesia's job as coordinator was to organise speakers to come and talk at the Wednesday Club. She organised for all kinds of people to come, including pianists, singers and violinists. Even the mayor of Glen Eira came. No one could ever say no to my wife.

In the Holocaust Centre, the permanent exhibitions on display consisted of photographs, objects and memorabilia. In the first few years, these exhibitions included *The Vanished World* (featuring photos of those who had perished during the war, including my sisters and parents), *The Rise of Nazism, Ghetto Life, The Camp System* and *Towards a New Life*. New exhibits and displays are now created on a regular basis, and survivors are always asked to offer our feedback. Many survivors, including myself, have donated photographs and documents to the centre. We know that the centre is a place where our stories, photos and memories will permanently be on display, and where people will be able to see and listen to our stories long after we are gone.

The centre evolved into a research and educational space, and it wasn't long before a constant stream of schools and students started visiting. For me, personally, this was the most fulfilling part of being a guide. In the beginning the guides were all survivors, or children of survivors, and we loved talking to the young people. Face to face contact with survivors like us is so important for students because it encourages a dialogue between the young and the old, the past and the present, and teaches tolerance, respect and understanding. We would show and tell these students, and older visitors, what it meant to live in an intolerant society.

The young people who came to the centre were always so respectful, and genuinely interested in our experiences, as well as stunned and horrified by what they were seeing and hearing. Many of them were unable to fully comprehend what we had been through and wrote us letters after they had left and gone home, telling us what an enormous impact we had had on them and the way they would now look at their lives. This was always the greatest reward for us, to know that we were making a difference by meeting these lovely and empathic young people.

Over the years, some of those students became teachers who then brought their own students to the centre. It always warmed my heart when one of these adults came over to tell us what a huge effect their visit to our centre had on them when they were a student.

I have met so many amazing people who have visited the Jewish Holocaust Centre over the years, and some of them have become very dear friends. I started talking to Mark Dent, and Janine and Ackie Callaghan one afternoon twenty-five years ago when they visited the centre, and we formed an immediate bond. I ended up standing in the one spot speaking with them for three hours until the centre was closing. They reluctantly left, but as soon as they got home, Mark and Janine both wrote to the centre saying how special it was to meet me and hear my story. Those letters led to a friendship that has now lasted a quarter of a century. Our families have shared numerous meals together and we have celebrated many birthdays, weddings, births, 21sts and bar mitzvahs over the years. We have also shared many sad times too. Our families are now entwined in each other's lives forever, and it all started one afternoon at the Jewish Holocaust Centre when they were lumped with me as their guide.

Over the past almost forty years, I have spoken to thousands of students, teachers, and visitors about my experience during the Holocaust. Talking about it day in and day out was of course very emotionally draining, and some days I would come home feeling exhausted and very sad. But talking about it was also therapeutic, especially in an environment like the JHC where there were so many others who knew exactly how I was feeling

The Strength of Hope

and how hard it was to recount certain stories.

In 1992, I filmed my testimonial for the centre, which involved sitting in a room with an interviewer and a camera person for over two hours as they asked me questions about my life during the war. It was quite harrowing, and I got very emotional, needing to stop to wipe away tears many times, but I got through it. I am glad that my testimonial will now be there forever, and that I have left a legacy for the centre. Many of us filmed our testimonies over the years. We wanted to tell these stories for the future generations to watch long after we are gone. My mum could never have imagined that her son would one day be sitting in a room, telling our family's story to a camera, but I think she would be so proud that I have done what I promised. Now tens of thousands of people have heard my story, both on video and in person, and I will keep telling my story until the day I die.

I love it when a student comes up to me after my talk to tell me that my story has made them appreciate their life, or when a teacher tells me they heard me speak when they were a kid and have now brought their class to the centre. I love that we are teaching the younger generations about tolerance and acceptance and showing them what could happen in a world where these things don't exist. I have received so many kind letters over the years from young people who have met me at the centre or heard one of my talks.

I am so proud of what we have built over the years. At the time of writing, the centre is being rebuilt and the new centre will reopen mid-2022. Bono and Aron's vision was for the JHC to be a platform that educates about humanity, which is why we must look towards the future and engage more people to help our centre continue to flourish. There are not many of us survivors left, and as the ranks thin out, we must look to the next generation who have received the message from their parents, grandparents and great-grandparents to continue our work. The centre has also been very important and healing for me personally. It is a place where myself and my fellow survivors have been able to share our stories, remember those we have lost and stay connected to our survivor community. Our dedication to the JHC is not a passion, it's a promise fulfilled, and it is these profound bonds between the Holocaust survivors that cemented its foundations and that continue today.

33

FACING THE PAIN

Bono passed away in 1995 while visiting his close friend, the Jewish writer Chava Rosenfarb, in Montreal. His body was flown home to Melbourne, and he was buried at the Chevra Kadisha Springvale Cemetery, with hundreds in attendance. Bono's close friend, the politician, Barry Jones, spoke at his funeral and described Bono as a 'dynamic orator, a man of passion, a unique mixture of idealism, pessimism, optimism and realism, an interventionist and an Australian patriot'. I wrote a piece called *One day in the Ghetto* as a tribute to my friend and the great man he was. Bono was an enormous inspiration to me and countless others, wherever and whenever they met him in the world. His courage in life should be used as an example for present and future generations. Losing Bono felt like losing a brother and I will always remember and miss him dearly.

Cesia's sister, Hela, also sadly passed away from pancreatic cancer in 1995 at the age of 70. Her death left a big hole in my wife's life. They had been so close all their lives and had been through so much together and Cesia was devastated when she died. Through this very sad time, my wife surrounded herself with family and friends to help her get through the grieving process.

Then, in 1996, Mumek's wife, Amelia, called to say that my old friend had passed away. It was incredibly sad news, but we felt lucky that we had had the opportunity to have so many good times with Mumek, both here and in Montreal, over the years. Mumek had requested that his ashes be deposited in the ruins of the number two gas chamber crematorium at Auschwitz on the 23rd of August. Mumek, his brother and mother had all been transported from the Łódź Ghetto on this date in 1944, and when Mumek visited Auschwitz a couple of years earlier, he'd found records detailing the gas chamber and crematorium, as well as the date his mother had been killed.

Amelia told us that she would be travelling to Auschwitz to scatter his ashes on this date. Without hesitation, I said that I would be there too. Cesia, Charlie and Helen all decided to come along. Cesia too had arrived at Auschwitz on 23 August 1944, and she had lost her mother on the exact same day Mumek lost his. Therefore, it would be the anniversary of her own mum's death on that date too.

Cesia had to steel herself for the journey. I was so proud of my wife. I knew that it took a lot of strength for her to go back when she really didn't want to return to Poland.

Charlie's father-in-law, Borje, drove down from Sweden to drive us around, and the four of us met Amelia, Joe – Mumek's son from a previous marriage – and Joe's wife in Warsaw on the morning of 21 August. From there we travelled to Auschwitz.

The storm in my heart was fiercer than ever that day, but as we stood near those rusted railway tracks outside Auschwitz-Birkenau, Charlie hugged us to him.

'Here you are, Mum and Dad,' he said. 'You are standing at the site of your greatest loss, with the family you created. Here is your victory.'

He was right. It did feel like a victory of sorts being back there all those years later.

We walked slowly through the camp to crematorium number two. Amelia held Mumek's ashes close to her, and for a few moments, I spoke lovingly about her husband and my friend and the many adventures we had had together. As Amelia struggled to open the box, Joe gently helped her remove the tape. Then, Amelia slowly poured Mumek's ashes out of the box and onto the ruins of crematorium number two. We all stood in silence for a few moments, thinking about Mumek and his reunion with his beloved mother.

May their souls rest in peace.

After this, we made our way around the various blocks in the camp. Cesia wanted to visit Blocks 4 and 5 in Birkenau, where she spent her time while she was incarcerated here, but it was very distressing for her.

Borje drove us to Auschwitz 1, where the buildings were different to those at Birkenau. These were more solid structures that were made of brick and cement, and they had tiled roofs. In one area we saw mounds of shoes, piled up to the ceiling, behind glass walls. There were thousands of them, all kinds, and sizes, each belonging to someone who was killed here. There were also combs, suitcases and coarse grey hair that had been shaved from the Jews on arrival. It was an eerie and disturbing sight.

'Maybe my shoes are in there,' Cesia said quietly.

We headed to the administrative offices so I could try and get some answers about what had happened to my sisters. I had brought with me a letter of introduction from the director of the Holocaust Centre in Melbourne, and a request to search the archives for any information they might have on Estera and Frajda, but unfortunately, they couldn't find anything.

Borje then drove us to the Warsaw Jewish Historical Institute, where the director said he would be happy to meet with me. Helen and I left the rest of our family outside and went into a room with him. The director asked me some questions about our family and my sisters' details and was very respectful and patient as I told him everything I could. I gave him dates and names and he took many notes. After this, he took me down a corridor to a library, where he began to produce many books that contained a lot of information on names, places and dates.

After some time searching through these books, he couldn't find anything about my sisters.

I knew that my sister Frajda had been staying in Koszyce, because of the letter we received in 1941, but he could only find an affidavit from a woman from Koszyce who witnessed 140 Jews being taken into the forest and shot. We can only assume Frajda was among them.

The next day, we said goodbye to Amelia, Joe and his wife and Borje drove us all to Krakow. We walked the streets near Wawel Castle looking for the house I stayed in back in 1940. I looked at

The Strength of Hope

every door and window, trying to remember which one it was.

It was here. I could sense it.

After a little while, I came upon an arched doorway and the memories came flooding back: sliding on the ice on the river Vistula, playing with the kids ... this was it. This was the house.

We knocked and an elderly man opened the door. When I asked him if he knew about the Alexandrovich brothers – my young playmates – he said he didn't know anything but that this was now a school for priests and had been since 1939. But I know I stayed in that house early in 1940 so it must have been taken over by the church very soon after that.

The letters I had from Frajda were from an address a few houses away at number 11, so we could only conclude that the family she had been staying with had had to move when the church took over.

Next, we went to visit the oldest Jewish synagogue in Krakow but found it closed. As we were walking away, we could hear music playing nearby – vibrant Yiddish folk music. The Jewish Quarter was alive with people, laughter and music.

Cesia's eyes lit up. The same eyes that had been full of so much grief and pain only yesterday.

'Shall we stay a little?' I asked.

'Yes,' she nodded, and in that moment, I saw the young girl I fell in love with.

We stopped to listen to a klezmer band that was playing outside a Jewish restaurant and Cesia clapped along with a huge smile on her face. It gave the children and me so much joy to see her this way. There is no greater joy than seeing the one you love happy, and right then, in that place, the music and atmosphere were making my wife so very happy.

We had lunch at another Jewish restaurant, a delicious garlicky cholent and borsht, where a violinist and guitarist were playing Yiddish songs like *Tumbalalaika* and *Der Rebbe Elimelech*.

'L'Chaim!' Charlie said, raising his glass.

'L'Chaim!' we echoed, clinking our glasses of vodka against his.

To life. Our lives. Lives we did not lose in that terrible place all those years ago, despite all the odds being against us.

A feeling of such joy and freedom suddenly came over me and I couldn't stop myself from joining in. I sang with gusto, tapping the table and looking over at Cesia who was singing along too. For a few moments, the two of us forgot the world around us. In that moment it was only the two of us at this table. Two free Jews enjoying a meal and singing songs from our childhood. We both felt it and were thinking the same thing; we are here, we survived, and we still have our culture, our music and our lives.

They tried to destroy us, but they failed.

The next day we went back to Łódź. Cesia was not looking forward to going back and claimed she 'felt nothing' for the place she grew up in, but I was eager to see it after so many years away.

When we arrived in Łódź we checked into the Grand, and oh how grand I felt. Only the rich people stayed there when I was a young boy, but there I was, walking into the lobby and up to the counter to get the key to my very own room.

Once we unpacked and had a quick bite to eat, Borje drove us towards the streets of the old ghetto. The tram line was the same and I could still remember the barbwire wall where the footpath was. We got out of the car to have a walk around, but it was a sorry sight. The buildings were old and dilapidated, and I could still feel the sadness and poverty from when I was there over fifty years ago.

'Where is my house,' Cesia began to ask, looking all around. 'This is where it was, but it's different. Where is the door in the middle? Where is my balcony?'

She was becoming more upset and anxious with every passing moment.

'It's gone,' she said. 'Where are the flowers? This street had so many flowers!'

Confusion, anger, frustration and disappointment washed over Cesia as she started talking about the poverty in the ghetto, the destruction of the synagogue, the bakery, the restaurant, and how many tears she used to cry. So many tears.

I knew Cesia was upset about seeing our hometown so rundown and neglected but I started to feel impatient. I too was frustrated, especially to see that no memorial existed here to honour the 233,000 Jews who had been locked in here, but I couldn't see the point of getting upset because what could we do?

We moved on and started to look for number 48 Zgierska Street, the house I lived in with my parents and three sisters before the ghetto was built. We eventually came to it and saw that the two wooden huts that had been in front of my old building had been demolished but the block remained. It was just as I remembered it – an old, dirty, rundown building with sheds and a stable in the cobblestoned yard.

I pointed up to the dirty windows on the third floor.

'That is where I lived,' I said to Charlie and Helen.

They laughed when I told them how shocked my mother was to see me climbing through our third-floor window after clambering up the scaffolding as a young boy. But even though I was thinking about this happy memory, I felt very sad to be there. This was once my home, but what was it now? A town that no one seemed to care about, its buildings and memories all crumbling into nothing.

'Let's go,' Cesia said, her face drawn and sad.

There was a heaviness in the air between the four of us as we started to walk back down the street again.

'We must find the Jewish Cemetery,' I told my family. 'I want to see Bono's parents' graves before we leave here.'

I knew they had been buried in the cemetery on the edge of the ghetto boundary.

Borje drove us around, looking for the entrance to the cemetery and soon found a gate but it was locked. Still, I refused to give up. Eventually, we found a small door hidden from the road. We walked through it into the cemetery, which had also been neglected even though there were new graves near the entrance. It seemed that Jews were still dying in Łódź and being put to rest in the one-hundred-year-old cemetery.

I began my search for the Weiner's graves, both of whom had died in the ghetto, like the 50,000 other Jews also buried here. We found a caretaker who helped us look through an area where the weeds had knotted together. But it was impossible to search there, and it was so overgrown that eventually we had

The Strength of Hope

to give up. I felt deeply sad, exhausted and despondent as we walked back to the car.

On our way back to the hotel we looked for Cesia's old school, but only passed more and more disintegrated buildings. It was too much. Too heartbreaking. Cesia and I could not look anymore and so we both turned our faces away from the windows.

Back at the Grand, we sat in the bar to regroup and gather our thoughts as a family. Helen and Charlie could feel our deep disappointment and sadness and did all they could to comfort their distressed parents.

As we stood up to leave, we heard someone behind us say in Yiddish, 'Abram Goldberg, is that you?'

I turned to see an old Jewish man who had been in the ghetto and invited him to join us. We started to reminisce about old friends, neighbours and loved ones, and he told me he decided to make Łódź his home again after the war. It was obvious that he was very lonely and desperate to connect with both Cesia and me because we represented another time for him. He could not stop talking about the past and the words spilled out of him for over an hour.

We finally left him, and I felt sad to think that he might spend his time looking closely at every tourist who visited Łódź, hoping to find other Jews who survived the war so he could while away some time in his lonely days. I knew I would never see him again as I knew for certain that I would never return here again. I could not wait to leave Łódź. It was a sad place now and there were too many bad memories for Cesia and me.

Łódź was my past and that is where it would now stay forever.

34

CESIA PART 2

We went back to Auschwitz-Birkenau in 1996. Oh, I will never forget. I didn't want to go back. I said to my family, 'I'm not going. Everything will burn under my feet if I walk there.' But two weeks before Abe and our children, Charlie and Helen, were to go on the trip, I couldn't sleep. I had a bad dream, and I was so nervous and thinking, 'My God, if my husband and children are going, I should go with them.' So, we all went together.

When we got to Auschwitz, I was walking with a stick and Abe and Charlie were angry that they didn't have a wheelchair for me. My body had started to give out on me a few years earlier. In Australia, my doctor's desk was covered in my X-rays, and he told me, 'A girl between ten- and fifteen-years old needs nourishment, which you did not have, Mrs Goldberg. That is why your bones are now like paper.'

The people at Auschwitz-Birkenau said they would open the gate for our car, but I said, 'No, I don't want any comfort. The car must stay outside.' I was determined not to take the car but to walk in by myself. When we walked in, I couldn't say a word. I couldn't talk at all. We went to the crematorium, where my mother was cremated, and left some flowers *and a candle. My son said a prayer.*

On the way back I didn't stop talking, I couldn't stop talking, not for a second. Everything came out. I told them every little thing, every little thing that happened. That was the only time I ever went back to Auschwitz-Birkenau and it will be the last.

LESSON LEARNED

There are some wounds that can never truly heal.

35

A LONG AND FULL LIFE

I took up golf when we were still running Goldy's and began looking forward to playing nine holes with my friends every Saturday morning. I enjoyed it so much that after I retired, I started heading to the golf course four or five times a week to play with a group of friends. The maximum number of people for a round of golf is usually four, but sometimes we had up to sixteen in our group. On those occasions we had to draw lots in order to work out who was playing with who.

Our golf group continued playing together for several years, but as our members got older and began passing away, I found myself running out of partners. I too was getting older of course and was busy with the Holocaust Centre. Rather than try to find new golfing buddies, I decided to stop playing.

Cesia and I also travelled a lot after retirement with our friend, Helen Jacobs. We visited America many times, at least eight or nine, as well as Canada and Europe. I eventually realised that we had spent so much time seeing other countries but hadn't yet seen the whole of our own.

'I won't travel overseas again until we have seen Australia,' I told Cesia.

The first place on our wish list was Western Australia so we flew to Adelaide and from there got a train to Perth because we wanted to experience travel through the desert. We had our own compartment with a sofa, bunk beds, a sink to wash our hands, a small table by the window and a separate ensuite. It was very luxurious train travel, and quite different to my days of hanging off the tops of trains by a military belt with my friends.

We stopped to visit the mines in Kalgoorlie, then back on the train again to continue to Perth. We took a bus tour up the west coast to Monkey Mia, 900 kilometres away and went to Shark Bay Marine Park where the dolphins swim right up to the beach. It was amazing to see these beautiful creatures up close and something I could never have imagined I would ever see in my life as a young boy growing up in Łódź.

From the mid-1980s until the early 1990s, Cesia and I travelled to many cities around the country until we had been to every state in Australia. Only then did we resume our overseas travels.

We went back, not only to America, but to Europe as well, this time with our grandchildren in tow.

Our family of four had grown over the years. Helen married Victor, a man she met in SKIF when they were both teenagers, and our two families have a long history together. Victor's grandfather was a friend of my father's back in Łódź, and I had known his father as a young boy too. In 1988, Helen and Victor's twins, Daley and Nastassja, were born, and Cesia and I were delighted to be grandparents. We loved spending time with our beautiful grandchildren, who learned to call us Bubba and Zaida.

Charlie married a lovely Swedish woman named Bettan in 1983, and they had a son, Daniel, in 1994. All our family spent a lot of time visiting the Holocaust Centre, and Charlie also volunteered as a guide there. His son, Daniel, spoke his first word at the centre when Bettan brought him there to visit me one day. He was nine months olds, and as soon as he spotted me, he pointed and said, 'Zaida!' What a wonderful moment for his grandfather.

In 1999, Helen and her family moved to America for Victor's job. Cesia and I were heartbroken that our grandchildren had gone to the other side of the world, but I promised Daley and Nastassja that I would come over and take them to Poland when they turned thirteen.

In 2001, I kept my word.

I met Helen, Victor and the kids in Poland, and we all travelled to Warsaw, Łódź, Chelmno and Auschwitz. Maryla's son, Heniek, now in his fifties, also joined us for part of the trip.

There was a commemoration of the Holocaust taking place when we arrived in Warsaw, with over seventy Israeli officers taking part. The kids spoke to the soldiers and told them I was a survivor, so they were very interested to talk to me. The soldiers invited me to the ceremony which was the commemoration of the Warsaw Ghetto Uprising in 1943. It was taking place near the Rapoport Monument on the grounds where the ghetto used to be, and we all went along. They asked me to lay the wreath as part of the ceremony, but I didn't want to take that honour away from the two officers who had been chosen to lay the wreath. They asked me to light the eternal flame instead. It was a very moving experience for all of us, but especially for me.

When we arrived at the site of the Treblinka death camp, something was happening there too. Two Israeli girls were performing a scene in Hebrew about a mother and daughter being sent to Treblinka and being gassed. It was very traumatic to watch this performance, especially in that place. Far more traumatic than anything Hollywood could ever produce. It was a dark, stormy day and as I stood with my grandkids, daughter, and nephew, a man came over to ask if I was a survivor. When I told him I was, he asked if I could speak with the girls who were in the performance and their classmates – they were part of a group of fifty girls from a youth organisation. I talked to them, and a member of Israeli parliament who was accompanying them. I told them who I was and about the Holocaust Museum in Melbourne – told them my story and what I promised my mother. It was a very moving scenario, especially in the thunder and rain.

The six of us then travelled back to Auschwitz-Birkenau where we spent almost seven hours. We visited the ruins of every crematorium, and my grandchildren both collected memorabilia from the fences around the camp to bring home so they would always remember the day.

An amazing and unexplainable thing happened while we were there. It started to pour rain and all of us became soaked through. Every part of our clothes was wringing wet. We looked around for shelter but could only see a small wall with a tiny ledge jutting out over the top of it. We ran over to try and huddle underneath the narrow ledge, when, out of nowhere, we all felt a hot wind blow on us and were completely dry within a few seconds. I am not a religious man, as you now know, so I cannot say this was an act of God. But to this day I have no idea how to explain that strange occurrence. Not even my daughter had a logical explanation for it, and she is a secular non-believer like her father.

Hela's husband, Herszel, passed away in 2004, and my dear sister died in 2011 at the age of ninety-three. I was very sad when she died but felt grateful for her long life and that she had been able to spend the last half of it with us in Australia. My sister had been troubled with ill health for a lot of her later years, which is why she never worked here, but I know that she was glad to see her two sons grown and happy with families of their own. We all stayed in each other's lives. Maryla's son, Danek, is now eighty-two years old and lives in Perth, while her other son, Herszel is in his early seventies. Hela's son, George, is seventy-six now and lives around the corner from us in Elsternwick. And Hela's daughter, Shirley, is seventy and lives just five minutes away. Cesia and I are still very close with all of them, as are our children.

Cesia and I have lost many friends and relatives in the years since the war, but we are still here and grateful for that fact. I have learned that life must go on, even when you suffer so much pain and loss that you cannot imagine how you will get up the next day, and that time heals most things. So, even in my late nineties, I am still learning. To continue learning in life is so important, no matter what your age. Learning something new every day has been the cornerstone of my philosophy. That and to give people hope for a better world, just like my father taught me.

As I have said many times in this book, I am a lucky man. In 2012, the Jewish Holocaust Centre nominated me for an OAM (Order of Australia Medal), and I felt incredibly humbled when I received the award in 2013. It was bestowed upon me in recognition of my life-long commitment and dedication to Holocaust memory and education, as well as my contribution to Yiddish culture. It was an incredible honour and one of those wonderful moments in life when I know that I am truly blessed.

I still have my beautiful Cesia, and my wonderful family all around me. I am so proud of my children and grandchildren. Charlie ran a successful restaurant business for many years before retiring a couple of years ago and is still heavily involved with the Jewish community. His wife, Bettan, has a great job as a senior interior designer for an architect's firm and is like a second daughter to Cesia and me. She takes such good care of us, and we are so lucky to have her in our lives. We are so glad Charlie didn't give up the chase to win her over all those years ago. They have now been married for thirty-nine years (together for forty-four) and are still very happy. Their son, Daniel, works as a speech pathologist and lives with his lovely girlfriend, Isabelle. He is still very involved in the Jewish community and was recently one of the co-organisers of the *In One Voice* Jewish Festival in Elsternwick.

Helen came back from America after eight years, to take on the role of principal at her old Kindergarten, Sholem Aleichem. A strong driver for Helen to come back was to help find ways for the Jewish community to connect and work together. She wanted to create a place with a strong sense of belonging for all ages, from birth to the elderly. She joined the board of the Kadimah and started working to bring the two organisations even closer, with their shared love of Yiddish, the arts, education, and culture. This dream has become a reality with the development of the JAQ (Jewish Arts Quarter) now in full swing in 2022. The JAQ is being built next door to the newly renamed Melbourne Holocaust Museum. The plan is for this area in Elsternwick to become a dedicated hub for the Jewish community, celebrating its culture, history, and education. It is a place, supported by government and the local community, where people can celebrate diversity, culture, and inclusion.

Helen is still the principal at Sholem Aleichem, and she and her second husband, Paul, have been together for over eighteen years now. He is from New Jersey, and luckily for us, Paul decided to join Helen when she came back to Melbourne in 2007. Daley and Nastassja are now in their mid-thirties, and doing well. Nastassja is married to a lovely man named Dean and they have a beautiful four-year-old daughter, Sienna, who Cesia and I adore. Nastassja works in digital marketing and is creative and well-organised just like her mum and grandmother. She also volunteers in the Jewish community and organised the art exhibition for the *In One Voice* Jewish Festival. Daley lives in Kansas City and is a US Marshall. He studied criminal justice, served in the army in Iraq and had many roles in law enforcement before becoming a US Marshall. Daley has always had a strong sense of justice and we have always been close, so I miss him a lot. As a young boy, he would always ask me questions about my life and the Holocaust, and whenever he comes back to visit, he always accompanies me to the Jewish Holocaust Centre to hear me speak to the students.

The best revenge Cesia and I could ever have on Hitler is the family we have created since the end of the war. My family is my proudest achievement in life. Family is so important. Family is everything.

LESSON LEARNED

Never stop learning.

36

ELSTERNWICK
MELBOURNE
17 JANUARY 2022

I have tested positive for Covid.
    Charlie and Bettan have it too. We don't know who we got it from, but it could be anyone. Covid is everywhere this summer. The two of them came over for Shabbat dinner on Friday night as usual and I wasn't feeling the best when they arrived. We always have the big dinner for Shabbat with the whole family, but Helen and her family were all away, and Cesia was in lockdown at Gary Smorgon House, so it was just the three of us.

    I had a runny nose and was coughing a little bit, which is very unusual for me, so when they arrived, I said I wanted to go for a Covid test. They agreed to take me after dinner. Bettan looked up the nearest testing sites and we found one near Chadstone Golf Course that was open until 8pm.

    After dinner we all bundled into the car and arrived at the testing site at 7.15pm, only to find it closed. We had no choice but to go back home. Charlie and Bettan said they'd give me a call the next morning to see how I was feeling and if I still wanted to go and test. But I woke feeling fine on Saturday. When they rang, I said there was no need to take me for a test after all.

I felt fine all day Saturday and that night too. Charlie and Bettan came over again last night and I was still in good form. Charlie and I were sitting on the couch and Bettan was at the computer, when a little while later they both started complaining of having sore throats. They ended up leaving early to go home to bed and then both woke the next morning with sore throats, runny noses and temperatures. Of course, their first thought was, 'We have Covid'. Their second thought was me.

I had just finished my breakfast this morning when Charlie rang to ask my carer, Basia, to do a test on me. It came back with a strong positive result. I couldn't believe it! I felt completely fine and had no symptoms at all, not even a temperature. But Charlie and Bettan both felt terrible and since then have returned positive results too.

So, here we are in isolation for seven days.

I was supposed to see Cesia today. This week I also had a session booked with Fiona, the woman who is helping me write my story. We've been meeting on a regular basis since August last year, and all the Goldbergs have become close with her and her whole family since then. We sit at my kitchen table, and she listens and takes notes and records me as I tell her my life story. A few years ago, a man named Alan Reid started writing my story, but he got sick and had to stop. It is sometimes very emotional for me, reliving such terrible memories, but I am grateful that my memory is still strong and that I can recall specific dates, people and details. My family always joke that I am a stickler for details, and I am. It is the way I have always been. I am the head and

Cesia is the heart. That is how it has been with us for seventy-five years. It is a combination that works well.

Cesia moved into Gary Smorgon House almost four years ago. I miss having her at home with me, but know she is happy there. In 2018, Cesia first told me that she wanted to go and live at the home.

'I need people around me, Abie,' she said. 'You are so tired when you come home from the Holocaust Centre in the afternoon, but that is when I have the most energy and want to go out and do things.'

She was right. After being up early and then spending the morning talking to students at the centre or attending committee meetings, I would come home to a big cooked lunch that our carer had made – chicken soup with noodles and beans or a schnitzel – and then was ready for a nap. I love talking to young people and sharing my experiences, but it is exhausting. There was rarely a day before the pandemic when I wasn't at the centre. It is being rebuilt now and I am missing going there very much. I also miss many of my old friends. From the original group of survivors, I am the last one left. I am still on the Board of Directors, and we continued having meetings over Zoom during lockdown. I also kept doing talks for students over Zoom, but it is not the same.

I intend to keep doing these things for as long as my memory allows.

My children made me stop driving when I was ninety-three, even though I never got a single fine or had an accident in my life. (Don't believe my children when they say I have little dents in my car. I am a better driver than them!) After that, I couldn't provide Cesia with the life we used to have – driving around and visiting friends whenever we felt like it. Cesia needs people around her. She is a very social person and needs the stimulation of other's company, but the older you get, the harder it is to get out and do things.

Now Cesia has friends all around her every day. Behind every door, there are people to chat and laugh with and there are endless activities on offer all day every day, so she is much happier. We all joke that Cesia is Queen Bee of Gary Smorgon. She knows everyone, plays bingo, dominoes, does the daily exercises and attends all the concerts, and everyone loves her.

Cesia has been starting to forget little things over the past few years now, but we have noticed that her memory and brain seem to have improved since she moved into Gary Smorgon. She has less anxiety there and is always being stimulated.

Cesia has always been such a people person. When we ran our restaurant, Goldy's, we would always close late on a Saturday night and then go out partying until the early hours of Sunday morning. Her various health issues over the years have never stopped my wife from going out and living life to the fullest. She has severe osteoporosis, and has had two shoulders, two hips and two knees replaced, so I call her the Bionic Woman. But it has never stopped her from doing anything.

Cesia has friends everywhere and her constant refrain is, 'I don't know why EVERYBODY loves me!'

She loves the atmosphere at Gary Smorgon, and the people who work there are lovely and take good care of her. But Cesia doesn't ask if I will move in there because she knows I will say no.

I am a social person who loves spending time with people too. Before the pandemic, I would go for a walk every day, but it would take twice as long as I expected because I met so many people I knew. Everybody wanted to stop me for a chat. But I would never voluntarily move into a communal home because I like my independence and always have. I want to keep my independence, living at home, for as long as I can, while I can.

Sometimes Cesia says she wants to come home because she worries that I am lonely without her. Also, she misses the contact with me and our daughter Helen (who lives with her husband Paul in the flat upstairs), but I know she would be restless after a few days back here.

Through the lockdowns over the past two years, it was much harder for Cesia to be her usual social self. Many times, the residents couldn't come out of their rooms to interact with each other. When we were allowed, all of us would go to see her to walk around the garden or have picnics and those times were very special and she never complained. My wife is a person who never complains about anything. Her response to everything is always, 'I'm fine'.

I won't complain about being in isolation now either because what is the point? I missed interacting with people over the past two years but didn't complain then either, because I knew there was nothing anybody could do about it. Also, I was safe in my home, with food, a TV, the phone, computer and everything I could possibly need. I had nothing to complain about.

My good friend, Jack Lewin, passed away in Los Angeles on 30 May 2022. He was ninety-four and had been sick for some time.

I was very sad to hear the news but was able to watch his funeral on Zoom. It was a beautiful send off for the friend I shared many wonderful and exciting adventures with when we were young boys.

I know my parents would be happy that I have survived this long, and that I kept my promise to never be silent, but there is still so much racial discrimination and antisemitism in the world, which pains me. When we were liberated, I expected humanity would learn. I was sure we were going to have a better world for ourselves, for our children and grandchildren and great-grandchildren. But it's the fourth generation and look at what is happening over in the Ukraine, even now in 2022.

I am so angry to see this kind of thing happening in the 21st century. I have spent my whole life talking about the damage tyranny and dictatorship can do to humanity, and now I see it again. This is the power of propaganda. People are brainwashed into murdering people. They say, 'If you don't believe what I believe and you don't convert to what we are, your life is worthless'. In this regard, much hasn't changed. It's devastating, but I'm used to devastation. I'm also very angry because it has been seventy-five years since the end of the war and what have we learned? I don't think anybody can explain why it's happening. We should know better, and we should value every human being's life. I had hoped the world would be a much kinder and tolerant place by the time I was ninety-seven years old.

But I am not ready to give up hope for humanity just yet. I am still trying to do what I did in the ghetto, which is to inspire and enlighten others to understand that life is precious and worth living. Many people were silenced by the Nazis and cannot speak now, but I can. As soon as I was liberated, I realised that the legacy of my family and of the innocent Jewish victims was to tell the world what happened, and to be a witness, so nothing like the Holocaust can ever be repeated against Jewish people or any other race or ethnicity. This is the message I give to students, grown-ups, children and visitors to the centre. It is the message I have given to my own children and grandchildren.

We all belong to the same race. It doesn't matter what the colour of your skin is, the shape of your eyes, your ethnicity or religion. We are all human beings. What hurts one human also hurts another. I believe you should always respect people even if they are different to you. Hitler rose to power on racially discriminative slogans about a superior race, but none of us are superior to anyone else. We must remember that.

There were times during the war when it would have been easier to give up, but I was determined to stay optimistic and hopeful. This mindset was instilled in me as a young boy and is with me now. My father taught me to never give up and to never give in to oppression. He dedicated his whole life to helping Jews out of oppression.

'Fight it with everything you have, Abram,' he told me.

This is what I did in the ghetto, even before the war. I didn't run from antisemitic trouble. I faced it head on. I still bleed inside because of what happened to me and the loved ones I lost. I will bleed for them until my last breath. The grief and trauma are with me all the time. So many years afterwards and even today, when I recount it again and again, it's so visible in my mind. Usually, I don't describe in detail what I saw and witnessed, but

The Strength of Hope

I do say to the visitors and students at the Melbourne Holocaust Museum that I could smell the burning flesh at Auschwitz-Birkenau because I was only 60 metres away from the chimneys. The images of that smoke belching out has never left me, and never will.

I did everything I could to survive the Holocaust and was lucky enough to be one of those who did. I lived when millions of others did not. This is something I have never forgotten, or ever taken for granted – not for a single day of my very long life.

I don't blame survivors who are angry and hold on to that anger forever. That is their choice, and they have a right to live their lives whatever way they want. But I did not see any point in holding on to the anger and bitterness. When I came to Australia, I wanted to live my life free from hatred and anger. People have often asked me, 'how can you live a normal life?'

'Of course, we can live a normal life,' I would tell them. 'But just because we are aiming for a normal life doesn't mean we should forget our past.'

I am not afraid to die because I grew up with danger in my life all the time, even before the war, and so that fear went away. I'm a realistic person and know death will come one day. I don't look forward to it, but I hope to live as long as possible and to always be happy and surrounded by the people I love. For young people reading this book, I hope you will understand why I wrote it and what my message is. I hope you might learn something from my experiences and take that lesson with you throughout your life. People should understand that this is the truth, and that life is beautiful and worth living.

I don't hate anyone, not even the Germans. There have been three or four generations of Germans born since the war, so how could I hate them? Hatred destroys people. I raised my children to believe there is no difference between people. I am not only Jewish, but I am also a human being, and this is what unites all of us, no matter what religion or race you are. There is only one race and that is the human race. We must never forget that.

Some people find it hard to understand how I have retained my positivity throughout my life, and been able to see the good in people, after what I experienced and endured. Now that you have read my story, you may have a better understanding of why I am this way.

I was twenty-six when my beautiful new bride, Cesia, and I left Belgium to travel across the world to Melbourne, Australia. We were fresh from a war that had stolen our families from us and destroyed parts of our souls and hearts forever; but when we arrived, I was determined to start again. The pain and memories will always be in my heart, but I needed to find joy in my life. I needed to know that I had left all the misery and horror behind so I could start again with my beautiful Cesia, my friends and my Jewish community in another land. I would never be free from the sadness and loss, but I could make a choice to not let the terrible experiences define me and rule the way I lived my life. I have had so much good luck in my life and that is what I choose to focus on instead of the bad. Hate and anger destroy you. I know that. I have seen it in my life during the war and since.

Let us always remember. And in the name of that memory, let us put out the call to stop bloodshed wherever it is happening in the world. We must do everything we can to reject tyranny and terrorism and murder and hate. And to hold on to hope. When I talk to students at the centre I always say to them, 'The most important thing for you now is your education, but as you grow up, you must always remember that not every day of your life will be sunny. There will be overcast days, but the sun will always shine afterwards.'

The strength of hope is a powerful force and one that kept me going in those first few days, weeks, then months and years of the war. It got me to the time and place I find myself in now. At my age, I know that I may not be able to go on telling people my story at the Holocaust Museum for much longer, so putting it all down in a book means it might just reach more people, long after I am gone.

I have already lived a life so much fuller and happier than I could ever have imagined in my wildest dreams, and with a woman who I love with all my heart. I share my story, no matter how painful it may be, because that is my tribute to my mother, and everyone else I know who suffered, including the millions of people I never got to meet. I am proud that I have never given in to hatred. The Nazis took so much from me already and so if I let them make me hate too, they would have just kept taking from me forever. Instead, I choose to live each day to the fullest and to try and spread joy and hope to everyone I meet. Eighty-three years after the invasion of Poland, *that* is my greatest resistance.

I am Abram Goldberg, a husband, a father, a grandfather, a friend, a teacher and a survivor. And this is my story.

37

CHARLIE

I was about four years old when I first remember hearing the word 'Holocaust'. My kindergarten was in the local church, and I gradually became aware of these older people called 'grandparents' who would sometimes pick up my friends. One day when Mum came to pick me up, I turned to her and asked: 'Where are my grandparents?'

She burst into tears.

When I was about ten, I asked Dad if he hated the Germans. Out came the index finger and that furrowed brow and I immediately thought, 'I'm in trouble here!'

'Don't you ever use that word!' he said.

'What word?' I asked.

'Hate!' he said. 'If you ever give in to that emotion, you become one of them.'

I believe it was those words that have been instrumental in shaping me and the way I live my life.

Dad also taught me to 'never take a backward step' if I was being confronted or challenged. 'Put your back against a

The Strength of Hope

wall and fight back.'

Once when I was in early high school, I was walking to my SKIF meeting in Wellington Street, St Kilda when I saw a group of seven boys my age walking towards me from the opposite direction. I often saw these boys when I was walking to SKIF, and they knew I was Jewish. I didn't like the way they were looking at me, but Dad's words echoed in my head, so I kept walking and didn't cross the road.

As I passed them, one of them said, 'Where are you going, you fucking little Jew?'

I backed myself up against the fence next to me as they started hitting me. I was a good swimmer at that age and fit, so nothing was really hurting that much until one of them kicked me in the face and broke my nose. That's when I started to fight back. As soon as I did, the cowards ran away, and I continued on my way to SKIF.

When I got home, I told Dad what had happened, and he immediately stood up.

'Did you recognise any of them?' he asked. 'Where was this? Let's go.'

We went looking for them, but they were long gone.

Growing up with SKIF meant that we were accustomed to socialist ideals, which helped to mould us.

In 1970, I went to Israel to live on a kibbutz, which was the ultimate scenario for a kid who had been brought up in a socialist organization like the Bund. The October War broke out in 1973 and all the men disappeared from the kibbutz, having been called up to the military. I made a commitment to stay until everyone came back, which took another nine months, then returned to Australia for a short while. But the bug had bitten me, so before long I was back on the kibbutz in Israel.

While I was there, I met a beautiful seventeen-year-old Swedish volunteer named Bettan. She had only planned to stay on the kibbutz for a few months but ended up staying for nine. I received my call-up papers for the Israeli Army just as Bettan was leaving and served with them for two and a half years.

I remember once finding a phone booth in Lebanon and calling home to speak to my parents. I called Goldy's and Dad answered. There was artillery and mortar fire in the background and so Dad asked what I was doing. I told him I was a sports instructor at one of the army bases in Israel, even though I was in binocular range of Beirut. I didn't want them to worry, and it was only years later that I told Mum and Dad the real story.

My son Daniel has an incredible sense of what is right, and of wanting to give back to the community. My father has had a huge impact on the way Daniel sees the world and travelling to Poland with him in 2011 was an experience he has never forgotten. 'It was a surreal experience being in the places that I had always heard about from Zaida,' Daniel said. 'Having him and Dad there also made it extra special and strengthened our bond. There was a sense of pride going back all together, a sense of the survival of a people as well as of my Zaida. It was the most emotional I have seen my Zaida. He is usually so stoic and strong in his recollections and when telling his story but being back during a chilly April with Dad and myself, on an especially emotional day, it was so hard seeing him break down.'

Overall, I know I have been enormously influenced by my dad. By his character, his determination and his consideration of others. I can also see that influence in my son. Dad is small in stature but larger than life. He is steadfast in his resolve to tell the world what happened to him, his family and the Jewish people during the Holocaust. His life has been devoted to fulfilling the promise he made to his mother in the last few seconds they had together on their arrival at Auschwitz-Birkenau in August 1944 before they were separated. He has never given in to hate, has always had hope and strength, and has imparted this to everyone he has met over his life. Abram Goldberg is a beacon of light, strength and positivity, and I feel so incredibly lucky and grateful that he is my father.

38

HELEN

Dad's character, his value system and his determination to succeed shaped our lives. Our parents used to talk about how they had missed out on an education and how important it was, and that always stayed with me. Even when I was little, I was always playing games where I was the teacher. When I left school, I went into teaching and am now a school principal. The values Mum and Dad taught me as a child are still with me, so much so that I have implemented them in the way I run my school. That sense of belonging, community, friends and family has been central to us, and even though we didn't have lots of blood family, so many people became aunts and uncles to Charlie and me because Mum was always inviting people over.

That sense of continuing traditions from the past has always been important to us as a family too. For example, Mum and Dad both went to SKIF when they were young, then Charlie and I, and then our own children. There is something in Yiddish called the Golden Chain, which is about the links of the past carrying forward through the present to the future, so there is always a connection. This is something that has been very important for Mum and Dad, especially because they both lost their parents.

My parents had a huge impact on me when it comes to giving back to the community. JAQ was originally my vision as I wanted to find a mechanism to bring the Jewish community together, support each other, share our vision, educate the wider Melbourne community about us, and develop a home for Jewish culture, art and education. The *In One Voice* festival was reborn when the then-president of Kadimah and I were having a coffee one day and discussing how we can bring a sense of community back and promote our organisations.

Both my parents have had an enormous impact on who we all are, what we believe in and how we conduct ourselves. They have taught us about having strength in difficult situations, putting things in perspective, empathy, resilience, a strong sense of identity, the importance of education, organisation and how one person can lead by example. More than anything though, they have taught us the importance of family.

Dad was always willing to talk about what happened during the war and the Holocaust; he never hid anything from us, and my son, Daley, was always asking him questions when he was young. Later, when we were living in America, Daley decided he wanted to join the US Army, and I said no. He kept on and on about it and I kept saying no, until one day he told me he had a strong sense of justice and wanted to protect and look after people. How could I refuse to let him do that? He is now a US Marshall with Homeland Security and I have no doubt that his drive and sense of what is right came from my father. My daughter, Nastassja, is different, but very family oriented, which she inherited from my parents as well. She also inherited Dad's gymnastic skills and was picked up by the Australian Institute of Sport when she was young, which unfortunately came to an end because of an elbow injury. She moved on to sport aerobics instead and ended up representing New Jersey in the American championships when she was fourteen. Much later she represented America in the American/Canadian competition.

Dad talks about his 99 per cent luck in surviving the war, but I believe it was more than that. I think it was also 99 per cent determination and 99 per cent believing he could be proactive in making that luck. And we are 99 per cent lucky to have him as our dad because he is such a special person. We are who we are because of Dad's influence and character. I look around at my circle of friends, many of whom are children of Holocaust survivors, and how successful they are as a group of people, and it is that determination that shines through, just as it does with our family. Charlie and I have asked ourselves over the years, 'How would we have coped if we were in our parents' position. What would we have done? But of course, there is no way of knowing.

39

CESIA PART 3

I love my life at Gary Smorgon House. I have so many friends here and I love playing dominoes and watching the concerts. Sometimes when singers or speakers come, they know me and say, 'Cesia! I remember you from the Wednesday Club!'

I love movies and I always go to the Jewish International Film Festival at the Classic Cinema in Elsternwick. My friend, Raquel, brings me and we take a sandwich and a coffee. We go and see lots of the films. Last time, I saw seven films at the festival. I watch all the films about the Holocaust. I cry a bit when I watch them, but I want to cry. Some people had had enough there but I need it. I need to let it out. Every person's story deserves to be heard and that is why I go to see these movies. Abram is different. He doesn't like to watch films about the Holocaust because he is all about the facts, and if they don't get something right, he gets upset. 'The Boy in the Striped Pyjamas' upset him because he said it's not real and that could not have happened that way. Those boys could never have gotten that close to each other, especially in Auschwitz. The commandant's son could never have got that close to a prisoner. Also, the barbed wire was electrified. Abram got very angry that people believed this would be true. He prefers a Holocaust documentary to a film.

I didn't believe that I would live until my age of ninety-two and could still talk and tell my stories. But I look around and see my children and grandchildren and to me it is a great achievement. I am sure all the survivors are thinking the same thing.

Deep in me, I don't hate, and I don't hate the people alive now, but in the beginning, I didn't buy anything made in Germany. My daughter bought a German car, which I wasn't happy about. But it's a different generation now. It still hurts me that all that horror and killing came from an intelligent country like Germany. How they must have studied ... to slowly kill people, to make pain for people. I can't say I forgive the Germans 100 per cent.

I don't know how I survived, but I'm paying the price for the starvation and the neglect now. I have had two shoulder replacements, two knee replacements and two hip replacements. I have also had breast cancer. But even as I'm getting older and less mobile, I still believe that life is beautiful. I have beautiful children, beautiful grandchildren and my beautiful great-grand-daughter, Sienna. Such a beautiful family I have got. I love everything here and am so glad we left Europe. Australia is a very good place. I am the happiest person in the world because I got Abie.

I still got Abie.

EPILOGUE

2022

'Happy anniversary, Bubba and Zaida!'

Our grandchildren, Daniel and Nastassja, take turns to lean down and give each of us a tight hug.

'Thank you, darlings,' Cesia says, beaming. 'Beautiful.'

Cesia and I are feeling very lucky today. It is our 75th wedding anniversary and we are here to celebrate our deep and long-lasting love for each other, surrounded by our friends and family. After all our many years together, and after everything we have endured in our lives, both separately and together, we are still here. My love for Cesia has only grown over the years, and I know what a lucky man I am.

I squeeze my beautiful wife's hand and lean over to give her a kiss on the cheek. She smiles back at me. It's a smile that has energised and illuminated me for nearly eight decades.

'How lucky we are,' she says, echoing my thoughts.

But we are not only here at the Kadimah in Elsternwick to celebrate our anniversary. Today, we have all come together to celebrate another very special occasion: our son Charlie's 70th birthday. Cesia and I were married on 10 June, and Charlie was born on 15 June, so we decided to organise a double celebration this year. Helen and Bettan organised everything for this special event. They had initially booked another venue, the Balaclava Hotel, but a few days ago the hotel got in touch to say they would have to cancel our booking for 'COVID-19-related' reasons. What to do? Even in the scheme of our long and eventful lives, the past two years have been remarkable.

Well, Bettan and Helen swung into action and organised for our big celebration to be held at the Kadimah, a place where the Goldberg family has made many wonderful memories over the years. What could be more fitting than Cesia and I celebrating our 75th anniversary, and Charlie his birthday, in this place that is so special to us?

There is a small dark cloud over today's festivities. My good friend, Jack Lewin, the man with whom I shared so many adventures post-war, including jumping on and off trains all through Europe, and being interrogated by Russians and kept in a cell overnight with Nazis, died in Los Angeles last week at the age of ninety-four. It is always so hard and painful to lose such old dear friends, and I am thinking about Jack today and wishing he could have been here with us on this special occasion.

There are over one hundred people here to celebrate with us today. There is an amazing feast of food and drinks but the most popular – for Charlie and me at least – is our favourite Żubrówka Bison Grass Vodka from Poland. My younger self would never have believed such a feast could be possible, or that we would be sharing it with our extended family.

The Strength of Hope

Excitingly, both of Maryla's sons are here: Heniek, who is now seventy-five, and Danek, who will be eighty-two this year. Danek and his wife, Ewa, have flown all the way from Perth to celebrate with us.

Charlie speaks to the crowd eloquently and says, 'I want to tell you all here today that life is wonderful. Friends and family are everything. Thank you all for being a part of my wonderful life.'

Cesia and I look to each other and smile. Our son has perfectly expressed how we feel too.

Daniel brings me up to the microphone and I look out over the faces of so many of our loved ones. Family, friends – old and new – and of course, the face I know and love so deeply, my Cesia. I look at my beautiful family, all sitting around the table together, arms around each other and big smiles on their faces.

'Cesia and I have such a lovely family, and now with little Sienna we are a fourth-generation Jewish family, which represents the ultimate triumph over the Nazis and everything they tried to achieve,' I say. 'I promised my mother all those years ago in Auschwitz that I would never be silent and that I would try to educate the younger generation. I have fulfilled that promise, and after this day I will continue to do so for as long as I'm able.

Here we are all together – hopefully we will have many more happy celebrations in the future, and I will see you all for many, many more years. Well, I'm only ninety-seven years old. I'm not giving in. I'm stubborn.'

Everyone laughs loudly as my family shouts, 'YES! YES!'

I laugh along, nodding my agreement.

When the speeches are over, Tomi Kalinski – a dear friend who is part of the well-known music group, Yid! – sits at the piano to play so we can all sing the Yiddish song, '*Lomir Ale Ineynem.*'

Cesia and I hold hands and our voices ring out, louder than anyone else's in the room:

> *Lomir ale ineynem, Lomir ale ineynem,*
> *Trinken a glezele vayn!*
> *Lomir ale ineynem, Lomir ale ineynem,*
> *Trinken a glezele vayn!*
> Let us all together, together
> Drink a glass of wine!
> Let us all together, together
> Drink a glass of wine!
> *Mazal Tov!* (Congratulations!)
> *L'chaim!* (To life!)